SHAKESPEAREAN MELANCHOLY

EDINBURGH CRITICAL STUDIES IN SHAKESPEARE AND PHILOSOPHY
Series Editor: Kevin Curran

Edinburgh Critical Studies in Shakespeare and Philosophy takes seriously the speculative and world-making properties of Shakespeare's art. Maintaining a broad view of 'philosophy' that accommodates first-order questions of metaphysics, ethics, politics and aesthetics, the series also expands our understanding of philosophy to include the unique kinds of theoretical work carried out by performance and poetry itself. These scholarly monographs will reinvigorate Shakespeare studies by opening new interdisciplinary conversations among scholars, artists and students.

Editorial Board Members

Published Titles

Rethinking Shakespeare's Political Philosophy: From Lear to Leviathan
Alex Schulman
Shakespeare in Hindsight: Counterfactual Thinking and Shakespearean Tragedy
Amir Khan
Second Death: Theatricalities of the Soul in Shakespeare's Drama
Donovan Sherman
Shakespeare's Fugitive Politics
Thomas P. Anderson
Is Shylock Jewish?: Citing Scripture and the Moral Agency of Shakespeare's Jews
Sara Coodin
*Chaste Value: Economic Crisis, Female Chastity and the Production of
Social Difference on Shakespeare's Stage*
Katherine Gillen
Shakespearean Melancholy: Philosophy, Form and the Transformation of Comedy
J. F. Bernard

Forthcoming Titles

Making Publics in Shakespeare's Playhouse
Paul Yachnin
Derrida Reads Shakespeare
Chiara Alfano
The Play and the Thing: A Phenomenology of Shakespearean Theatre
Matthew Wagner
*Shakespeare and the Fall of the Roman Republic: Selfhood, Stoicism and Civil War in
Julius Caesar and Antony and Cleopatra*
Patrick Gray
Conceiving Desire: Metaphor, Cognition and Eros in Lyly and Shakespeare
Gillian Knoll
Shakespeare's Moral Compass: Ethical decision-making in his plays
Neema Parvini
Shakespeare and the Truth-Teller: Confronting the Cynic Ideal
David Hershinow
Revenge Tragedy and Classical Philosophy on the Early Modern Stage
Christopher Crosbie

For further information please visit our website at edinburghuniversitypress.com/series/ecsst

SHAKESPEAREAN MELANCHOLY

Philosophy, Form and the Transformation of Comedy

◆ ◆ ◆

J. F. BERNARD

EDINBURGH
University Press

Edinburgh University Press is one of the leading university presses in the UK. We publish academic books and journals in our selected subject areas across the humanities and social sciences, combining cutting-edge scholarship with high editorial and production values to produce academic works of lasting importance. For more information visit our website: edinburghuniversitypress.com

Edinburgh University Press Ltd
The Tun – Holyrood Road,
12(2f) Jackson's Entry,
Edinburgh EH8 8PJ

Typeset in 12/15 Adobe Sabon by
IDSUK (DataConnection) Ltd, and
printed and bound in Great Britain.

A CIP record for this book is available from the British Library

ISBN 978 1 4744 1733 4 (hardback)
ISBN 978 1 4744 1734 1 (webready PDF)
ISBN 978 1 4744 1735 8 (epub)

CONTENTS

ACKNOWLEDGEMENTS

I have been thinking about melancholy, comedy and Shakespeare for eleven years, ever since I took a graduate seminar with my master's advisor, Kevin Pask, at Concordia University. My first debt of gratitude is thus his for having put me on this path. From Concordia, I also thank Louis-Patrick Leroux and Meredith Evans.

I have incurred many more debts along the way and will do my best to acknowledge them here.

I owe quite a lot to my doctoral advisor at the University of Montreal, Joyce Boro, for her guidance, wisdom and support. I also thank Heike Harting, Lianne Moyes and Heather Meek.

I am also incredibly grateful to two friends with whom I had the pleasure (and pains) of going through the doctoral program while at U de M. The encouragement and timely insight given by Maude Lapierre and Frederik Byrn Køhlert live in the margins of this book.

As a graduate student, I was fortunate enough to hold two research assistantships with the Shakespeare Performance and Research Team at McGill University, as well as to present some of my work at their various meetings, which proved an invaluable learning and growing experience, both personally and professionally. I thank Wes Folkerth, Leanore Lieblein, Denis Salter and Paul Yachnin to that effect.

I have presented excerpts of this project over the years at various meetings of the following organisations: The Renaissance Society of America, The Shakespeare Association of America, The North East Modern Language Association, The International Society for Humor Studies and The Ohio Valley Shakespeare Conference. I had stimulating and challenging conversations with colleagues at these events over the years that solidified a lot of my claims and kept me honest. With that in mind, I thank Russ Bodi, Kent Cartwright, Lars Engle, Amir Khan, Katherine E. Maus, Jennifer McDermott, Neema Parvini, Mary Thomas Crane, Richard Van Oort and Adam Zucker. Likewise, a symposium on *The Two Noble Kinsmen* at Xavier University, organised by the amazing Niamh O'Leary, provided me with the crucial base for my discussion of the play in Chapter 5. I am very grateful to Niamh and to everyone who participated in the event.

In May of 2016, I had the opportunity to partake in a month-long seminar at the University of Michigan thanks to the Early Modern Conversions Project. Though the work I did there pertains to another project, the informal and thought-provoking discussions with colleagues over food and drinks (so much food) were most welcome and have helped shape parts of the argument of this book. My heartfelt thanks go to Alison Searle, Stephen Spiess and Lieke Stelling.

Michael Bristol's mentorship and friendship over the years has brought me more than can be expressed here. As evidenced through my critical framework, his work has had a strong influence on mine. His nod, if I can indulge in a baseball metaphor, is equivalent to Sandy Koufax telling me I can pitch. Thanks, Mike.

I am very grateful to everyone at Edinburgh University Press, Commissioning Editor Michelle Houston and Assistant Commissioning Editors Ersev Ersoy and Adela Rauchova, as well as my two anonymous readers, whose comments helped enhance the overall quality of the manuscript. In particular, I wish to thank the series editor, Kevin Curran, for his insight and support throughout this project. The book could not have come to fruition without him. I wish to thank Emily Bernard and Diana Verrall, as well as Diana Neate, for attentive readings of portions of the manuscript. Josie Panzuto also undertook a generous and insightful reading of the introduction at a timely juncture. I thank the amazing (and dare I say magical) Nisha Coleman for her unbelievable insight and diligent reading of the manuscript near the end.

I thank my family and friends for their love and support over the years. Je vous aime tous très fort.

A portion of Chapter 3, on *The Merchant of Venice*, appeared previously in *Renaissance Studies* ("*The Merchant of Venice* and Shakespeare's Sense of Humour(s), 28 November 2014, p. 5). I thank them for the permission to reproduce the material here.

SERIES EDITOR'S PREFACE

Picture Macbeth alone on stage, staring intently into empty space. 'Is this a dagger which I see before me?' he asks, grasping decisively at the air. On one hand, this is a quintessentially theatrical question. At once an object and a vector, the dagger describes the possibility of knowledge ('Is this a dagger') in specifically visual and spatial terms ('which I see before me'). At the same time, Macbeth is posing a quintessentially philosophical question, one that assumes knowledge to be both conditional and experiential, and that probes the relationship between certainty and perception as well as intention and action. It is from this shared ground of art and inquiry, of theatre and theory, that this series advances its basic premise: Shakespeare is philosophical.

It seems like a simple enough claim. But what does it mean exactly, beyond the parameters of this specific moment in *Macbeth*? Does it mean that Shakespeare had something we could think of as his own philosophy? Does it mean that he was influenced by particular philosophical schools, texts and thinkers? Does it mean, conversely, that modern philosophers have been influenced by him, that Shakespeare's plays and poems have been, and continue to be, resources for philosophical thought and speculation?

The answer is yes all around. These are all useful ways of conceiving a philosophical Shakespeare, and all point to lines of inquiry that this series welcomes. But Shakespeare is philosophical in a much more fundamental way as well. Shakespeare is philosophical because the plays and poems actively create new worlds of knowledge and new scenes of ethical encounter. They ask big questions, make bold arguments and develop new vocabularies in order to think what might otherwise be unthinkable. Through both their scenarios and their imagery, the plays and poems engage the qualities of consciousness, the consequences of human action, the phenomenology of motive and attention, the conditions of personhood and the relationship among different orders of reality and experience. This is writing and dramaturgy, moreover, that consistently experiments with a broad range of conceptual crossings, between love and subjectivity, nature and politics, and temporality and form.

Edinburgh Critical Studies in Shakespeare and Philosophy takes seriously these speculative and world-making dimensions of Shakespeare's work. The series proceeds from a core conviction that art's capacity to think – to formulate, not just reflect, ideas – is what makes it urgent and valuable. Art matters because unlike other human activities it establishes its own frame of reference, reminding us that all acts of creation – biological, political, intellectual and amorous – are grounded in imagination. This is a far cry from business-as-usual in Shakespeare studies. Because historicism remains the methodological gold standard of the field, far more energy has been invested in exploring what Shakespeare once meant than in thinking rigorously about what Shakespeare continues to make possible. In response, Edinburgh Critical Studies in Shakespeare and Philosophy pushes back against the critical orthodoxies of historicism and cultural studies to clear a space for scholarship that confronts aspects of literature that can neither be reduced to nor adequately explained by particular historical contexts.

Shakespeare's creations are not just inheritances of a past culture, frozen artefacts whose original settings must be expertly reconstructed in order to be understood. The plays and poems are also living art, vital thought-worlds that struggle, across time, with foundational questions of metaphysics, ethics, politics and aesthetics. With this orientation in mind, Edinburgh Critical Studies in Shakespeare and Philosophy offers a series of scholarly monographs that will reinvigorate Shakespeare studies by opening new interdisciplinary conversations among scholars, artists and students.

Kevin Curran

To Emily, who made this possible by sharing in the mirth and melancholy of this long journey.

I love you so very much.

CHAPTER 1

WHAT'S SO FUNNY ABOUT HUMOURS? MELANCHOLY, COMEDY AND REVISIONIST PHILOSOPHY

Tragedy is when I cut my finger. Comedy is when you fall
into an open sewer and die.   (Mel Brooks)

In the induction to *The Taming of the Shrew*, Christopher Sly
is tricked into thinking that he is a wealthy Lord who 'these
fifteen years . . . have been in a dream' (Induction, II, 79).
A servingman subsequently informs him that

> Your honour's players, hearing your amendment,
> Are come to play a pleasant comedy,
> *For so your doctors hold it very meet,*
> *Seeing too much sadness hath congealed your blood,*
> *And melancholy is the nurse of frenzy.*
> Therefore they thought it good you hear a play
> And frame your mind to mirth and merriment,
> Which bars a thousand harms and lengthens life.
> (Induction, II, 125–32, emphasis mine)[1]

In its broadest sense, the scene plays out an elaborate jest on
Sly, who gullibly accepts whatever information his 'attendants'
provide. Servants convince him to watch the play by asserting
that doing so has been recommended for him by his physicians to offset a medical condition: his blood is apparently too

cold, contaminated by the bodily substance known as melancholy. The implication of such a diagnosis is that exposure to
the merriment of comedy will nurse him back to health. In
actuality, the above-quoted speech offers dramatic exposition
to frame the *actual* comedy about to unfold. Yet the casual
conflation of theatre and medicine suggests a familiarity that
resonates beyond *Taming*'s induction. Dramatically, Sly is
about to witness the same play as Shakespeare's audience, and
the detailed description the servingman provides, along with
Sly's willingness to accept it, suggests a broader early modern
awareness – at least culturally – of the physician's prognosis
concerning his melancholic state. This deceptively informal
dovetailing of theatre and medicine provides a point of departure for the analysis of melancholy in Shakespearean comedy
that I undertake here.

Michael Bristol perhaps said it best when he wrote that
'nothing is more idiosyncratic than melancholia, and yet
nothing is more public and histrionic in its expression'.[2]
Melancholy is ubiquitous and paradoxical. Its daunting and
intrinsically contradictory nature epitomises life itself. Over-
lapping through the ages, its oxymoronic definitions form a
truly eclectic tapestry of human behaviour. Melancholy is at
once a principle of health and a catalyst for disease, an emblem
of genius, a symptom of madness, a marker of grandiose interiority and a sign of feeblemindedness. It infers a seemingly
endless constellation of human emotions, mores and states
of being. Melancholy beckons sin, sloth, ingenuity, loss, lust,
excess, depression and black bile. It proves highly malleable
and incredibly adaptive, effortlessly seeping into cultures,
ideologies and philosophical discourses. Its ever-present spectre within the realm of artistic creation is equally astounding. To chart the history of melancholy as a literary subject
is to assemble a veritable who's who of artistic ingenuity that
yokes together classical Greek philosophy and modern-day

graphic novels, channelling Aristotle, Shakespeare and Keats as much as Byron, Benjamin and Kurt Cobain. Its critical staying power is just as remarkable. Consistently mined but never exhausted, melancholy remains a potent analytical tool that transcends disciplines and epochs, as works such as Anne Cheng's *The Melancholy of Race*, Peter Schwenger's *The Tears of Things: Melancholy and Physical Objects* or Eric Wilson's *The Melancholy Android: On the Psychology of Sacred Machines* suggest. As both a marker of emotional turmoil and a token of intellectual gravitas, melancholy never goes out of style.

Surprisingly, its comic potential remains largely unexamined, particularly in literary studies, where tragic icons such as Hamlet and Young Werther inevitably relegate the idea of a comic sense of melancholy to an afterthought. One does not expect to encounter many comic characters professing inexorable sadness, other than perhaps as a farcical foil to the spirits of mirth and revelry that generally characterise the comic genre. Nevertheless, the notion pervades the Shakespearean comic corpus in an astonishing variety of ways, from deceptively casual mentions, such as the one discussed at the outset of this introduction, through more obvious incursions (the melancholy Jaques in *As You Like It*) to downright perplexing utterances (Antonio's inexplicable sadness at the onset of *The Merchant of Venice*). Such instances have received a fair share of critical attention over the years, but seldom have they been placed in dialogue with one another as part of an explicit consideration of their comic functionality.

In this book, I argue that Shakespeare performs dual revisions of comedy and melancholy that shape the philosophical afterlife of both notions. I contend that Shakespearean comedy reappropriates tenets from prevalent definitions of melancholy that emerge out of classical Greece: the humoral conception of the idea, advocated by Hippocrates and Galen, as well as Aristotle's more spiritually inclined counterpart, which positions melancholy as a symptom of creativity and intellectual genius. Shakespearean comedy repeatedly blends the two philosophies as it rethinks melancholy through comic theatre and, conversely, retheorises comedy through melancholy. Characters rely on explicitly humoral lexicons to express themselves and, likewise, frame their melancholic dispositions as markers of a unique sense of interiority and wisdom. Conversely, this sustained focus on melancholy reshapes Shakespearean comedy away from its farcical or romantic heritage and into the more emotionally complex dramatic efforts of later tragicomedies. Comic melancholy in Shakespeare underscores the dramatic limits of this psycho-humoral dimension as it transforms the genre of comedy. The plays dislocate the notion of melancholy from individual, bodily characterisations and recast it as a more liminal, emotional imprint that proves at once painful and pleasurable.

Though Shakespeare draws substantially from established traditions, the sense of comic melancholy he extracts from them proves extraordinary, even within the plethora of meanings that early modern culture ascribes to melancholy. This book thus understands Shakespearean comic melancholy not as a fixed ideology but rather as a multivalent dramatic concept that results from the distillation of various classical and early modern sources. It underlines the productive site of analytical friction that a comic tradition of Shakespearean melancholy affords. As I will argue, the more wistful sense of melancholy that emanates from Shakespeare's final plays marks an endpoint of sorts in the transformation of melancholy within Shakespearean comedy from an understanding of the emotions as dichotomised and towards one of them as cyclical. Through their sustained engagement with melancholy, the plays foster a perception of these seemingly oppositional sentiments as equally integral components of the affective response process; to be merry *and* melancholic, the plays suggest, is to be human. Ultimately, the deceptively potent sorrow at the core of Shakespeare's comedies, what I come to define as their 'melancomic' quality, forges previously unnoticed links between Shakespearean comedy and modern theories of melancholia. Under these terms, Shakespearean comedy can be conceived of as a prism that fundamentally alters melancholy as it runs through it, taking in the philosophies of Galen, Aristotle, Robert Burton and others and refracting out our modern understanding of the idea.

Shakespeare's development of melancholy proves simultaneously anchored in the prevalent scientific discourses of his time and remarkably innovative as he hopscotches between several authoritative sources available to him. His theatre displays significant opportunism in reworking various sociomedical understandings of melancholy while developing a comic philosophy of the concept that, while very much in tune with its predecessors, proves unique to the period's dramatic output. The classical binary of galenic and Aristotelian melancholy is a well-rehearsed one that clearly delineates the concept's rich history. Galen's work on anatomy provides the underpinnings of a humoral understanding of melancholy, while Aristotle introduces the connection to intellectual proficiency and creativity. However, such a dichotomy misleadingly glosses over the prevalence of melancholy within classical discourses, as the notion is discussed with remarkable frequency by philosophers, physicians and poets over the centuries. The two traditions intertwine through the ages to shape the primary doctrines of melancholy that wind up at the core of an early modern understanding of the subject. Ever opportunistic, Shakespearean comedy borrows indiscriminately from both traditions in developing a comic sense of melancholy for the Renaissance stage. In the same fashion that Shakespeare drew from Ovid, Holinshed, Greene and Plautus in creating dramatic plots, he channels elements from Galen, Aristotle, Ficino and Timothy Bright to create his own sense of comic melancholy.

No Laughing Matter: A Psycho-humoral History of Melancholy

References to black bile and its effects on human anatomy appear ubiquitously in scientific work produced in antiquity. In the 'Nature of Man', Hippocrates explains how 'the body of a man has in itself blood, phlegm, yellow bile and black bile [and] these make up the nature of his body and through these he feels pain and enjoys health'.[3] Plato writes in his dialogues that when humours

> wander up and down [man's] body without finding a vent to the outside . . . they produce all sorts of diseases of the soul, [and] each of them produces a multitude of varieties of bad temper and melancholy in the region it attacks.[4]

The Stoics similarly acknowledge the 'phantastic groundless attraction [that] occurs in the melancholic and in madmen'.[5] These descriptions find common roots in the theory of humorality, which stipulates that the universe is composed of four basic elements: fire, air, water and earth. According to humoral theory, each of these elements possessed a dominant characteristic (heat, cold, moisture and dryness, respectively). Such an understanding formed the basis of the classical conception of anatomy, in which the body was comprised of four humours, substances that embodied a specific combination of the elements and traits listed above: blood (hot and dry), phlegm (cold and wet), choler (hot and wet) and melancholy (cold and dry). The governing principle of the humoral doctrine was one of balance, both within the body and in relation to the universe, in which harmony implied 'a concordance in the movements of air and fluid [where] everything is in sympathy'.[6] The body was thought to contain various other substances and tissues, such as bones and nerves, but the interplay among the four humours, during which 'the nutriment becomes altered in the veins by the innate heat, [where] blood is produced when it is in moderation, and the other humours when it is not in proper proportion',[7] represented a central tenet in the understanding of human health. The preponderance of a given humour would determine a person's overall temperament. Melancholy, from the Greek words for black (*melas*) and bile (*khole*), was thought to produce a sorrowful demeanour that was deemed 'least enviable, for cold and dryness are opposite to the vital qualities'.[8] Melancholy thus existed first as a necessary constituent of normal human physiology rather than as a physical or mental affliction. Greek thinkers effectively differentiated between what they deemed a natural state of melancholy (an abundance of the black bile within the body) and its unnatural, diseased manifestation. Much like the Stoics' theoretical conception of the wise man as an 'ideally virtuous' model to emulate, classical philosophy conceded that perfect humoral balance constituted a hypothetical ideal rather than a physical reality, one that lent itself to a broader range of discourses than a strictly anatomical conceptualisation.[9]

Despite a Hippocratic focus on health and balance, the idea of melancholy as disease rapidly came to dominate medical writings on the subject. Essentially, the humours became diseased in cases of extreme imbalances, when passions such as anger and despair would heat bodily humours and produce noxious vapours that could harm the brain through the process of adustion. The works of Galen grew synonymous with a humoral philosophy of melancholy, to the point where Galenism became, as Gail Kern Paster puts it, a 'dominant physiological paradigm', a widespread cultural construct that endured well into the seventeenth century in spite of Galen gradually being forsaken as a medical authority.[10] The treatises also display a surprising awareness of readership in offering anecdotal examples of outrageous symptoms and bodily side effects that seek to inform as much as they do entertain. In 'On the Affected Parts', Galen recalls a melancholic's overwhelming fear that 'Atlas who supports the world will become tired and throw it away'.[11] The story is repeated almost verbatim, and without any reference to Galen, in a list of melancholic symptoms found in Johann Weyer's *Of Deceiving Demons* (1562).[12] This detailing of outrageous bodily and psychological symptoms offers a prime example of the merger of medical and literary practices that begins in antiquity, a kind of scientific sensationalism that subsequently informs many early modern humoral writings.[13]

The disease of melancholy always proves difficult to characterise definitively since it channels an overwhelming plethora of symptoms and putative causes that render any treatment onerous. Indeed, a multitude of factors, ranging from diet and exercise through natural elements such as air or flora to a penchant for vice or luxury, were thought to influence melancholy.[14] As might be expected, the prescribed remedies were as varied as the causes and symptoms of the illness, but similarly revolved around the physical evacuation of humoral excesses. The one element that proves a staple in most discourses is the idea that melancholy produces a sense of fear and sadness without apparent cause. As Galen writes, 'although each melancholic patient acts quite differently than the others, all of them exhibit fear or despondency'.[15]

This particular understanding of melancholy resonates through the Middle Ages as various writers tailor the notion to their respective geographic and cultural concerns, introducing lexical variants and subdivisions of the aforementioned doctrine of fear and sadness. Writing about the life of desert coenobites in the fifth century, Cassian introduces the notion of accidia, a 'mental state of despondency, lethargy, and discouragement'[16] to describe the languor that often plagues his subjects. 'Of the Spirit of Accidie' builds on galenic theories through its sustained focus on the dangers of idleness and antisocial behaviour that strongly reverberates in early modern representations of melancholy. The work on melancholy by the famed Arab physician Avicenna (c. 1170) offers a more medicalised account that further bridges classical and early modern discourses on the subject. Though Avicenna's contention innovates on the classical model, the galenic influence still appears strong, both in its grounding of the notion in physiological principles and in its inference that melancholy, in its natural state, is a necessary and useful anatomical component. For Avicenna, melancholy becomes a touchstone of disposition, a reactionary agent for other fluids to interact with, a combination which, in turn, creates the melancholic disease. 'If it were pure black bile,' he writes, 'then there would be a great deal of deliberation, and a reduction of frenzy; unless it was stirred and upset, or unless there were enmities which could not be forgiven.'[17] Around the same time, Hildegard of Bingen (c. 1151-8) introduces a gendered distinction to the discussion of melancholy, depicting melancholy women as 'heedless and dissolute in their thoughts and of evil dispositions if they are grieved by any irritation'.[18] Again, Bingen's text recuperates galenic discourse to establish her male–female dichotomy of melancholy. It is the sustained galenic presence more than each individual argument of melancholy that is worth noting here. The definitions these authors put forth earmark the permutations that the concept of melancholy undergoes from its classic inception towards early modernity, under the paradoxical guises of a primarily physical ailment concealing powerful psychological underpinnings.

Shakespeare's most direct sources for an understanding of the melancholic influence remain early modern, but the humoral tradition expounded here shapes the contemporary discourses he draws from. Though well suited to tragedy, the overarching association with fear and sorrow does

not serve the comic genre as fruitfully; Shakespearean melancholy always implies a sense of sadness, but the galenic
model and its fluid repartee between physiological, psychological and behavioural undertones allows the comedies to
integrate melancholy into multiple iterations. Shakespeare
borrows heavily from the galenic discourse when having
characters explain, refer to or advocate for their melancholy.
The humoral lexicon becomes a representational stage tool
that immediately communicates a character's makeup to
audiences. Shakespeare eventually disengages from individual humoral characterisations in developing a comic sense of
melancholy, but principles of Galen's humoral philosophy,
such as balance and excess, loom large in his early comedic
efforts. The plays are never locked into such an ideology,
however, as they borrow as heavily from the Aristotelian tradition of genial melancholy.

Sad Clowns, Tortured Artists and Savvy Philosophers: The Genial Melancholy Tradition

Genial melancholy does not so much oppose its galenic
counterpart as it complements it through the belief that
melancholy can denote creativity, depth of character and
intellectual genius. The idea is best represented in Aristotle's
interrogation in 'Problem XXX': 'Why is it that all those
men who have become extraordinary in philosophy, politics,
poetry, or the arts are obviously melancholic, and some to
such an extent that they are seized by the illness that comes
from black bile?'[19] Whether Aristotle did in fact write the
seminal classical discussion of melancholy does not matter much in the wake of his sustained association with it
throughout history. Much in the way that Galen becomes
the figurehead of a larger physiological imagining of melancholy, Aristotle is positioned as genitor to its intellectual

tradition by 'Problem XXX'. Aristotle's definition of melancholy finds its root in the idea that mingling (of hot and cold, of disease and natural temperament and so on) can produce a number of effects in an individual, both internal and external. He remarks that

> in most people, therefore, arising from their daily nutrition, it produces no differences in character, but only brings about some melancholic diseases. But those in whom such a mixture has formed by nature, these straightaway develop all sort of characters each different in accordance with the different mixture; for instance, those in whom (the black bile) is considerably cold become sluggish and stupid, whereas those in whom it is very considerable and hot become mad, clever, erotic, and easily moved to spiritedness and desire, and some become more talkative.[20]

Aristotle conceives of melancholy as a linchpin of possibilities, a spinning wheel of symptoms, causes and behaviours that cover the near-entirety of human attributes, from the negative (mad, sluggish and stupid) to the positive (clever, erotic and spirited). Yet his understanding somewhat disregards the body to focus primarily on intellectual features. He writes that individuals whose intelligence is affected by the heat of melancholy

> are affected by diseases of madness or inspiration . . . those in whom the excessive heat is relaxed toward a mean, these people are melancholic, but they are more intelligent, and they are less eccentric, but they are superior to the others in any respects, some in education, others in arts, and others in politics.[21]

'Problem XXX' lists a few classical heroes and philosophers who have suffered from such a condition before surmising that 'in many such men diseases have come from this sort of mixture in the body, whereas in others their nature clearly inclines toward these conditions'.[22] Thus, the natural state of melancholy does not suggest an ailment that occasionally plagues the philosopher or artist but rather, as Julia Kristeva suggests, is understood as the 'very nature [and] ethos' of the thinking man.[23] This understanding offers a somewhat self-serving validation for those suffering from melancholy who happen to be writing about it. One cannot help but notice the irony of a melancholic philosopher declaring melancholy to be a marker of excellence in arts such as philosophy and poetry. This tendency towards self-identification becomes a common tenet of genial melancholy, one that Robert Burton eventually perfects in the seventeenth century and that informs much of the dramatic engagement with the idea, where countless characters attempt to justify their melancholy as a sign of intellectual and emotional gravitas.

Though the Middle Ages somewhat cast aside Aristotle's conception of melancholy in favour of Avicenna's physiological understanding, the idea re-emerges in the medical discourse of the fifteenth-century Italian physician Marsilio Ficino. Though his focus is primarily humoral, being concerned with the diagnosing, cataloguing and treatment of the diseases of the back bile, Ficino's discussion of the ways in which melancholy affects the scholar in 'On Caring for the Health of Students' borrows from Aristotle's figure of the melancholic genius. Ficino identifies astrological, spiritual and anatomical sources of melancholy in scholars and thinkers alike. The acknowledgement of the planets' influence on behaviour predates Ficino, but its iteration in *The Book of Life* solidifies the idea that the fragile microcosm of human temperament stands at the mercy of external factors.[24] It is when discussing the natural and anatomical source of scholarly melancholy that Ficino touches on genial melancholy most directly. He writes that

because the pursuit of knowledge is so difficult, it is necessary for the soul to remove itself from external things
to internal as if moving from the circumference to the
centre. While one is looking at this centre of man . . . it
is necessary to remain very still, to gather oneself at the
centre, away from the circumference. To be fixed at the
centre is very much like being at the centre of the earth
itself, which resembles black bile. Contemplation itself,
in its turn, by a continual recollection and compression,
as it were, brings on a nature similar to black bile.[25]

Ficino legitimises the melancholic man by inscribing him in
the elemental world. Much in the way that melancholy lies
at the core of our planet through its association with earth;
one must turn back towards oneself in order to truly excel
intellectually.[26] Melancholy thus invites a closing in on oneself, a withdrawal from the social dimension of life in order
to achieve intellectual and spiritual excellence, all the while
paradoxically connecting the melancholic individual to the
world he inhabits. Ficino nevertheless acknowledges the
disastrous effects that black bile exerts. For him, the act of
thinking does violence upon the body since 'in thinking, the
spirit is also continually broken by such movement'.[27] The
condition is at its worst in philosophers since, as he explains,
'their minds get separated from their bodies and bodily
things'.[28] The conception of 'the melancholy scholar', characterised by Ficino as a sensitive intellectual whose depth of
character dwarfs others, gained tremendous popularity during the Renaissance.

The idea of melancholy as a necessary evil in the pursuit
of knowledge further impresses the notion of sacrifice in the
name of excellence. Genial melancholy becomes the asking
price for attaining mastery and superiority within a given
field of study, a notion which eventually fosters the archetypical representation of the tortured artist or genius who

suffers through his craft for the benefit of others. As far as comedy is concerned, this idea is best encapsulated by the twentieth-century allegorical story of the sad clown and the psychiatrist: 'someone once visited a doctor to find a cure for depression. "Do something amusing," said the doctor, "like going to the circus – the great clown Grock is in town." The patient looked infinitely sad. "But you see, doctor, I am Grock"'.[29] The clown figure is at once intrinsically connected to the world by the laughter he elicits and yet desperately isolated by his crippling melancholy. The clown figure is thus destined to wallow in misery to everyone else's amusement. The performative potential attached to genial melancholy offers Shakespearean comedy a clear avenue in which to develop its own sense of melancholy, both as a clownish foil (à la Jaques in *As You Like It*) and as a way to infuse emotional complexity into comic plots.

No Business Like Sad Business: Early Modern Melancholy

The majority of critics agree that the Renaissance represents a 'golden age of Melancholy'[30] during which a fascination with the concept informs much of the period's literary and scientific output in England, to the point of its cultural appropriation as a distinctively English trait. As Robert Burton eventually writes in his quintessential *The Anatomy of Melancholy*, 'we are of the same humours and inclinations as our predecessors were; you shall find us all alike, much at one, we and our sons'.[31] Discussions of melancholy thus relied on a blending of galenic and Aristotelian philosophies, being couched in the humoral terminology of purgation and balance while repeatedly bringing up the notion's spiritual dimension and propensity for ingenuity. A fixation with diagnosing and treating melancholy, apparent as early as Thomas Elyot's *Castel of Helth* (1539), also became a staple of English melancholy. Although foreign discourses on the subject by the likes of Jaques Ferrand and André Du Laurens were eagerly translated, domestic studies of melancholy, such as Burton's or Timothy Bright's, gained tremendous popularity and eventually came to play a crucial role in appropriating melancholy within specifically English norms. The insertion of political nationalism within philosophical enquiries mirrors a broader conflation of medical and literary aspirations in early modern treatises seeking to capitalise on the large-scale popularity of melancholy to satiate their developing readership. These early modern efforts to theorise melancholy provide a potent source of inspiration for Shakespeare's comic revision of the concept.

Timothy Bright's *Treatise of Melancholy* (1586) builds on galenic philosophy in order to offer an exhaustive portrait of English melancholy, oscillating between being a medical oeuvre and providing a theological discourse on the properties of the soul. Bright describes melancholy as the 'fullest of variety of passions [causing] strange symptoms of fancy and affection'[32] before positioning his anatomical model within an explicitly dogmatic framework that identifies the soul as the optimal connective site between mankind and God. For him, the detriment that melancholy can inflict on the soul proves worse than any form of bodily harm it may cause. Consequently, despite an extensive display of medical knowledge, the treatise identifies divine intervention, where faith leads the physician to successful treatment and spiritual health takes precedence over physical well-being, as the overriding cure for melancholy. In his concluding remarks, Bright conflates Christian doctrine and medical prognostication, asserting that the

> discrete application of the wise physician (who is made of God for the health of men) shall bring [God's help] unto you . . . for medicine is like a tool and instrument of the

sharpest edge, which not wisely guided nor handled with that cunning which thereto appertaineth, may bring present peril instead of health.[33]

In other words, purges, diets and concoctions may help to alleviate melancholic symptoms, but the ideal remedy is found in virtue and piety; the physician (and writer) must defer to divine will when apprehending the calamity of melancholy. In terms of outlining potential sources of influence for Shakespeare's revision of melancholy, the success of Bright's devout endeavour is not as important as his straddling of medical and literary spheres.

Likewise, André Du Laurens' *Discourse on the Preservation of Sight* (c. 1594, translated 1599) presents itself as both a private medical compendium (Du Laurens served as a physician for the duchess of Uzez) and as an exhaustive survey of melancholy aimed at a larger readership. The work opens with a general condemnation of the contemporary world, in which disease seemingly runs rampant, asking his readers to consider

> the lamentable times and miserable days, that are come upon us in this last and weakest age of the world, partly by reason of the commonnes and multitude of infirmities, partly by reason of the strangeness and rebelliousness of diseases breaking out more tediously than heretofore.[34]

The treatise offers relief in the form of instruction on how to alleviate or prevent diseases, among which is counted 'the store of histories, and means of dispelling the mournful fantasies of melancholic moods'.[35] Du Laurens acknowledges the existence of several types of melancholy, but his *Discourse* eschews a discussion of the melancholic disposition itself, as it is found in what he refers to as 'sound melancholic persons',[36] in favour of examining the disease of melancholy – what he defines in explicitly galenic terms as 'a kind of dotage without any fever, having for his ordinary companions, fear and sadness, without any apparent occasion'.[37] Du Laurens' treatise also offers another example of the scientific sensationalism previously alluded to, where the symptoms of melancholic patients are offered up as entertainment. At the onset of a chapter concerned with 'certain melancholic persons' and their 'strange imaginations', he writes that 'it behoves me now . . . (to the end that I may somewhat delight the reader) to set down some examples of such as have had the most fantastical and foolish imaginations of all others'.[38] The works of Bright and Du Laurens make significant contributions to the cultivation of melancholy as an object of interest that warrants serious empirical analysis while concurrently offering a potent source of entertainment. Their treatises attest to the growing versatility of melancholy as a subject of discourse in the period. Both physicians advocate its eventual eradication, but the fact that their work achieves great success in print speaks to a cultural entrenchment of melancholic philosophies within the early modern psyche that outlasts any medical reservations.

Both Robert Burton's *The Anatomy of Melancholy* (1621) and Jaques Ferrand's *A Treatise on Lovesickness* (1623, translated c. 1640) exert a great degree of influence on early modern conceptions of melancholy, presenting nearly exhaustive compendiums of the subject matter. Though published after Shakespeare's lifetime, both texts represent syntheses of prevalent and widely circulated melancholic discourses in early modern England throughout the sixteenth century. Ferrand's work is remarkable in that it focuses explicitly on the condition of lovesickness, maintaining a primarily medical focus in diligently expounding the methods of diagnosing, treating and, eventually, curing the illness. The result is a thoroughly early modern view of love-melancholy that combines a robust classical framework with innovative scientific approaches detailing 'pharmaceutical treatments specifically intended for love melancholy'.[39] Love-melancholy plays a crucial role in Shakespeare's comedies, particularly at the turn of the century, when works such as *Twelfth Night* mark the apogee of his comic revision of melancholy. Nevertheless, in its strict differentiation of natural and deviant incarnations of melancholy, its caution against idleness and its final praise of 'the honing and perfection of wisdom',[40] Ferrand's treatise adopts a generally moralistic view of melancholy that recalls the one propounded by Bright, which similarly blurs the boundaries between scientific, spiritual and literary intentions.

With five editions during his lifetime and nearly a dozen throughout the seventeenth century, Burton's *Anatomy* remains the epitome of the early modern literary enthralment with melancholy. 'I write of melancholy, by being busy to avoid melancholy,' Burton famously writes, '[since] there is no greater cause of melancholy than idleness.'[41] Immensely popular in England, *The Anatomy* delivers a study of gargantuan proportions that incorporates a plethora of sources, including lengthy sections on romantic and religious forms of melancholy. It proves encyclopaedic in the meticulous collection of sources and the examples it produces in delineating the rampant presence of melancholy in seventeenth-century society. For Burton, melancholy is a national concern that extends beyond the individual, evidenced by the fact, as he writes, that 'kingdoms, provinces, and politic bodies are likewise sensible and subject to this disease.'[42] Such a focus accounts for the larger preoccupation with both social and political reform in Burton's work. Simultaneously, the work adopts an introspective focus on the scholarly form of melancholy from which Burton professes to be suffering. *The Anatomy* is thus no different from contemporaneous treatises in its fluctuating between literary and scientific intentions. The fact that the overall study is embedded within a fictional narration by 'Democritus Junior' alerts us to the inherent dangers of treating Burton's work as a purely scientific encyclopaedia of melancholy. It remains, however, the most renowned and sustained discussion of the subject. In addition to providing an invaluable wealth of information on the complex and often dizzying subject, it presents melancholy as fundamentally paradoxical, its remarkable discursive staying power equalled only by its incredible philosophical versatility.

Michel de Montaigne's essays offer a potential Continental source of influence for Shakespeare's comic melancholy that similarly attests to the concept's dualistic nature. Montaigne's essays express a certain disdain for sadness or, more precisely, for its excessive posturing alongside attributes such as wisdom, virtue and conscience as a 'stupid and monstrous ornament'.[43] The essays criticise the more superficial and easily remedied sense of sorrow, noting that little can be gained or learned from '[mediocre] passions that allow themselves to be savoured and digested'.[44] Conversely, for Montaigne, true grief, the kind that dumbfounds 'the whole soul', serves an important purpose in its aftermath since it relaxes the soul 'into tears and lamentations, [causing it to] unbend, extricate itself, and gain more space and freedom'.[45] The essays remain too anchored within their own genre to be of direct influence on dramatic texts, yet both Shakespeare and Montaigne's works suggest that melancholy and mirth can (and should) exist in paradoxical symbiosis within the individual. Montaigne's idea that the 'soul is often agitated by diverse passions' recalls the humoral model of anatomy, in which the ideal of a dominant governing humour often gives way to a contested mingling of substances owing to the inherent 'volatility and pliancy' of our constitutions.[46]

The comedies nod to this understanding of emotions without necessarily drawing explicitly from it. Early modern conceptions of melancholy are constant in their scientific underpinnings yet fundamentally unstable in their definitions of their subject, which acts for them as a referent for a whole gamut of afflictions, from severe mental disturbances through physical ailments to a more mundane sense of sadness. Much like their classical ancestors, the works discussed here are representative of a broader social understanding of melancholy. Several critics have posited that Shakespeare would have been familiar with Bright's work[47] and, concurrently, with Thomas Wright's *Passions of the Minde* (1601), which examines the wide-ranging effects engendered by various extremes of passion such as sadness or fear, several of which can be tied to melancholy. All of these works provide multiple templates for Shakespeare to rework melancholy through the prism of comedy. Though I refer to specific works throughout this book, my dominant critical commentary revolves around Shakespeare's opportunistic distilling of various philosophies of melancholy throughout his comic canon.

The plays recuperate such a dovetailing of scientific and literary aims through their development of a comic sense of melancholy predicated upon performance and public fascination with the concept. The medical knowledge in Shakespeare remains subservient to dramatic intentions; scientific accuracy and medical rigour routinely give way to more colourful examples that extreme symptoms can procure. Even when characters express themselves with reference to humours, their melancholy simultaneously operates on a different level. Shakespeare never endorses a dominant doctrine for melancholic dramatisations, positioning the writings of Aristotle and Galen on the same level as the various early modern medical treatises on the subject: as easily recognisable signposts of melancholy that can be subsequently adapted to suit specific dramatic requirements. As the following chapters will demonstrate, comic melancholy in Shakespeare can seldom be accommodated solely through medical prognosis and cure, nor can it be strictly understood as a revision of the Aristotelian philosophy of genial melancholy. The plays both rely on and work against such traditions in developing comic characterisations of melancholy. Likewise (as a result of it, more precisely), Shakespearean comedy proves simultaneously to be anchored in the genre's rich history and to depart from it in innovative ways.

Comic History Through the Shakespearean Prism

As their mythical founders Thespis and Susarion suggest, Tragedy and Comedy have seemingly always existed as binary opposites of one another.[48] Aristotle's brief discussion of comedy in *Poetics*, as an 'imitation of men worse than the average; worse, however, not as regards any and every sort of fault, but only as regards one particular kind, the Ridiculous, which is a species of the Ugly',[49] should not be considered as a dismissal of the genre but rather, as Andrew Stott argues, as evidence of its position as 'a counterpoint to tragedy . . . for the purposes of producing a symmetrical literary system that reflects a conception of humanity as an amalgamation of two competing facets of character'.[50] The idea further suggests a set hierarchy between the two genres that inevitably undercuts the value of comedy (even as a valid counterpoint, comedy actually helps define what tragedy is by showcasing what it is not). The understanding of comedy as an imitation of human faults and limitations already conflates with characterisation (rather than plot), where specific flaws create a corresponding stock figure. Theophrastus' seminal *Character*, offering an array of short descriptions of character types meant to reflect 'the vicissitudes' of fourth-century Athens, exemplifies the association of comedy and characterisation that was to become one of its salient features through the ages.[51]

This sustained focus on characters helped usher in the shift in antiquity from the older comic model of Aristophanes and its dramatisation of current Athenian affairs, towards the New Comedy of Menander, whose depictions of stock characters and plots repositioned the genre as a more 'social comedy questioning contemporary Greek *attitudes*'.[52] The works of Menander solidify the shift by moving away from previous chorus-centric works, focusing instead on 'individual voices on stage' and catering to 'the audience's superior knowledge of what has really happened but with no means of apprising those on stage'.[53] It is this focus on comic characterisation that Plautus and Terence recuperate when they later develop their Roman 'comedy of manners'.[54] The lineage discussed here bears a strong influence on Renaissance comedy in general and on Shakespearean comedy in particular. Shakespeare routinely draws from stock figures (such as the melancholic) and classical plot structure (such as Plautus' *The Brother Meneachmi* when writing *The Comedy of Errors*). Yet, as will be discussed in greater length in the following chapters, Shakespearean comedy rapidly supersedes such classical models in fashioning its own comic characterisation of melancholy. The humour is rarely a mere counter to revelry but rather is an integral component of a character's comic ethos.

The prevailing early modern conceptualisations of comedy remained for the most part anchored in their Aristotelian underpinnings, depicting the genre primarily as a tragic foil that could educate audiences to proper mores and behaviours. Sidney's *Defense of Poesy* echoes Aristotle in defining comedy as

> an imitation of the common errors of our life, which he representeth in the most ridiculous and scornful sort that may be, so as it is impossible that any beholder can be content to be such as one. Now, as in geometry the oblique must be known as well as the right, and in arithmetic the odd as well as the

even, so in the actions of our life who seeth not the filthiness
of evil wanteth a great foil to perceive the beauty of virtue.[55]

Comedy serves a valid literary and humanistic purpose,
according to Sidney, as long as 'the comical part', he cau-
tions, 'be not upon such scornful matters as stir laughter
only, but, mixed with it, that delightful teaching which is
the end of poesy'.[56] The *Defence* similarly levies a widespread early modern criticism of works seeking to blend
tragic and comic genres into what Sidney describes as the
'mongrel tragicomedy', in which 'neither right tragedies
nor right comedies, mingling kings and clowns . . . so as
neither the admiration and commiseration nor the right
sportfulness is . . . obtained'.[57] As this book will suggest,
Shakespearean comedy undercuts such an attitude from its
onset through its development of comic melancholy, con-
structing in its place a melancomic model that moves away
from comical stereotypes and towards more emotionally
nuanced dramatic works. Though Shakespeare is not the
only playwright to resist such attitudes, his comic engagement with melancholy fundamentally alters the afterlife of
both notions by suggesting their oscillatory (and complementary) comic qualities.

There's No Crying in Comedy! An Overview of Non-Shakespearean Melancholy

The beginnings of English comedy, rooted in the modes and
practices of Christian morality drama, betray a preoccupation with the mitigation of its characteristic topsy-turvy revelry, one that anticipates the medicalised language quoted
earlier from *The Taming of the Shrew*. Nicholas Udall's
Ralph Roister Doister (c. 1552) opens on such a pre-emptive
defence of the mirthful jesting that is to follow. Its prologue
claims that it is

Used in an honest fashion:
For Mirth prolongeth life, and causeth health,
Mirth recreates our spirits and voideth pensiveness,
Mirth increaseth amity, not hindering our wealth,
Mirth is to be used both of more and less,
Being mixed with virtue in decent comeliness.

						(Prologue, 7–12)

The passage stresses the health benefits of the merriment that will follow, using medical allusions to validate the comedy that will be staged. Thus, Matthew Merrygreeke opens the play by discussing the value of mirth, declaring that 'as long as liveth the merry man (they say) / As doth the sorry man, and longer by a day' (I, i, 1–2). In early English comedy, being funny seemingly is not enough; the play must also prolong life and engender well-being. The imbued medical vernacular remains mainly tongue-in-cheek and plays such as *Ralph Roister Doister* and *Gammer Gurton's Needle* (printed 1575) prove more concerned with the farcical potential of gender clashes, sexual innuendos and the general clownery of their characters than with melancholy *per se*. Still, the extolling of the virtues associated with the comic genre carries into the works of pioneering early modern playwrights, such as George Peele's *The Old Wives Tale* (printed in 1595), where stories (on and off the stage) become a means by which to 'drive away the time trimly' (86) as Old Madge entertains three brothers with an outlandish tale of wandering knights, evil conjurers and damsels in distress. Peele's comedy, a wonderfully odd blend of magic, romance and theatrics which never directly addresses melancholy, suggests that storytelling itself counteracts tragedy and that even the telling of a 'heavy tale, / Sad in mood and sober in thy cheer' (182–3) can bring about merriment. Although melancholy abounds within revenge plays and other tragedies that populate the decade (Thomas Kyd's *The Spanish Tragedy* and Christopher

Marlowe's *Doctor Faustus* are prime examples of such a phenomenon), it does not receive any substantial comic treatment at this time.

A sustained comic reliance on melancholy emerges in the
1590s, most notably in the courtly drama of John Lyly. Lyly's
interest in the notion revolves primarily around its purported inferences of nobility and intellectualism, as well as
its already burgeoning popularity as an affectation. His characters, anchored soundly within the tradition of courtly love,
show a clear propensity for melancholy, generally developed
within the supernatural auspices of magic or divine intervention. Plays such as *Endymion* (1591) epitomise Lyly's
showcasing of grief-stricken characters whose seemingly
hopeless longings are resolved ultimately through regal or
godly intervention. *Endymion*'s titular character, desperately
in love with the moon, Queen Cynthia, incurs the jealous
ire of her lady-in-waiting, Tellus, who casts a spell on him
and plunges him into an inescapable sleep for decades. The
play draws on the potential for derision of its protagonist's
love-melancholy by underscoring the hindrance that such
excessive displays represent. Endymion's extreme bouts of
lovesickness (though he sleeps for the better part of the play)
clearly stress the need for their eradication. As his friend
Eumenides puts it early on, 'that melancholy blood must be
purged, which draweth you to a dotage no less miserable
than monstrous' (I, i, 22–4). Queen Cynthia eventually inter-
cedes and restores him to good health, eradicating his melancholic tendencies in the process. *Endymion* not only offers
one of Lyly's most extensive engagements with melancholy,
it also provides a perfect example of the lack of any comic
treatment of the humour in his works. Though melancholy is
linked to the courtly affectations of the protagonist, the bulk
of the comedy resides within the subplot, which depicts the
misadventures of the braggard Sir Tophas, an old knight figure in the same tradition as Don Quixote. Melancholy holds

centre stage in Lyly's comedy but also appears disconnected from the play's comedic undertones, a pattern that repeats itself in other comedies such as *Gallathea* (1592), in which the central plot of cross-dressing shepherdesses falling in love lends itself to potent melancholic pangs, while the subplot of three brothers seeking to become apprentices supplies most of the comedic moments.

Lyly's drama contributes to the already established popularity of melancholy as an affect, while casting it explicitly within the scope of the romanticised depictions of nobility. In *Midas* (1591), the servant Licio answers Motto's affirmation that he is 'as melancholy as a cat' by advising him to 'say heavy, dull, and doltish [instead]. Melancholy is the crest of / Courtiers' arms, and now every base companion, / Being in his muble fubles, say he is melancholy' (V, ii, 101–4). Lylian drama remains a notable precursor to, rather than a prime example of, comic melancholy as this book understands it. Nowhere does it showcase the degree of complexity and revisionism that Shakespearean comedy demonstrates in its dramatic development of melancholy. Both the romanticising of melancholy and its potentially troublesome social ubiquity resonate within Shakespearean comedy, particularly in plays such as *Love's Labour's Lost* and *Twelfth Night*, which explore the comic intricacies of love-melancholy and the dangers of excessive emotional longings. The frequency of such allusions alone suggests that Shakespearean comedy loosens the term's ties to nobility while it morphs into a multivalent designation of *dramatic* sadness.

The first substantial comic engagement with melancholy originates within the genre of the humour play, a subset of English comedy that enjoyed scintillating albeit brief popularity on the early modern stage at the close of the sixteenth century. As Peter Womack explains, the comedy of humours, predicated on the exacerbation of the tenets of the four bodily humours, is produced when the incontinence manifests itself in the arbitrary predominance of one of them, a systemic disorder which gives rise to temperament bias in moderate cases, and extremely to disease and madness. To the extent that this happens – and consequently that the typing serves to distinguish dramatis personae from one another – the humorous individual becomes a monster, because the flow of humour is governing the affections of the heart . . . and because the overrunning of the stable distinction between containing and contained produces uncontrolled appetites and discharges.[58]

While several dramatists dabble in the genre, the works of George Chapman and Ben Jonson embody the English humour play, where the critiquing and purging of humours, manners and a plethora of quirky behaviour traits become the predominant dramatic focus. Both Jonson and Chapman help to grow melancholy's dramatic popularity while pigeonholing its development as a source of ridicule on the early modern stage. Chapman is credited with the genre's inception with plays such as *The Blind Beggar of Alexandria* (1595), which survives in fragments, and *A Humourous Day's Mirth* (1599), considered the first complete comedy of humours.[59] Ben Jonson's humour comedies are of greater importance in terms of establishing a dramatic framework to depict humours onstage. *Every Man In his Humour* (1598) and its companion piece, *Every Man Out of His Humour* (1599), stage a parade of unruly humours that end up methodically purged by witty trickster figures. The process elicits laughter, but also offers a vehicle for Jonson's clear distaste for the perceived governing powers of humoralism. In the Prologue to *Every Man Out of His Humour*, the Jonsonian mouthpiece, Asper, deplores how a humour may

By metaphor, apply itself
Unto the general disposition:
As when some one peculiar quality

Doth so possess a man, that it doth draw
All his affects, his spirits, and his powers,
In their confluctions, all to run one way.
But that a rook by wearing a pied-feather,
The cable hat-band, or the three-piled ruff,
A yard of shoe-tie, or the Switzers' knot
On his French garters, should affect a humour!
O, it is more than most ridiculous.

(Prologue, 103–14)

Jonson's characters are colourful and engaging, but his approach to humours remains largely satirical. His critique predominantly takes aim at the evasion of responsibility that comes with humorous affectations. For him, humours not only exert a totalising effect on the individual, they also morph into absurd behavioural traits that can be triggered by wearing certain items of clothing. Asper recognises that a man may exhibit a 'peculiar quality' superseding his behaviour, but refuses to accept that it can be remedied by any physical or medical mean. As Richard Dutton puts it, humours in Jonson stand as

a moral condition as much as a mental one, reducing [character's] full status as human beings. In their folly they have lost touch with reality, creating for themselves private worlds of fantasy and illusion which, however comic, are not harmless; they attack the fabric of social harmony, creating the friction and mistrust which run through the play.[60]

Melancholy is never dealt with extensively and appears as one of several traits being paraded onstage and ultimately curbed, its comic potential inevitably trumped by that of jealousy, braggardery or puritanism. Jonson's humour plays also offer a synecdochic example of the dramatic veering off that the genre itself eventually undertakes. The genre gradually transforms 'humours' into a bloated tapestry of behavioural quirks, mannerisms, attitudes and accessories that become the target of dramatic ridicule. As their popularity increased, humour plays moved away from the philosophies of humoralism, to the point where, in some cases, the mention of 'humours' in a play's title amounted to an early modern marketing ploy more than a dramatic device.[61]

The dramatic landscape of the seventeenth century bears witness to a return of sorts towards humoral interest, as the comedies of playwrights such as John Fletcher, Francis Beaumont, John Ford and Phillip Massinger show an increasingly medicalised approach to the dramatisation of humours. In plays such as Fletcher's *The Humourous Lieutenant* (1619) and Massinger's *A Very Woman* (1619–22) the diagnosis, treatment and eventual cure of humoral afflictions by medical practitioners holds as much dramatic importance as the comedy that ensues from various characters' humoral extravagances. *The Nice Valour* (1615–25) presents an intriguing protagonist, known as the Passionate Lord, who

> Runs through all the Passions of mankind,
> And shifts 'em strangely too one while in love,
> And that so violent, that for want of business.
> He'll court the very Prentice of a Laundresse,
> Though she have kib'd heeles: and in's melancholy agen,
> He will not brooke an Empress, though thrice fairer
> Than ever Maud was.   (I, i, 50–6)

The performative nature of humoral affectation comes across strongly in this description; the speech alerts the audience to the humours the Lord will subsequently enact onstage. The Passionate Lord, through his numerous appearances onstage, exhibits the various bodily humours in sequence. The Lord's problem, in effect, is not related to an excess of certain humours but, rather, to an endless fluctuation between them.

Humours succeed one another and 'the taile of his melancholy / Is alwayes the head of his anger' (III, iv, 5–6). The play impresses the connection between humours and theatrical performances. Beaumont and Fletcher's plays rely increasingly on the scientific diagnosis, treatment and cure of humoral ailments, as opposed to the social correctives heralded by humours plays. Melancholy appears extensively in such comedies, epitomised in John Ford's *The Lover's Melancholy* (1628), where a physician (Corax) is asked to cure the melancholy that afflicts Palador, ruler of Cyprus. The entire play revolves around the proper diagnosing and treatment of Palador's melancholy, which, Corax tells us, 'is not as you conceive, indisposition / Of body, but the mind's disease' (III, i, 109–10). The physician eventually triumphs after having Palador witness an elaborate masque depicting the varied strains of melancholy that can afflict an individual. Posing the correct diagnosis magically lifts the melancholic veil that afflicted the patient. Here, melancholy is intrinsically connected to the comedy it occupies, but its treatment is firmly encased in the medicalised tradition described earlier; the physician more than his patient stands as the comic hero.

Interestingly, given the ongoing popularity of humours on the English stage under various permutations, Shakespeare never writes a humour comedy, either in the Jonsonian sense or in the seventeenth-century medicalised vogue described above. Critics such as Giorgio Melchiori have suggested that *The Merry Wives of Windsor* represents Shakespeare's response to the humour play genre.[62] Portions from the play invitingly lend themselves to a parody of humour comedies, such as when Corporal Nym delivers this assessment of Falstaff:

> And this is true. I like not the humour of
> lying. He hath wronged me in some humours. I
> should have borne the humoured letter to her; but I
> have a sword, and it shall bite upon my necessity.

He loves your wife; there's the short and the long.
My name is Corporal Nym; I speak and I avouch 'tis
true. My name is Nym, and Falstaff loves your wife.
Adieu. I love not the humour of bread and cheese,
and there's the humour of it. Adieu.   (II, i, 122–30)

The repeated mentions of the word 'humour' in nine lines
of text point to a critique of the genre, depriving the concept of any meaningful dramatic impact by exacerbating its
potential uses. Other than a few key moments such as Nym's
speech, *The Merry Wives,* much like the rest of Shakespeare's
comic canon, never seems to follow the humour play model.
None of his comic works include the word 'humour' in
their titles, nor do they approach the subject (melancholy
especially) under similar farcical underpinnings. His comedy achieves greater complexity by weaving the melancholy
into the dramatic fabric. In charting out the dual revisions
of melancholy and comedy that Shakespeare undertakes,
this book aims to address such a critical oversight in Shakespeare studies, where melancholy is seldom considered as an
intrinsic comic element.

Why so Serious? The Problem of the Melancomic in Shakespeare Criticism

The idea that Shakespearean comedy bears witness to an
ongoing clash of mirthful and sorrowful elements is well
established in critical history. As early as 1765, Samuel
Johnson remarked that

Shakespeare has united the powers of exciting laughter
and sorrow not only in one mind, but in one composition.
Almost all his plays are divided between serious and ludicrous characters, and, in the successive evolutions of the
design, sometimes produce seriousness and sorrow, and
sometimes levity and laughter.[63]

This affective polarity, predicated on a distinction between amiable and antagonistic characters, lies at the heart of archetypical studies of Shakespearean comedy by C. L. Barber and Northrop Frye and their perception of the genre as inherently exclusionary, a dramatic world in which the driving comic force sharply divides characters who embrace celebration from those who oppose it. Their studies of festivity, rites and the communal dimension of comedy provide the original caveat on which to interpret Shakespearean comedy as the contrast of mirthful and pessimistic forces.

Within this model, melancholic characters are depicted as nemeses to merriment. Barber writes of Jaques in *As You Like It* that his 'factitious melancholy, which critics have made too much of as a "psychology," serves primarily to set him at odds both with society and with Arden and so motivate contemplative mockery'.[64] There is nothing wrong *per se* with such a reading of the character, but it drastically overlooks the incredible potency of melancholy in the play, which goes beyond individual characterisation. Likewise, Frye places Shakespearean melancholics within a category of characters he terms comic *idiotes*, dramatic figures representing 'the focus of the anticomic mood [and a] withdrawal from the comic society'.[65] Frye maintains that such characters not only hinder but actually threaten the process of self-discovery that characterises the genre. As he explains, the *idiotes*

> is usually isolated from the action by being the focus of the anticomic mood, and so may be the technical villain, like Don John, the butt, like Malvolio and Falstaff, or simply opposed by temperament to festivity, like Jaques. Although the villainous, the ridiculous, and the misanthropic are closely associated in comedy, there is enough variety of motivation to indicate that *idiotes* is not a character type, like the clown, though typical features recur, but a structural device that may use a variety of characters.[66]

Though diminutive, Frye's interpretation gets us closer than Barber's to a proper understanding of the function of melancholic characters in Shakespearean comedy. As will become clear in later chapters, the characters listed in the passage above (save Falstaff) are all relevant to an exploration of comic melancholy in Shakespeare, suggesting that the idea may indeed be conceived of as a structural device on the level of characters. Still, the binary of inclusion and exclusion present in these understandings of Shakespearean comedy fails to properly delineate the dramatic function of melancholy, which is never easily or successfully excluded from comic celebrations.

The dichotomy of comic characterisation outlined above informs much of the scholarship that follows, be it concordant or reactionary. Even analyses that account for the darker undertones of Shakespearean comedy seek to designate characters as either facilitating or impeding comic resolution, whether they be Frye's *idiotes*, Levin's 'playboys' and 'killjoys' or, as Kenneth Muir writes, downright 'evil [characters] who threaten the comic resolution'.[67] Again, such readings perform a disservice to melancholic characters by absorbing them into the larger category of anticomic foils. Shakespearean melancholics transcend such classification. They permeate countless designations within the plays; they are men, women, merchants, dukes, jesters, heiresses, lovers, heroes or villains. Melancholic characters become emblematic of the blend of mirthful and unhappy elements that characterise Shakespearean comedy in general. They provide evidence that the genre finds its nexus in tonal dissonance, in the symbiotic conflation of comic and uncomic elements. In other words, if comic scenes can populate Shakespeare's tragedy and history plays – the porter scene in *Macbeth* or Falstaff's involvement in the history plays, for example – the reciprocal association may hold true as well, if only on the level of dramatic makeup. From this thwarting of generic structures we may infer that some elements found in Shakespearean comedy are not intrinsically comic, *nor do they need to be*. To construe Shakespearean comedy as an amalgamation of different thematic and tonal fragments permits the understanding of comic melancholy as a valid mode of self-representation that is not only viable but dramatically necessary. This interpretation echoes that of Karen Newman, who contends that Shakespeare's characters 'are marked by what we might call a residue beyond their function . . . as agents, beyond their relation to specific actions'.[68] For Newman, the inherent opposition found in comic characters (dating back to Samuel Johnson) is best understood as a strategy towards more realistic characterisations. As she writes, the real conflict in Shakespearean comedy transpires 'between two different and opposing conventions, one which foregrounds itself and its artifice, the other which conceals itself by seeming "real"'.[69]

Newman's understanding of dovetailing methods of characterisation in Shakespeare relying on artificial constructs to produce more 'life-like' representations resonates with the dual revisionist process that this book ascribes to Shakespearean comedy. This idea also recalls Katherine Maus's discussion of what she terms the 'radically synecdochic' nature of early modern theatre when contrasting the genre's physical limitations with its fervent appeal to the imagination.[70] By using the artifices of stage melancholy, Shakespeare manages to create a more complex representation of the humour which, in turn, reshapes its philosophical underpinnings. Thus, in an attempt to chart the dual rethinking of comedy and melancholy that Shakespeare undertakes as early as in *The Comedy of Errors*, I focus not so much on melancholic characters but on comic characters that are melancholic.

While individual melancholic characters in Shakespearean comedy have received a substantial amount of critical attention over the years, this effort has been mainly undertaken within larger interpretations of specific plays. Most readings of *The Merchant of Venice*, for example, offer a cause for Antonio's sadness, but they do so in a manner that betrays a certain critical anxiousness in their urge to address the issue and move on to other concerns, treating melancholy as a stepping stone towards other lines of enquiry. I do not necessarily reject this interpretive strategy, but I seek to move beyond it by considering the functionality of melancholy within the genre of Shakespearean comedy, rather than within a given play. In doing so, I echo Jeremy Lopez's vision of a systemic comic failure in Shakespeare denoted by the absence of certain characters from a play's conclusion – 'characters', Lopez writes, who serve as 'a reminder of the fact that the comedy has not entirely neatly tied up loose ends'.[71] These characters, 'whose bizarre energy', he adds, 'is allowed to pervade the play to the point where they have an interpretative effect disproportionate to what the genre would seem to require of them', represent an analogous dramatic process to that of the intersecting rethinking of melancholy and comedy that Shakespeare undertakes throughout his career.[72]

'To tell sad stories': Sorrowful Terminology

'How canst thou part sadness and melancholy?'

Armado's question to his page in *Love's Labour's Lost* (I, ii, 7) introduces a potential roadblock that a study of melancholy in Shakespearean comedy might encounter: are all references to sadness to be considered as melancholy? It is certainly true that not every utterance of sorrow in comedy immediately translates into a melancholic affectation that seriously complicates comic structures. Going as far back as Frye, the genre has often been perceived as 'a structure embodying a variety of moods, the majority of which are comic in the sense of festive or funny, but a minority of which, in any

well-constructed comedy, are not'.[73] Not only can a sorrowful premise exist in comedy, but it may also serve to
intensify the eventual celebratory climax (as it often does in
Shakespeare). On some level, early modern dramatists use
terms such as 'melancholy', 'sorrowful' or 'sad' as somewhat homologous variants within the larger lexicon of sadness. This practice develops concurrently with a widespread
reliance on humoral language as a dramatic tool of self-
representation that further complicates the issue. Hence,
Mistress Ford's question to her husband, 'why art thou /
Melancholy?' (II, i, 135–6), in *The Merry Wives of Windsor* and Antonio's declaration at the onset of the *Merchant
of Venice*, 'I know not why I am so sad' (I, i, 1) both hint
at a similar emotion. Yet Mistress Ford's question is soon
dismissed – 'I melancholy? I am not melancholy' (II, i, 137)
– while Antonio's unresolved melancholy, as I argue later,
represents one of the play's salient features. Similarly, in *A
Midsummer Night's Dream*, Theseus' order to 'awake the
pert and nimble spirit of mirth [and] Turn melancholy forth
to funerals; / The pale companion is not for our pomp'
(I, i, 13–15) suggests a rigid binary of mirth and melancholy
similar to the one alluded to by Berowne near the end of
Love's Labour's Lost when he declares, 'to move wild laughter in the throat of death? / It cannot be. It is impossible. /
Mirth cannot move a soul in agony' (V, ii, 845–7). Theseus'
speech, however, does not carry the more ominous quality
of Berowne's in the wake of the French king's passing.

Though the word 'melancholy' and its derivations are
used extensively within Shakespeare's comic canon, I focus
on instances that carry a larger function at the level of form,
to the extent that they operate as an essential cog in the
mechanism of Shakespearean comedy. I use the lexical fields
of melancholy and sadness somewhat reciprocally within
this frame, as I do with 'wistfulness' in later chapters when
referring to the spectral sense of melancholy that pervades

Shakespeare's final group of plays. Conversely, since this book attempts to extricate humour (in the generic sense) from the humoral (in its larger philosophical sense), I wish to avoid for my readers the sort of confusion that brought on blank stares from colleagues when mentioning my work on comic humour. For the purpose of clarity, I will use the term 'humour' only in reference to matters of humoralism, so as to not confound it with its alternative connotation (as a synonym for comedy). The latter connotation emerges from the concept of bodily humours, but it appears near 1680, where possessing a 'sense of humour' begins to refer to 'that quality of action, speech, or writing, which excites amusement; oddity, jocularity, facetiousness, comicality, fun'.[74] Shakespeare's comic treatment of melancholy both enables and adds complexity to the genre by moving away from the obvious dramatic avenues of mockery and derision. In distilling various philosophical discourses of melancholy into an unprecedented dramatic and affective incarnation, Shakespeare places the tenets of comedy and melancholy in a close dialogical relationship that effectively alters both of their theoretical afterlives.

In this sense, Shakespeare's dual revision of comedy and melancholy anticipates Joseph Addison's eighteenth-century aesthetics of laughter and its inherent shift from a 'transgressive category [within] a moral discourse . . . into an aesthetics of pleasurable response, sympathetic laughter, and comedy'.[75] Critics such as Ronald Paulson have linked Addison's theory to Cervantes (and, tangentially, to Shakespeare), suggesting that *Don Quixote* undercuts 'the conventional definition of comedy as satire [and] of laughter as ridicule'.[76] It is not my intention to dwell extensively on such lineage as yet another potential source of Continental influence for Shakespearean comedy, but to hold it as further proof that Shakespeare's melancomic undertaking happens at a time when both concepts undergo systemic ideological upheavals.

Shakespeare's development of comic melancholy belongs in such a conversation but also represents its clearest and most influential embodiment within early modernity.

This framework requires a novel understanding of melancholic characters that pushes off from the seminal humoral criticism concerned with early modern melancholy. The contributions of Michael Schoenfeldt and Gail Kern Paster in this regard have been instrumental in outlining the ways in which humoral theory pervades the discursive, social and scientific spheres of early modern England, not merely in moments of emotional or physical trauma but also, as Schoenfeldt puts it, in the realm of 'mundane activities' such as eating and bodily evacuation.[77] For Schoenfeldt, these daily acts are as much conducive to self-fashioning as extraordinary moments of revelry and excess since early modern humoral theory stresses control over one's desire more than their fulfilment.[78] Within Schoenfeldt's frame, Shakespeare's plays provide a particularly salient reflection of an 'inner reality via external demeanor',[79] a reliance on physiology to properly sketch out human emotions, desires and intricacies. Using the sonnets as his primary example, Schoenfeldt argues that a drive towards the regulation of desires informs much of the period's conceptualisation of selfhood. 'The Renaissance', he writes,

> seems to have imagined identity to emerge from the success one experiences at controlling a series of undifferentiated and undifferentiating desires. To give way to one's various passions is to yield the self to the kinds of inconstancy with which the Sonnets themselves continually battle on a variety of fronts.[80]

The oppositional dynamics Schoenfeldt describes resonate in the binary of self-control and emotional release that characterises Shakespearean comedy. Schoenfeldt comes close to uncovering the functionality of comic melancholy, particularly in his idea that the optimal aim of Shakespearean comedy 'is to find a way to direct such desire to socially approved ends'.[81] Still, his model does not engage with comic melancholy in any significant way, highlighting once more the critical shortcomings that come to define the issue. Though Schoenfeldt accurately identifies the opposition that melancholics encounter throughout Shakespearean comedy – through the medium of characters like *The Merchant of Venice*'s Nerissa, who preaches self-control and regulation to her mistress in her first appearance on stage (II, i) – Shakespeare's revision of melancholy escapes such a definition. Even in *Merchant*, there exists a strong impression that Antonio's melancholy, though bothersome to other characters, serves a vital purpose within the comedy beyond advocacy for regulation. Shakespeare's comic melancholy eschews self-regulation because the characterisations it offers are never strictly humoral.

Gail Kern Paster's writings on humours contrast Schoenfeldt's conception of the body as embedded in daily regulatory practices by stressing its basic instability. As she explains, 'the humoral body should be characterized not only by its physical openness but also by its emotional instability and volatility, by an internal microclimate knowable ... more for changeability than for stasis'.[82] For Paster, passions are unruly and inevitably threaten the subject's mastery of his abilities, but such fluctuations are to be expected in the course of everyday life. More central to her contention is the notion of humoral subjectivity, in which humours not only provide individuals with 'characteristic ways of responding to their worlds', but form the basis of what she terms 'a fluid form of consciousness inhabited by, even as it inhabits, a universe composed of analogous elements'.[83] Paster's work unearths the fundamentally social nature of early modern humoralism, when emotional experiences always transpire within a dense cultural context. Early modern drama relies on this sociocultural realm as a way of understanding, navigating and affirming oneself within the early modern world.[84] Yet, such a framework only tells part of the story as far as Shakespearean depictions of melancholy are concerned. As Paster accurately points out, for Shakespeare's comic characters, 'humoral thinking is the basis for self-understanding and self-justification in a hostile world'.[85] These subjection systems reflect the dialogical relationship of melancholic characters *within* each play, but Shakespeare's treatment of comic melancholy exceeds this interpretative level. It allows for a symbiotic rethinking of melancholy in conjunction with the underpinnings of comic theatre so as to understand the profound transformation that melancholy and comedy undergo concurrently in Shakespeare. This divergence is particularly salient in later comic plays, which eventually do away with individual characterisations of melancholy in favour of an intangible sense of wistfulness that resituates them as generic concerns.

There is commensurate value in both critics' reinterpretation of humoral theories. Thinking back to the passage from *Taming* cited earlier, the lexicon of comic characters in Shakespeare is by and large humoral, a fact that validates the cultural systems that Paster and Schoenfeldt illustrate. If there is a drawback to their analyses as far as comic melancholy is concerned, it is that it nudges subsequent critical efforts into a similarly constricted scope of research, where the notion is understood mainly as a synecdochic embodiment of larger ideological movements within the period. This focus is best exemplified by works such as Adam Kitzes' *The Politics of Melancholy from Spenser to Milton* and Douglas Trevor's *The Poetics of Melancholy in Early Modern England*. Each author devotes a chapter to examples of Shakespearean melancholy (in *As You Like It* and *Hamlet*, respectively), but neither text capitalises on the potent friction that comic melancholy offers. Most recently, Drew Daniel's *The Melancholy Assemblage: Affect and Epistemology in the English Renaissance* and Erin Sullivan's *Beyond Melancholy: Sadness and Selfhood in Renaissance England* broke new critical ground in offering definitions of early modern melancholy as a fundamentally multivalent concept. *The Melancholy Assemblage* contends that the affect cannot be understood without an 'epistemologically framed account' that considers both sufferer and witness under manifold incarnations.[86] For Daniel, early modern melancholy thus exists both individually and as 'a plural social and material assemblage of bodies being together'.[87] Conversely, Sullivan situates melancholy as a one of several iterations of the 'complex emotional identity' tied to ideas of sadness in the period.[88] In doing so, she examines the way early modern writers understood 'seemingly contradictory approaches to sadness and selfhood [and] how they attempted to divide this capacious passion into related, but nevertheless theoretically distinct, categories of grief or worldly sorrow, melancholy, godly sorrow, and despair'.[89]

My work benefits importantly from such scholarship, as I join my voice to theirs in arguing for the pluralistic nature of early modern melancholy, which cannot be restricted to any particular niche, be it cultural, scientific or theological. I align myself with Daniel's key methodological understanding of melancholy, but I depart from him by attending overtly to comedy and making a sustained argument about the relationship between melancholy, philosophy and theatrical form, which is not a primary concern of *The Melancholy Assemblage*. Similarly, though Sullivan's work touches on comic depictions of melancholy (Shakespeare's particularly), she does so mainly in a humoral context, drawing attention to 'the raucous comedy that could arise from melancholy's very earthy connection to digestion, scatology, and the viscera'.[90] My work acknowledges such a focus but departs from it in suggesting that Shakespearean comedy presents multiple versions of melancholy which significantly transform the affect's relationship to the comic genre in the process.

The philosophy of comic melancholy this book eventually sketches out is in itself plural. The consideration of what I term the fundamentally melancomic quality of Shakespeare's comedies stems from their astounding revision, interpretation and rethinking of classical and early modern philosophies of melancholy. It stands at the intersection of social, medical and literary engagements with the ideas outlined above. The melancomic thus represents the dramatic, aesthetic and emotional endgame of the ongoing transformation of Shakespearean comedy that this book uncovers. As I see it, by reworking and eventually rejecting traditional philosophies of melancholy, Shakespeare orients his comic style towards the melancomic as a fundamentally plural concept. As a generic mode, it offers a novel way to denote Shakespeare's late works that centre on their generic hybridity and substantial melancholic character. Conversely, the term articulates both the complex dramatic tenor of Shakespeare's later comedies and the emotional response that they invite. The play brings its audience to delight in the intangible sense of sorrow it promulgates through the staging of powerful traumas and their miraculous resolutions. Ultimately, the melancomic bridges the aesthetic and theoretical gaps between Shakespeare's comic transformation of melancholy and our modern understandings of nostalgia, melancholia and a range of affective and performative concepts.

Melancholia and the Shakespearean Comic Spectre

As this book eventually suggests, there exist interesting interplays between psychoanalytic accounts of melancholia and Shakespeare that need to be redirected into a dialogue with comic melancholy. The works of Sigmund Freud show his interest in Shakespeare both culturally and scientifically; *Hamlet* looms large in his seminal essay 'Of Mourning and Melancholia', notably in the definition of melancholia as 'the loss of an object that is withdrawn from consciousness'.[91] Yet, Freud seldom engages with comedies within his psychoanalytic interpretations of the notion.

On the whole, I argue against reading backwards, from psychoanalysis *into* Shakespearean melancholy, a practice that still permeates relevant criticism with surprising frequency. The early modern concept of melancholy and its psychoanalytic counterpart of melancholia cannot be dealt with interchangeably despite obvious theoretical, historical and philosophical kinships.[92] Shakespeare's development of melancholy, comic or otherwise, resides on the theatrical stage, oscillating between inner reality and performed exteriority. Moreover, the comic vein of melancholy that Shakespearean drama puts forth resists psychoanalytic interpretations through its recuperation of the notion as an intrinsic element of comic theatre that transforms the genre itself. Freud's theory of melancholia does intersect with the Shakespearean philosophy of melancholy outlined here at various critical junctions. The description of melancholia as a combination of mourning and narcissism that 'behaves like an open wound, drawing investments to itself from all sides . . . draining the ego to the point of complete impoverishment',[93] echoes comic characterisations of melancholy such as those of Antonio or Jaques in their suggestion that such an excessive degree of self-investment proves harmful to the afflicted individual. More importantly, comedy seemingly provides the 'high counter-investment' that Freud deems crucial in countering the forces melancholia.[94] Comic melancholy, as developed here, allows us to rethink more theoretical definitions of melancholy within emotional and theatrical dimensions.

This book aims to redirect melancholia's Shakespearean heritage so as to account for its comic ancestry, suggesting that the *transformation* of melancholy throughout Shakespearean comedy finds strong echoes within modern conceptions of melancholia. My contention is that the altered notion of melancholy that ultimately appears in Shakespeare informs psychoanalytic theories of melancholy as much as – if not to a greater degree than – tragic examples such as *Hamlet*. The ethereal, ubiquitous sense of longing it suggests can be understood in similar fashion as the subconscious and unnameable void created by melancholia. More recent engagements with the gendered, performative and emotional implications of melancholia bear a similar emotional imprint.[95] As I argue later on, the works of Judith Butler and Sianne Ngai both take a cue from the powerful wistfulness of later plays such as *Twelfth Night* and *The Winter's Tale*. Definitions of gender such as Butler's, which argues that the notion denotes 'a constructed identity, a performative accomplishment which the mundane asocial audience, including the actors themselves, come to believe and to perform in the mode of belief' benefits from a connection with Shakespearean comic melancholy since the plays ultimately advocate for a validation of the affect as a necessary component of emotional life.[96] The process of recuperating undesirable emotions that Sianne Ngai outlines in *Ugly Feelings* will also be reconceptualised through its purported comic heritage. Though she distances her work from melancholia, Ngai's recuperative effort towards 'negative affects for their critical productivity' yields an interesting parallel with later explorations of melancholy in Shakespeare's career.[97] Her consideration of tone in literary works and the related 'category that makes these affective values meaningful with regard to how one understands as a totality within an equally holistic matrix of social relations' will be of particular use in examining the late stages of Shakespeare's comic investment in melancholy.[98]

This book effectively bridges the gap highlighted here in its introduction between the rich amalgamation of philosophical conceptions of melancholy forming its early modern incarnation and its contemporary permutations in psychoanalysis, affect studies and performance studies. Without disregarding the long and insightful lineage of tragic melancholy, Shakespeare's comic revision offers us the opportunity to alter our current theoretical gazes to that effect. The nine plays I examine effectively sketch out the progressive rethinking of melancholy and comedy that Shakespeare undertakes and the lasting impact that such a process exerts on the philosophical afterlife of both concepts.

Shakespearean Melancholy

The following chapters attest to the mutual transformation of comedy and melancholy that Shakespeare develops. They first point to the gradual breakdown of traditional representations of melancholy in Shakespeare before turning their attention to its transformation into what I come to refer to as a comic philosophy of melancholy. I initially consider the ways in which early Shakespearean comedies interrogate established conceptions of melancholy such as lovesickness, mourning and interiority. Both *The Comedy of Errors* and *Love's Labour's Lost*, I suggest in Chapter 2, apply pressure on these melancholic expressions by developing them within explicitly comedic settings. In *Errors*, we encounter idealised descriptions of melancholy that recall its Aristotelian roots (Antipholus of Syracuse's intellectualised profession of interiority) and romanticised undertones (Egeon's stoic recounting of the loss of his family). Conversely, *Love's Labour's* depicts a more physiological sense of melancholy, anchored in the philosophies of lovesickness, climatology and ethnology. The chapter underscores the critique that Shakespearean comedy performs in reworking such philosophical notions, which culminates in the ambiguously happy resolution put forth. In both plays, there exist parallel efforts to neutralise and rehabilitate melancholic characters. The humour is not easily purged away through medical expertise, nor is it ultimately celebrated as a sign of interiority. There remains a perceptible sense of doubt as to whether characters eventually do away with the melancholy they express. *Love's Labour's Lost* in particular, with the jarring announcement of the King's death, suggests that the melancholy of early comedies shatters established classification. In its initial form, the chapter suggests, Shakespearean comedy already rejects traditional definitions of melancholy.

In Chapter 3, I build on this notion by arguing that *Much Ado About Nothing* and *The Merchant of Venice* underscore the limits of a psycho-humoral definition of melancholy, highlighted by the refusal of certain characters to address, define or temper their melancholic dispositions. Don John's participation in *Much Ado* offers a blueprint of such a process since his villainy proves subsidiary to his melancholic countenance in clashing with the festive spirit that otherwise infuses Messina. This pattern is fully developed in *The Merchant of Venice*, where the troubled melancholic figure is one of the comedy's protagonists. I argue that rather than seeking a clear cause for it, the merchant's melancholy needs to be understood as a vital part of the comedy; the *why* of Antonio's sadness does not matter as much as the fact that he consistently strives to retain the characteristic. The insistent clamouring of both Don John and Antonio on the irremediableness of their melancholy brings attention to the incompatibility of traditional definitions of melancholy with the comic genre. This revisionism disassociates melancholy from the psychophysical binary offered by traditional understandings. It undertakes a turn towards a more multifocal emotional imprint; Shakespearean comedy eventually offers an envisioning of melancholy as a liminal emotional tenet that uproots the concept from its classical underpinnings.

Chapter 4 underscores the powerful emotional ambiguity that characterises the final moments of *As You Like It* and *Twelfth Night*. This alteration, evidenced by the exaggerated depictions of melancholy offered by characters such as Jaques or Orsino, introduces a new understanding of melancholy that revolves around ideas of mood, time and setting.

No longer tied to physical characterisations but grounded instead in the languor elicited by the inevitable passage of time, melancholy impresses itself into the very fabric of the plays it occupies. It finds particular resonance within the various musical interludes they contain, as well as in the several allusions to the bittersweet temporal perception that characters express. In *As You Like It*, Arden Forest appears as a repository for melancholy, where various characters can discard their woes and transform themselves prior to a return to court. Within this context, Jaques, the hyper-melancholic figure *par excellence*, functions as a siphon that feeds off others' melancholy. Similarly, melancholy affects most characters in *Twelfth Night*, but the individual characterisations give way to the sustained sense of wistfulness that gradually takes over the play. In both plays, the sense of a comic ending is seriously problematised by the growing sense of wistfulness that develops. Despite the promise of a return to court, the multiple loose ends in *As You Like It* undercut the otherwise joyful resolution. Similarly, a strong sense of this more spectral melancholy, embodied in Feste's closing ballad, sweeps through the final act, coating it in a wistful longing for times past. The powerful emotional ambiguity of these final moments underscores the symbiotic revisions of melancholy and comedy into a melancomic theatrical and philosophical affect.

Late Shakespearean drama, Chapter 5 suggests, develops this melancomic philosophy, predicated on the yoking together of past memories of sorrow and a present sense of gratification. The late plays' dovetailing of tragic and comic underpinnings (the staging of powerful trauma in a play's first half which is miraculously resolved in the final act) is common critical knowledge, yet the strangely wistful tone that characterises the ending of such works stems from taxonomies related to comic melancholy rather than from the tragic overtones of their initial premises. In late Shakespeare, irreparable past tragedies, exacerbated by lengthy time gaps, haunt seemingly joyous conclusions. The melancholy we find here suggests a voluntary sense of comic failure, since the melancomic quality of the plays infers both the legitimising of melancholy as a valid comic emotion and the nostalgic impossibility of return to a dramatic state of bliss. Doubts remain as to the potential for happiness at the end of *Pericles* despite a miraculous family reunion. The play brings its audience to delight in the intangible sense of sorrow it promotes. Likewise, *The Winter's Tale* epitomises the idea of a miraculous resolution, yet the intensity of the trauma that has developed coats the ending in an ambiguous emotional response. This emotional response transcends generic quagmires in representing a highly pleasurable feeling that can be understood as a precursor to nostalgia. Lastly, the chapter examines *The Two Noble Kinsmen* (a collaborative effort by Shakespeare and Fletcher) as evidence that, despite its transformative achievements, Shakespeare's comic melancholy loses out in the dramatic landscape of the seventeenth century, being supplanted by works predicated on a focal return to the humoral and the increased dramatic presence of medical practitioner characters. This shift is best exemplified by the tragicomedies of John Fletcher and his various collaborators (Francis Beaumont and Philip Massinger) as well as John Ford's *The Lover's Melancholy*. The play highlights the transition, as it were, from Shakespearean comic melancholy to the alternative that Fletcher's subplot dealing with the Jailer's Daughter puts forth.

The concluding chapter charts out potential critical links between Shakespearean comic melancholy and modern conceptualisations of melancholia in the works of Freud, Butler and Ngai. I argue that the comic philosophy of melancholy and of the melancomic I elaborate here, through its performative and affective dimensions, is consistent with the theoretical frameworks of all three writers. The chapter positions the representation of melancholy as a productive emotional marker akin to nostalgia in its conflation of sorrow and pleasure, as well as the artistic and creative repercussions that such a connection suggests over the years.

In closing this introduction, I must caution somewhat against my own methodology. There is an obvious danger in offering what amounts to a chronological reading of Shakespeare's comedies, the implication being that a qualitative progression coincides with the aforementioned temporal one. There is value in examining the comedies chronologically, since Shakespeare's conception of melancholy and comedy does evolve over time. I do not intend any such assessment of quality. I would not declare *The Merchant of Venice*, for example, to be 'inferior' to *Twelfth Night*, comically or otherwise, nor do I wish to the convey the argument that the late plays amount to a 'perfecting' of earlier comic efforts. I understand comic melancholy as an ongoing development throughout Shakespeare's writing career, in which the concept progressively morphs into the elusive yet overarching presence it holds in the tragicomedies. Conversely, I do not endorse a biographical reading of Shakespearean melancholy that would envision the playwright consciously reworking the concept across his career until he finally achieves the desired melancholic effect in his final plays (and breaks his staff). The comedies discussed here are written concurrently with history plays and tragedies, both of which similarly abound with melancholic references. Yet there remains a marked progression in depictions of comic melancholy that warrants specific consideration.

Additionally, in its linking of comedies and late plays, this project overlooks the problem plays and tragedies, creating a dramatic void that needs to be pre-emptively acknowledged. As stated, my interest lies specifically in the ways in which melancholy transforms the comic form of Shakespearean drama. Shakespeare's turn away from pure 'comedy' after

Twelfth Night does not necessarily imply his abandonment of melancholy as a dramatic concept. In essence, my decision to gloss over the mature tragedies and so-called problem comedies (*All's Well that Ends Well, Measure for Measure* and *Troilus and Cressida*), pertains to scope as much as it does to context. While most tragedies and problem plays contain their share of melancholy, the relationship to dramatic structure operates differently. Melancholy is expected from tragedies; the genre compels various forms of despair as characters suffer loss, injuries or death. If anything, one should be wary of characters incapable of grief or sorrow (those who profess not to be what they are). In the problem comedies, Shakespeare's focus is diverted to different concerns as an altogether separate set of darker images centring on notions of corruption and disease erupt. This trope resonates in tragedies such as *Hamlet* and *Othello* more than it does in the mature romantic works that preceded them. Shakespeare never exists in a vacuum, but the idea of comic melancholy as I understand it does not find any particularly compelling echoes in tragedies or problem plays.

Finally, I also want to address the bleak reading of Shakespearean comedy that my book may sometimes suggest. Inevitably, peering over yellowed play-texts within the confines of a windowless library on grey winter afternoons, incessantly seeking out their melancholic undertones, can skew one's appreciation of how funny Shakespearean comedies truly are. If anything, that last statement speaks to my point: melancholy can be understood as an integral, non-comic component of Shakespearean comedy, and while it does not necessarily yield laughter in itself, it heightens actual comical moments. The transformation of comedy that I identify here rests simultaneously on both ends of the affective spectrum that constitutes it. Robert Burton declared early on in *The Anatomy* that 'even in the midst of laughter, there is sorrow'.[99] This assertion is undeniably true, but a more appropriate epitaph for this study would probably be a revision of the old adage 'dying is easy; comedy is hard' into a caution that, as arduous as comedy may be, writing about its inherent melancholy is to be done carefully and with a strong sense of humour(s).

Notes

1. All Shakespearean quotations are taken from Bevington, *Complete Works of Shakespeare*.
2. Bristol, 'Shakespeare's Sonnets and the Publication of Melancholy', 193.
3. Hippocrates, 'Nature of Man', 11.
4. Plato, 'Timaeus', 1286.
5. 22: Aëtius 4.12 1–6, *Stoic Reader*, 49.
6. Galen, 'On the Natural Faculties', I, 13.
7. Galen 193.
8. Babb, *Elizabethan Malady*, 9.
9. 'Glossary', *Stoic Reader*, 211.
10. Paster, *The Body Embarrassed*, 2.
11. Galen, 'On the Affected Parts', 67–8.
12. Radden, *Nature of Melancholy*, 98.
13. For discussions of the coalescence of medical and literary aspirations in the period, see Lyons, *Voices of Melancholy* and Wells, *Secret Wound*.
14. See Galen, 'On the Causes of Diseases', 157–79.
15. Galen, 'On the Affected Parts', 90.
16. Radden, *Nature of Melancholy*, 69.
17. Radden, *Nature of Melancholy*, 78.
18. Hildegard of Bingen, 'Book of Holistic Healing', 79–85.
19. Aristotle, 'Problem XXX', 277.
20. Aristotle 287.
21. Ibid.
22. Aristotle 279.
23. Kristeva, *Black Sun*, 7.

24. The association is found within the Arabic scientific tradition, in the works of philosophers such as Abû Ma'šar, going as far back as the first century. See Klibansky et al., *Saturn and Melancholy*, 127.

25. Ficino, *Book of Life*, 6.

26. Radden credits Ficino's work as 'distinctive in developing the astrological significance of melancholy, particularly its relation to the planet Saturn', *Nature of Melancholy*, 87. However, its association with earthiness was already acknowledged in galenic writings and, as Klibansky et al. write, 'nearly all the writers of the late Middle Ages and the Renaissance considered it an incontestable fact that melancholy, whether morbid or natural, stood in some special relationship to Saturn and that the latter was really to blame for the melancholic's unfortunate character and destiny', 127.

27. Ficino 7.

28. Ibid.

29. Watson, *Heresies and Heretics*, 77.

30. Starobinski, *History of the Treatment of Melancholy*, 38.

31. Burton, *Anatomy of Melancholy*, 53.

32. Bright, *Treatise of Melancholy*, 123.

33. Bright 323.

34. Du Laurens (1599), 'To the Reader'. This address to the reader was possibly written and added to Du Laurens' text by Surphlet.

35. Du Laurens, 'To the Reader'.

36. Du Laurens 86.

37. Du Laurens 86–7.

38. Du Laurens 101.

39. Donald Beecher and Massimo Ciavolella note such innovations as the primary concern in Ferrand's work, 'Introduction', 135.

40. Ferrand, *Treatise on Lovesickness*, 366.

41. Burton 20.

42. Burton 79.

43. Montaigne, 'Of Sadness', 6.

44. Montaigne 9.

45. Montaigne 8.

46. Montaigne, 'How we cry and laugh for the same thing', 209.

47. See Hoeniger, *Medicine and Shakespeare*, 50–1. In *The Melancholy Muse: Chaucer, Shakespeare and Early Medicine*, Carol Falvo Heffernan identifies allusions to both Bright and Du Laurens in *Hamlet*, intimating Shakespeare's familiarity with both works, 125–35. In discussing Bright's treatise, Jennifer Radden mentions an anecdote suggesting that Shakespeare's familiarity with the text possibly stems from his work as a proof reader in the small London publishing house of Thomas Vautrolier, which printed Bright's treatise, *Nature of Melancholy*,119.

48. Walton and Arnott, *Menander and the Making of Comedy*, 1.

49. Aristotle, 'De Poetica 5, 31–4', *The Basic Works of Aristotle*, 1459.

50. Stott, *Comedy*, 20.

51. Theophrastus, *Characters*, 2. Theophrastus' work is crucial to the advent of the popular literary genres in England such as sixteenth-century Jest Books and seventeenth-century character books such as Samuel Butler's *Characters* [1667–9], ed. A. R. Walker (Cambridge: Cambridge University Press, 1908).

52. Walton and Arnott 18 (my emphasis).

53. Walton and Arnott 52; 58.

54. Walton and Arnott 39.

55. Sidney, 'The Defence of Poesy', 27.

56. Sidney 48.

57. Sidney 46.

58. Womack, *Ben Jonson*, 49–50.

59. Spivack, *George Chapman*, 64.

60. Dutton, *Ben Jonson*, 32.

61. Works such as *Day's Humours Out of Breath* (1608) or James Shirley's *The Humourous Courtier* (1631) have little to do with bodily humours (let alone melancholy). One can also think of the anonymous *Every Woman in her Humour* (c. 1598–1608) as an indicator of the popularity of Jonson's humour comedies.

62. Melchiori writes that the play 'is Shakespeare's ironical tribute paid to the new theatrical genre of the comedy of humours',

Shakespeare's Garter Plays, 107. Likewise, although he suggests that 'Shakespeare seems to have been responding to the newest dramatic genre of the 1590s', Bevington adds that 'Shakespeare characteristically does not satirise affectation so much as cherish it', 'The Merry Wives of Windsor', 253.

63. Johnson, *Preface to Shakespeare's Plays*, 9.
64. Barber. *Shakespeare's Festive Comedies*, 228.
65. Frye, *Natural Perspective*, 93.
66. Ibid.
67. Levin, *Playboys and Killjoys*. Muir, *Shakespeare's Comic Sequence*, 52.
68. Newman, *Shakespeare's Rhetoric of Comic Character*, 2.
69. Newman 5–6.
70. Maus, *Inwardness and Theater*, 32.
71. Lopez, *Theatrical Convention*, 208.
72. Lopez 210–11.
73. Frye 92.
74. According to the *OED*, 'humour' can also refer to one's ability to comprehend or appreciate such amusement, hence the expression 'possessing a sense of humour'.
75. Paulson, *Don Quixote in England*, xii.
76. Paulson xi.
77. Schoenfeldt, *Bodies and Selves in Early Modern England*, 15.
78. Schoenfeldt 19.
79. Schoenfeldt 75.
80. Schoenfeldt 89.
81. Schoenfeldt 90.
82. Paster, *Humouring the Body*, 19.
83. Paster, *Humouring the Body*, 135; 137.
84. Paster devotes a chapter to Shakespearean melancholy in *Humouring the Body*, but her examples and analysis do not address the comic functionality of humours. See 135–88.
85. Paster, *Humouring the Body*, 24.
86. Daniel, *Melancholy Assemblage*, 5.
87. Daniel 15.
88. Sullivan, *Beyond Melancholy*, 4.
89. Sullivan 16.

90. Sullivan 110.
91. Freud, 'Of Mourning and Melancholia', 205.
92. See Radden, 'Melancholy and Melancholia', 231–50.
93. Freud 212.
94. Freud 218.
95. See Kristeva's *Black Sun*; Schiesari, *Gendering Melancholia*; Butler, *Gender Trouble*, 73–83, *Bodies that Matter*, 169–84 and *The Psychic Life of Power*, particularly 1–30.
96. Butler, 'Performative Acts and Gender Constitution', 520.
97. Ngai, *Ugly Feelings*, 3.
98. Ngai 28.
99. Burton 144.

CHAPTER 2

COMIC SYMMETRY AND ENGLISH MELANCHOLY

On the subject of comedy, Baudelaire remarks that 'pour trouver du comique féroce et très féroce, il faut passer la Manche et visiter les royaumes brumeux du spleen' (One must cross the English Channel and visit the foggy kingdoms of spleen in order to encounter a ferocious kind of comedy).[1] Baudelaire post-dates this book's period of interest, but his description of England as the kingdom of the spleen (the organ generally thought to produce melancholy) in relation to the native's distinct comic style attests to the paradoxical status of the humour in early modern England. Scientifically, melancholy was a foreign concept that was culturally and intellectually appropriated as a marker of sophistication. The belief that geographical location and climate could help determine an individual's dominant humour, introduced by Hippocrates in *On Airs, Waters and Places*, was on an almost equal footing with Galen's anatomical model in the Renaissance. Works such as Jean Bodin's *Six Bookes of the Commonwealth* and William Harrison's *The Description of England* generally agreed that melancholy was characteristic of southern countries, where the inhabitants' darker skin was thought to reflect their prevalent humour (black bile).[2] England's northern climate, characterised by cold and moisture was thought to render its population mainly phlegmatic. Harrison writes that

> the Britons are white in colour, strong of body and full of blood, as people inhabiting near the North and far from the equinoctial line, where the soil is not so fruitful and therefore the people not so feeble . . . [they are] commonly taken by foreign historiographers to be men of great strength and little policy, much courage and small shift, because of the weak abode of the sun, whereby our brains are not made hot and warmed.[3]

The in-between nature of the phlegmatic, where any positive trait is immediately mitigated by a less desirable one, led the English to seek new ways of representing themselves that went beyond classical humoral descriptions.

England's appropriation of melancholy as a distinctively English trait can be understood as a reactionary effort against such a portrayal. Ethnologically speaking, early modern England was a far cry from Baudelaire's kingdom of spleen. As Mary Floyd-Wilson writes, the English melancholy vogue represents 'the northern nation's ambivalence toward a temperament recognised by many to be indigenous to the south, while some northerners aimed to cultivate the inward blackness of melancholy, others condemned its appearance in England as a foreign affectation or inflection'.[4] The English thus rejected melancholy's association with barbarous southern behaviour, turning instead towards its Aristotelian and Ficinian associations with genius, creativity and intellectual depth. Nowhere was this shift more apparent than in the period's dramatic output. The comic genre especially was a potent arena in which, as Floyd-Wilson puts it

> the multivalent nature of theatrical power nourished and fed on the English people's perception of their natural complexion as defective, in need of amelioration, and

exceedingly susceptible to all kinds of external influences from the heat of rhetoric to the chill of their own
climate.[5]

Comic stagings of melancholy both reaffirmed its appropriation as an English marker of interiority and offered an ideal
vehicle for mocking its feigned affectations. English comedy
also allowed for the counter-ethnological process of ridiculing
foreign characters for their attempts to purport melancholy as
a way to further affirm and strengthen its English appropriation on the stage.

Drawing on this ethnological model, this chapter suggests that Shakespeare anglicises the foreign settings of both
The Comedy of Errors and *Love's Labour's Lost* through
his early development of comic melancholy. Each comedy
explores concepts traditionally associated with melancholy
(identity, ethnology, humoralism and lovesickness) as a way
to position itself as an English comedy. Both plays also present the humour as a marker of masculine comic identity. In
Errors, melancholy links all three male members of a dis-
jointed family scattered around Ephesus. Both Egeon and
his sons see their identities challenged throughout the play,
and the melancholy they each affect tethers them through
the chaos of the mistaken identity plot. Conversely, the men
of Navarre's Academe in *Love's Labour's Lost* all affect
love-melancholy in a bid for social and romantic validation. Through its games of courtship, the play develops a
critique of masculine ideas of melancholy as a placeholder
for intellectual depth and genuine emotion. This accrued
melancholic focus represents a distinct Shakespearean addition to the sources he draws from.

Each work closely follows established structures in terms
of theories of melancholy and comic conventions. The comedies are predicated on a symmetrical model of characterisation as suggested by critics such Northrop Frye or Harry

Levin, one that emphasises acts of couplings and doubling. This model is intended to reflect the 'real world', as Harry Levin explains, and 'to act as an aid to self-correction',[6] but it also operates, as Frye suggests, as an inherent dramatic device which, through structure, dictates the comic mood.[7] The multiple melancholic iterations help further the plays' symmetry while catering to the expectation of the humour's eventual purgation. In each case, the drive to dispel melancholy becomes inexorably conflated with ideas of comic resolution and closure. In this sense, the plays acquiesce to traditional galenic philosophy in advocating for balance, suggesting that the comic crises they explore can be resolved through heterosexual symmetrical pairings.

Yet, these early comic works also push back from classical notions of melancholy by bringing attention to their incongruity within the comic genre. While the efforts to circumvent melancholy are, for the most part, carried out successfully (in as much as male characters are relieved from the torments of confused identity and troubled emotion), the ending of each play hints at the incompatibility of classically understood melancholy and Shakespearean comedy. *The Comedy of Errors* manages to dispel the melancholy afflicting Egeon and his sons through the reunion scene, but in presenting melancholy as a family trait with ties to the mercantile lifestyle, the play also creates reasonable doubt as to the humour's eradication. Alternatively, the abrupt ending in *Love's Labour's Lost*, ushered in by the announcement of the French king's death, undercuts its own playful critique of love-melancholy and shatters the possibility for a joyful conclusion. In this sense, both plays can be thought to draw from classical understandings of melancholy but also to interrogate their value within Shakespeare's comic style. In suggesting the purgation of melancholy but never explicitly staging it, each play hints at the paradoxical nature of melancholy in early Shakespearean comedy.

All in the Family: Melancholic Identities in The Comedy of Errors

Long heralded as the prime example of 'Shakespeare's apprenticeship', *The Comedy of Errors*, much like its characters, suffers from a mistaken-identity crisis.[8] The play is often dismissed as an imitation of Roman New Comedy, whose levity does not offer much in the way of complexity or comic innovation. Recent critical efforts to address the play's more serious elements and read it as both 'simple or pure comedy [and containing] dark and disturbing elements', have begun to amend this oversight, but the play's treatment of comic melancholy remains largely untouched and the play's focus on the farcical implications of its mistaken-identity crisis is usually thought to phase out the humour.[9]

The play relies on melancholy as a way to legitimise itself as an English comedy, in relation both to its Roman source material (Plautus' The *Menaechmi* and New Comedy more generally) and to the foreign setting of Ephesus it presents. The melancholic (and masculine) lineage found at the heart of the play helps to anchor it as an early modern English comedy by capitalising on the ethnological anxieties surrounding foreign affects and travel practices, drawing attention to the inherent threat that melancholy poses. The play also integrates melancholy within its symmetrical comic structure, in which the sense of self-division the characters undergo through the mistaken-identity crisis is resolved through the recognition scene and subsequent heterosexual unions. If the play is to be understood as a quest for self-identification and the recovery of a fragmented familial unit, melancholy reveals itself as its adhesive agent linking together the multiple masculine identity crises that develop throughout.

The Comedy of Errors borrows heavily from Plautus' *The Menaechmi* in spinning its tale of long-lost twin brothers. Plautus' version provides the basic plot structure and comically ripe character types that form the core of Shake-speare's revision. Both plays rely on the long-standing comic trope of the stranger in a strange land who, through a cri-sis of mistaken identity, 'fulfils the comic dream [of getting] everything for nothing'.[10] While it draws substantially from its roman counterpart, Shakespeare also performs extensive revisions. He transforms the general backstory (offered by Plautus in a short Prologue) into an intricate subplot involv-ing the twins' father, Egeon, which turns their moment of loss (being kidnapped at a public market) into a tale of a terrible shipwreck that tears the family apart.[11] He also emphasises the paradoxical conflation of doubling and self-division by including dual pairs of lost twins: merchants (The Antipholi) and their servants (the Dromios), who were separated along with their masters following the wreck at sea. The doubling extends to suitable romantic partners for each brother (sisters Adriana and Luciana), as well as their long-lost parents, who are both present in Ephesus with concealed identities at the beginning of the play. This exten-sive doubling is meant to raise the stakes ahead of the comic resolution, which takes on the air of a large-scale family reunion. This framework, I argue, allows the play to thread a sustained melancholic presence through its masculine lin-eage of characters that both serves and questions the comic structure within which it develops. Whereas Plautus elabo-rates a contrast between the Roman antipodes of business (the forum) and pleasure (the festival), *The Comedy Errors* shifts its opposition towards comedy and melancholy. The inherent tension in such a conflation harks back to Plautian comedy and the way in which, as Kathleen McCarthy puts it, Plautus draws attention to 'the separability of form and content by exaggerating rather than minimizing the contra-dictions'.[12] Yet, by situating its friction within the uneasy coexistence of melancholy and the comic genre, Shakespeare makes his first early modern comedy entirely English.

The play seemingly opens at its end point, with the Syracusan merchant Egeon about to receive a death sentence from Duke Solinus for trespassing on Ephesian soil. Condemned to die at sunset 'unless a thousand marks be levièd' (I, i, 21), Egeon relates his life story to the duke, and in doing so, provides both the expository framework for the comedy at hand and begins its conflation of melancholic tropes and comic conventions:

> A heavier task could not have been imposed
> Than I to speak my griefs unspeakable.
> Yet, that the world may witness that my end
> Was wrought by nature, not by vile offense,
> I'll utter what my sorrow gives me leave.   (I, i, 31–5)

The Comedy of Errors thus begins with professions of unspeakable sorrow in the wake of impending death. As Barbara Freedman and other critics have noted, the play draws on a narrative framework steeped in romance traditions, with its allusion to spectacular grief and melancholic longing for death.[13] Yet the play alters what Helen Cooper terms the typical romance narrative pattern of 'an opening disruption of a state of order, followed by a period of trial and suffering, even an encounter with death, [before] a final symbolic resurrection and better restoration' by beginning with Egeon's impending death, transforming the trials and suffering that came before into an expository backdrop for the comedy at hand.[14] Freedman, who identifies Egeon as the figurehead of what she terms the play's 'remarkable drive toward closure through a romance plot of the separation and reunion',[15] suggests that presentations of the grieving merchant bookend the play. Structurally, his disappearance after this first scene, along with his re-entrance in the last act, being led by the duke to the 'melancholy vale, / The place of death and sorry execution' (V, i, 120–1) indicates as

much. I would push her idea further by arguing that Egeon
encases the comedy in melancholy. His tale sets up the play's
crucial masculine melancholic lineage. The first scene introduces several of the notions that the play will go on to associate with melancholy.

Though it becomes clear – as soon as Antipholus of
Syracuse enters in the following scene and makes explicit mention of his possessing a thousand marks – that all will ultimately end favourably, *The Comedy of Errors* opens on the
powerfully melancholic situation through which Egeon sees
his 'misfortunes . . . by life prolonged, / To tell sad stories of
my own mishaps' (I, i, 119–20). The speech underscores the
play's ongoing fascination with acts of doubling, in particular
to their potential linking of mirthful and melancholic elements
in delicate oscillation:

> In Syracusa was I born, and wed
> Unto a woman, happy but for me,
> And by me, had not our hap been bad.
> With her I lived in joy; our wealth increased
> By prosperous voyage I often made
> To Epidamnum, till my factor's death
> And the great care of goods at random left
> Drew me from kind embracement of my spouse.
>
> (I, i, 36–43)

The passage draws attention to Egeon's mercantile lifestyle
as a source of anxiety. The polyptotonic alignment of marital happiness (good fortune) with the etymologically related
bad hap (poor fortune) alerts us to such an idea, which is
then solidified by the fact that Egeon's business ventures, the
'great care of goods at random left' that the death of his commercial agent created, is what initially separates him from
his family. Critics such as Lynn Enterline have denoted the
fruitful connections between early modern melancholy and
the merchant craft that *The Comedy of Errors* puts forth.

For Enterline, self-identification in the play is directly tied to ideas of property and 'the disappearance of either identity or value', she argues, 'produces what is explicitly called "melancholy."'[16] As a linchpin of early modern commercial ventures, maritime travel (and the threats of storms and shipwreck it always implied) strengthened the connections between melancholy and loss of identity, particularly in the sea's frightening capacity for total erasure and dissolution.

The association between melancholy and the oceanic landscape, predicated on the loneliness and isolation brought by maritime travel, was already present in Arabic astrology as far back as AD 800. Abû Ma'šar writes that the God Saturn 'presides over . . . sea travel and long sojourn abroad [as well as] being withdrawn into one's self . . . loneliness and unsociability', while Alcabitius adds that Saturn presides over 'respectable professions which have to do with water like the commanding of ships and their management . . . But when he is evil he presides over . . . far travels, long absences [and] preferences for solitude'.[17] These ideas were prevalent ones in early modern England. Michel Foucault notes that 'the Classical era was content to blame the English melancholy on the influence of a maritime climate: the cold, wet, fickle weather and the fine droplets of water that entered the vessels and the fires of the human body made a body lose its firmness'.[18] Drawing on Pierre De L'Ancre's *De L'Inconstance des Mauvais Anges* (Paris, 1612), *The History of Madness* outlines the rich connection between melancholy, liquidity and mercantilism. Before acquiring a direct connotation to madness, the figure of the sea wanderer, Foucault explains, was perceived as a bad omen:

> the uncertain furrow of the wake, the exclusive trust placed in the stars, the secret knowledge that passed from mariner to mariner, the distance from women and the ceaselessly shifting plain of the surface of the sea made men lose faith

in god, and cast off the shackles of their attachment to their homeland, thereby opening the door to the Devil and the ocean of his ruses.[19]

The implied threat here relates to a putative loss of identity engendered by the ocean's ever-shifting waters. For Enterline, the terrible storm and its 'warrant of immediate death' (I, i, 68) that sinks Egeon's ship and splits his family confirms her idea that the play's concerns with identity are inherently materialistic.[20] Enterline's argument delineates the correlation in *Errors* between masculine melancholy and a putative loss of identity; the comedy goes a step further in depicting the merchant lifestyle not only as carrying the potential for melancholy (in subscribing to a model of high risk and high reward) but as capable actually of generating it and potentially spreading it to other cities and their inhabitants. Egeon's capture in Ephesus results from a decree barring Syracusan merchants from doing business in Ephesus, an idea that draws on philosophical and political anxieties tied to the mercantile profession and maritime travel dating back to antiquity. On the subject of correct modes of governance, Plato, in his *Laws*, remarks that

> for a country to have a sea nearby is pleasant enough for the purpose of everyday life but in fact it is a "salty-sharp and bitter neighbour" in more sense than one. It fills the land with whole-sailing and retailing, breeds shifty and deceitful habits in a man's soul, and makes the citizens distrustful and hostile, not only among themselves, but also in their dealings with the world outside.[21]

In cautioning against what he terms 'the disgraceful copying of enemies [which] occurs when people live by the sea', Plato stresses the idea that the sea thus represented a point of entry for foreign threats (ideas or behaviours) to enter a city or state.[22] Though travel was thought of as a potential early modern cure for melancholy, it also embodied Plato's threat of contagion.[23] In his essays, Francis Bacon writes that upon returning home, a young Englishman 'should let it appear that he doth not change his country manners for those of foreign parts but only prick in some flowers of that he had learned abroad into the customs of his own country'.[24] Despite (or perhaps because of) a desire to appropriate it as English trait, melancholy remained a potentially noxious foreign element. As Laurence Babb explains, the great English interest in melancholy was thought to have grown out of the imitation of Italian affectations and vices by returning travellers. 'Melancholic were so numerous in Elizabethan London', he writes, 'as to constitute a social type, which was augmented by persons who took up the affectation even though they had never been abroad.'[25] For Babb, the figure of the discontent traveller is a fundamentally classical one displaying a galenic (external) appearance through being 'black-suited and dishevelled, unsociable, asperous, morosely meditative [and] taciturn' while claiming an Aristotelian internal disposition as a 'person of intellectual or artistic talent'.[26] The detaining of Egeon by Ephesian authorities alludes to such anxieties, as the mercantile lifestyle and its association with melancholy are defined by travel abroad. The opening of the play capitalises on these familiar notions by drawing on the threat of foreign affectations and alluding to a more acceptable English sense of melancholy.

Egeon's description of the wreck itself furthers the conflation of comedy and melancholy that the play undertakes. The story establishes the idea that the doubling of his sons is a melancomic one:

> My wife, more careful for the latter-born,
> Had fastened him unto a small spare mast
> Such as seafaring men provide for storms;
> To him one of the other twins was bound,

Whilst I had been like heedful of the other.

. . .

We were encountered by a mighty rock,
Which being violently borne upon,
Our helpful ship was splitted in the midst,
So that in this unjust divorce of us
Fortune had left to both of us alike
What to delight in, what to sorrow for.   (I, i, 78–82; 101–6)

The shipwreck creates new identities for them as they find themselves 'violently borne upon' the rocks. The allusion to birth underscores the idea that the brothers' identities are not erased in this moment but inexorably fused together along a tragicomic axis. The passage emphasises division, with both mother and father taking charge of one set of twins (Antipholus and Dromio) but in doing so, it doubles each brother as both rescued and lost. In a sense, each Antipholus becomes, for the parent, a beacon of joy in the aftermath of horrendous loss as well as a sorrowful reminder of what has been claimed by the sea. Each Antipholus embodies both what to delight in and to sorrow for. Egeon's story establishes this central framework of a melancomic doubling of its twin protagonists. The stage is thus set – literally – for the arrival of his 'youngest boy [and] eldest care' (I, i, 124) in the next scene.

Antipholus of Syracuse draws an immediate melancholic parallel with Egeon. Upon arriving in Ephesus, 'stiff and weary' from a lengthy sea voyage (I, ii, 15), he offers a description of his servant Dromio to a fellow merchant as 'a trusty villain, sir, that very oft, / When I am dull with care and melancholy, / Lightens my humour with his merry jests' (I, ii, 19–21). Despite acknowledging it as a passing ailment, the comment, on the heels of Egeon's introductory lament, maintains melancholy at the play's forefront. Before we can even ascertain that Antipholus is, in fact, Egeon's son, the play reiterates the previous connections between melancholy and maritime travel. Moreover, the underlying implication suggests a relational humoral binary between the master Antipholus and his servant Dromio that yokes together comedy and melancholy. As Paster explains, in early modern England, humoral distinction 'guaranteed that the structure of humoralism would reflect hierarchical social values and could be used powerfully to naturalize them. Affect . . . was expected to mirror the social hierarchy because both were built into the analogical order of things'.[27] The play draws on such knowledge to suggest that Dromio is often called upon to counter his master's melancholy with an equivalent display of mirth.

Dromio of Syracuse can be conceived of as a source of comic energy that emancipates the melancholic Antipholus from bearing the brunt of generic expectations. *The Comedy of Errors* combines mirth and melancholy but maintains the latter at a distance from its comic moments. Much as with his father, melancholy remains Antipholus' dominant trait throughout the play. Left alone onstage near the end of the scene, he delivers a soliloquy on identity, estrangement and family, declaring that

> He that commends me to my own content
> Commends me to the thing I cannot get.
> I to the world am like a drop of water
> That in the ocean seeks another drop,
> Who, falling there to find his fellow forth,
> Unseen, inquisitive, confounds himself;
> So I, to find a mother and a brother,
> In quest of them, unhappy, loose myself.   (I, ii, 33–40)

The passage, compassed round by notions of being 'content', then 'unhappy', echoes the dovetailing of mirth and melancholy established in the previous scene by Egeon's griefs unspeakable. Antipholus expresses a sense of genial melancholy concordant with the ethnographic construction discussed earlier, one that moves away from humoralism to centre on stoic grief and depth of character. Antipholus echoes Babb's figure of the discontent traveller who affects melancholy wherever he goes, recalling the ethnological threat of a foreign invasion of melancholy. Yet, rather than intimate a Ficinian return towards the self, the passage hints at a loss of identity, correlating Antipholus' sadness with his anonymity upon setting foot in Ephesus. In Plautus' version, the metaphor of drops of liquid is used to stress the brother's identical appearance. Upon seeing them reunited onstage, Messenio the slave declares 'I never did see two men more alike. / No drop of water, no drop of milk, is more like another' (V, i, 478–9). In Shakespeare, the water metaphor implies the incommensurability of Antipholus' disposition. The failure to maintain a distinct identity that he articulates, much like a drop of water losing itself in the sea's impenetrable vastness, bespeaks a profound sense of alienation, made worse by the fact that this proves to be his only recourse in searching for his family. For Antipholus, melancholy is a limitless ocean, an overwhelming force where he must lose himself in hopes of recovering his identity.[28] This paradoxical self-perpetuating cycle, where one must risk becoming further afflicted in hopes of curing himself, mirrors the play's treatment of melancholy both as foil to comedy and an inherent element of its structure. Antipholus' arrival in Ephesus performs an act of doubling similar to the one found in Egeon's story. It also stresses the fact that the eventual resolution of the mistaken identity crisis would double as a cure for Antipholus' melancholy. From its onset, the play builds towards a recognition scene that is also expected to purge away melancholy.

The drop of water metaphor is repeated in the following act by Adriana, Antipholus of Ephesus' wife, who, upon encountering the Syracusan merchant, mistakenly addresses him as her husband:

> As easy mayst thou fall
> A drop of water in the breaking gulf,
> And take unmingled thence that drop again
> Without addition or diminishing,
> As take from me thyself and not me too.   (II, ii, 124–8)

Adriana's turmoil is not grounded in melancholy. Her use of the simile is meant to convey loyalty, devotion and commitment to her husband (even if she is addressing the wrong person). While Antipholus speaks of his passive dissolution into the gulf of his existential angst, the relationship she envisions is that of an equal partnership without addition or diminution. The repetition of the metaphor highlights the gendered contrast that the comedy develops, in which only the male characters rely on melancholy as a mode of self-expression. This distinction is made more evident once the Ephesian brother appears onstage. As the solution to both the mistaken identity crisis and Adriana's marital woes, he furthers the play's development of a masculine sense of melancholic identity.

Though Antipholus of Ephesus' identity is challenged once his brother sets foot in Ephesus, he otherwise enjoys a much more grounded sense of self. When Antipholus of Syracuse wonders at the strange events he has experience in Ephesus, we gain a glimpse of his brother's life:

> There's not a man I meet but doth salute me
> As if I were their well-acquainted friend,
> And everyone doth call me by my name.
> Some tender money to me; some invite me;
> Some other give me thanks for kindness;
> Some offer me commodities to buy.
> Even now a tailor called me in his shop

And showed me silks that he had bought for me
And therewithal took measure of my body.   (IV, iii, 1–9)

The musings sketch out extensive and celebratory social relations that suggest that Antipholus of Ephesus' identity is socially and professionally validated. One of his fellow merchants later describes him as being

Of very reverend reputation, sir,
Of credit infinite, highly beloved,
Second to none that lives here in the city.
His word might bear my wealth any time.   (V, i, 5–8)

At first, Antipholus of Ephesus differs from his father and brother since his ties to merchant craft are grounded in the city of Ephesus (as opposed to being at sea), endowing him with what they each lack: a favourable and recognised Ephesian reputation and financial means. Likewise, he does not affect the melancholic disposition that they both display. His involvement in the mistaken identity crisis, becoming locked out of his house, threatened with imprisonment and subjected to a mock exorcism at the hands of the bumbling physician Pinch position him firmly on the comic side of the doubling process that the play sets up between him and his brother. The play conversely caters to the expectation that his troubles will also be solved through the impending recognition scene.

The final act challenges the melancomic doubling of Antipholi by introducing the idea that Antipholus of Ephesus also suffers from melancholy. When questioned by the Abbess of the Priory about her husband's condition, Adriana replies that

This week he hath been heavy, sour, sad,
And much, much different from the man he was;

But till this afternoon his passion
Ne'er brake into extremity of rage.

(V, i, 45–8, emphasis mine)

The second part of her speech describes the aftermath of being mistreated by Pinch in the previous act. Yet, the time-frame supplied by Egeon's impending execution allows for an interpretation of Adriana's revelation as evidence that Antipholus of Ephesus is also inherently melancholic. The play has transpired over less than a day and her description of him as sad and different from who he is the past week echoes his brother's earlier admission of being intermittently 'dull with care and melancholy'. As the play verges on resolving the identity crisis, melancholy is once again brought to the forefront. While the manoeuvre validates the ongoing conflation of melancholy with masculine identity and comic symmetry, offering a dramatic 'strategy that serves to extend their physical similarities [and] . . . their mental character', it also challenges the mirth and melancholy binary that the comedy previously established.[29] The reveal pertaining to Antipholus of Ephesus' melancholy hints at the complication that the recognition scene will engender as far as their melan-comic doubling is concerned. The Abbess subsequently questions Adriana on what could have caused this behaviour:

Hath he not lost much wealth by wrack of sea?
Buried some dear friend? Hath not else his eye
Strayed his affection in unlawful love –
A sin prevailing much in youthful men,
Who give their eyes the liberty of gazing?
Which of these sorrows is he subject to?   (V, i, 49–54)

Her questions offer several concrete sources for Antipholus of Ephesus' melancholy, and her final supposition regarding his infidelity seemingly hits the mark given his interactions with the courtesan. When Adriana rejects all of them, the Abbess concludes that

> Thereof came in that the man was mad.
> The venom clamors of a jealous woman
> Poison more deadly than man's dog tooth.
> . . .
> Thou sayst his sports were hindered by thy brawls.
> Sweet recreation barred, what doth ensue
> But moody and dull melancholy,
> Kinsman to grim and comfortless despair,
> And at her heels a huge infectious troop
> Of pale distemperatures and foes to life?   (V, i, 68–70; 77–82)

The Abbess' speech focuses on marital relations, accusing Adriana of hindering her husband's recreation, an inherently galenic diagnosis, tying idleness to 'moody and dull melancholy'. Her prognosis paves the way for a reconciliation between husband and wife, but it does not account for the depictions of melancholy as a multivalent mode of masculine self-expression shown throughout the play. Whatever the actual cause may be does not matter as much given that it now links the three male figures ahead of the resolution. If the brothers could simultaneously embody what to delight in and sorrow for as long as they were not onstage together, their reunion hints at developing incongruities between melancholy and comic closure.

The final act gathers everyone before the Priory doors, as Adriana, Luciana and Antipholus and Dromio of Ephesus are joined by Antipholus and Dromio of Syracuse (seeking to avoid unlawful imprisonment) and Duke Solinus leading his prisoner, Egeon, to the 'melancholy vale, / The place of death and sorry execution' (V, i, 120–1). The Abbess's revelation that she is Emilia provides the audience with the final plot piece to anticipate a joyful reunion. Her matriarchal status, both as the long-lost mother and the head of the convent, grants her the dramatic authority to untangle the identity crisis and restore symmetry once and for all. By producing the two brothers together onstage for the first time, Emilia validates Antipholus of Syracuse's affection for Luciana, reconciles the Ephesian merchant with his wife and spares Egeon's life, effectively putting an end to the play's farcical accumulations of errors and misunderstandings. Reuniting with Egeon, Emilia renders 'his morning story right' (V, i, 357) and, with her newly reacquired maternal status, grants her sons another birth, one with distinct and socially validated identities. As she summarises herself,

> The duke, my husband, and my children both,
> And you the calendars of their nativity,
> Go to a gossips' feast, and go with me;
> After so long grief, such nativity!   (V, i, 404–7)

Enterline notes that, through Emilia, the Priory is seen as 'a specifically female' space of recognition. 'It is the site both of female chastity (an abbey)', she writes, 'and of reproduction (a place of childbirth)'.[30] Emilia proves an ideal candidate to assuage all woes not only by producing both twins onstage at the same time but also by reacquiring her roles as mother and wife. The melancomic twins, once 'violently borne upon' a mighty rock, as Egeon explains at the onset of the play (I, I, 102), are now born anew at the Priory, as Emilia invites everyone inside, promising to 'make full satisfaction' of the day's errors (V, i, 400).

The play's final words belong to the Dromios, whose warm reunion befits a comedy (V, i, 415–27) more than does their masters', which proves lukewarm at best. On a dramatic level, ascribing correct identities to each brother effectively ends the comedy, but it does not account for the male characters' ongoing connection with melancholy. At the end of *The Brothers Meneachmi*, the twins profess a wish to return to their home country (V, viii, 1676). There is no such mention here. The play remains insularly in Ephesus and the insistent association of melancholy with the merchant craft lingers on. Comic symmetry and the reinstatement of correct identities do not eradicate the potentiality of shipwrecks, of losing one's sense of self or of intermittent bouts of melancholy.

Melancholy is admittedly peripheral to *The Comedy Errors*. Its presence never truly complicates the development of the farcical mistaken identity plot. Yet, as a marker of masculine identity-in-crisis, it proves integral to overwriting the would-be foreign features of the play as English and to establishing comic symmetry. It also hints at a gendered contrast in which characters such as Adriana and Emilia prove more adept at dealing with the sorrows that plague them than their male counterparts (a notion that looms much larger in subsequent Shakespearean engagements with comic melancholy). In the end, melancholy in *The Comedy of Errors* poses more questions than it answers, but in brushing up against the burgeoning style of Shakespeare's comic apprenticeship, it already raises doubts as to its compatibility with traditional comic models.

Wild Laughter and Love's Labour's Lost *Shattered Symmetry*

Love's Labor's Lost, I once did see a Play,
Ycleped so, so called to my paine
. . .
To every one (save me) twas Comicall
Whilst Tragick like to me it did befall.[31]

Robert Tofte's, poem 'Alba: The Month's Minde of a Melancholy Lover (1598)', detailing his witnessing of a performance of *Love's Labour's Lost*, does not only provide the earliest critique of the play, it also hints at its problematic merging of comic and tragic elements (particularly in its closing scene). Though Tofte implies that his own love-melancholy rendered the play unfunny to him, the fact remains that *Love's Labour's Lost*'s relationship to the comic genre is paradoxical. On one hand, the comic structure in which it operates, hinging on a series of symmetrical heterosexual couplings, is even more palpable than it was in Ephesus. The comedy also furthers the ethnological reversal of English and foreign affectations of melancholy through the character of Don Armado, whose affectation of melancholy as a bid for social status in Navarre's Academe proves a target of constant ridicule in the play. On the other hand, the play's deliberate thwarting of comic expectations in its final act and its persistent reliance on melancholy throughout undercuts the otherwise festive atmosphere it promulgates.

Similarly to *The Comedy of Errors*, the play's foreign setting is rendered English through an extensive development of love-melancholy centred on an octet of young lovers engaged in games of wit and courtship. Rather than maritime travel and identity crises, lovesickness becomes the *de facto* mode of self-expression for male characters. The play develops its representation of lovesickness around its intrinsic association with the emerging early modern print culture, particularly as it relates to the Petrarchan sonnet tradition and the advent of what Michael Bristol defines as a 'melancholy public' in England, one 'composed of solitary, isolated subjects connected only by the attention given to the expressive lives of others'.[32] In its exploration of comic melancholy and lovesickness, *Love's Labour's Lost* is astutely conscious of this public in offering a dramatic representation of this widespread phenomenon. This idea is reinforced by the play's allusions to literary English sources such as Sydney's *Defence of Poetry* and topical references to English figures,[33] which, while not explicitly concerned with melancholy, interlink with the familiar association of the humour with print and writing more generally. As Carla Mazzio writes of the play's fascination with print,

> the melancholy of love articulates a melancholy of speech in a world dominated by technologies of writing and print. That is, love melancholy, the most prominent disease in the play, is at once a dramatic realization of well-known Petrarchan conceits . . . and a historically specific ailment, articulating the oral and psychic self-estrangement of speakers living in a culture in transition to print.[34]

Though Mazzio's focus on print culture diverges from the concerns of this chapter, the idea that the play's melancholy channels a familiar sense of loss for the people experiencing it in the theatre echoes the ethnological process I detail here. Her conflation of the affliction of lovesickness with its putative artistic iterations, the idea that 'the melancholy of love can be seen . . . as a nostalgia for speech',[35] renders it a predominant component of the highly regimented structures of courtship and romantic expression that the play mocks. The melancholy of unrequited love reiterates the conflation of the humour and comic symmetry that early Shakespearean comedy undertakes, since it appears easily remediable through romantic pairing (as it did in Ephesus). Yet, the news of the French king's death brings the comedy to an abrupt end and negates the possibility of a happy ending. As Drew Daniel suggests, the play undertakes 'an exploration of the generative disturbances within melancholy, with Shakespeare raiding its richly contradictory heritage of medical and social knowledge only to stop short before the unknowable somatic abysses which melancholy also occasions'.[36] This tonal and thematic shift at the end the play brings attention the purported incompatibility of comedy and melancholy. The songs of spring and winter that close *Love's Labour's Lost* can be understood as a final commentary on the inherent tensions found in such a conflation.

The opening scene details an oath undertaken by Ferdinand, King of Navarre, and three young lords (Berowne, Longueville and Dumaine). Intent on turning his court into an academy for the pursuit of knowledge, Navarre calls for a rejection of romantic endeavours and the mastery of their dispositions:

> Let fame, that all hunt after in their lives,
> Live registered upon our brazen tombs,
> And then grace us in the disgrace of death,
> When, spite of cormorant devouring Time,
> Th'endeavour of this present breath may buy
> That honor which shall bate his scythe' keen edge
> And make us heirs of all eternity.
> Therefore, brave conquerors – for so you are,
> That war against your own affections
> And the huge army of the world's desires –
> Our late edict shall strongly stand in force.   (I, i, 1–11)

Couched in images of honourable death and eternal glory in the face of 'cormorant devouring time', the speech appears better suited for a history play. Navarre encourages the 'brave conquerors' before him to wage war against their affectations using military rhetoric to incite his young lords to self-control. Navarre's speech makes use of the poetical trope of the wooer as military conqueror (particularly prevalent in sonnet writing). It also depicts masculine self-expression as being predicated on extremes rather than temperance, on the conceit that men must forcibly tame their innate desires. Only Berowne appears sceptical of the pledge Navarre asks of them and its advocacy for abstinence, fasting and sleep deprivation. 'These are barren tasks', he says of Navarre's oath, 'too hard to keep, / Not to see ladies, study, fast, not sleep!' (I, i, 48–9). Berowne comes across in this first scene as the voice of balance and caution. 'Every man with his affects is born', he professes later on, 'not by might mastered, but by special grace' (I, i, 150–1). According to him, affects and passions are not so easily conquered, nor should they be forcibly manipulated out of their natural sequence. 'At Christmas I no more desire a rose', he declares to his companions, 'Than wish a snow in May's newfangled shows, / But like of each thing that in season grows' (I, i, 105–7). Berowne's reticence in this first scene stands in for the play's larger critique of excessive masculine behaviour and the self-defeating proposition of attempting to master their affects. The oaths taken in this first scene are rapidly discarded when the Princess and her attending ladies arrive and each member of the Academe becomes lovesick.

Lovesickness was one of the most prevalent forms of melancholy in early modern England. Jacques Ferrand's *A Treatise on Lovesickness* underscores its humoral underpinnings by ascribing to it the classical definition of a 'form of dotage, proceeding from an inordinate desire to enjoy the beloved object, accompanied by fear and sorrow'.[37] More generally, it was understood as immoderate affection grown diseased. Burton writes on the subject that 'love indeed . . . first united provinces, built cities, and by a perpetual generation makes and preserves mankind, propagates the Church; but if it rage, it is no more love, but burning lust, a disease, frenzy, and madness, hell'.[38] The inherent danger of lovesickness was its gradual morphing into an all-encompassing madness. Ferrand explains the process by which one becomes love-melancholic as one through which 'the passions that preoccupy the soul are imprinted there by the bad habits that generate them. These habits . . . become natural forces that are activated by the least occasion, [and] can be erased only

with the greatest of effort'.[39] As with melancholy generally, the scope and effects of lovesickness were also believed
to vary depending on climate and geographical location.
Ferrand notes that

> the symptoms arising from love bring on different species
> of love melancholy . . . as well as the various influences of
> different regions and climates. The orientals run slavishly
> after the thing desired without any moderation or discre-
> tion. Those who live in southern countries love with impa-
> tience, rage, and fury. Those of the western countries are
> industrious in their courting, and those of the northern are
> slow to woo at all.[40]

Though it draws on classical sources, Ferrand's assessment
performs a similar ethnological revision as the one discussed in this chapter. The treatise does not explicitly mention England, other than the allusion to northerners being
slow to woo. Even then, when Ferrand elaborates, he uses
'the cold German' as an example rather than the Englishman.[41] Again, geographical ramifications move the notion
away from strict humoralism. As a form of melancholy subject to galenic logic, lovesickness underwent a similar ethnological and intellectual recuperation in England. Burton's
Anatomy explains that lovesickness 'rageth with all sorts
and conditions of men, yet it is more evident amongst such
as are young and lusty, in the flower of their years, nobly
descended, high fed, such as live idly and at ease'.[42] The
quartet of young lords that open *Love's Labor's Lost* by
discussing self-mastery of their passions channels the stereotypical conception of a melancholy lover within an intellectualised English discourse.

The play's most comical depiction of melancholy stems
from outside the four pairs of young lovers, in the figure of
the foreigner Don Adriano de Armado. Before appearing

onstage, the character is positioned as a source of entertainment and ridicule for other characters. Navarre informs the other men in this first scene that his court

> Is haunted
> With a refinèd traveler of Spain,
> A man in all the world's new fashion planted,
> That hath a mint of phrases in his brain;
> One who the music of his own vain tongue
> Doth ravish like enchanting harmony;
> . . .
> How you delight, my lords, I know not, I,
> But I protest to love to hear him lie,
> And I will use him for my minstrelsy.   (I, i, 161–6; 173–5)

The 'child of fancy', Armado is presented as the perennial comic foil. The king's description expounds the various attributes the Spanish traveller brings into the Academe that can prove a potent source of entertainment for them. Though the character reflects the growing hostility between English and Spanish monarchies at the time, Armado also echoes Babb's traveller figure who picks up and appropriates the world's fashions but proves oblivious to the ridicule he incurs for doing so. For Navarre and his men, the mocking of such a figure promises delights 'like enchanting harmony'.[43]

In his insistent bid for social status and refinement, Armado too embodies immoderate behaviour. Holofernes describes him later as being too 'picked, too spruce, too affected, too odd, as it were, / Too peregrinate, as I may call it' (V, i, 13–14). The character also furthers ethnological critique of foreign melancholy outlined at this onset of this chapter. Though he does not appear onstage during this first scene, he manifests his presence through a written inquiry to Navarre, which the king reads aloud to the lords:

So it is, besieged with sable-colored
Melancholy, I did commend the black-oppressing humour
To the most wholesome physic of thy health-giving
Air, and, as I am a gentleman, betook myself to
Walk.   (I, i, 227–31)

The lines betray Armado's clumsy manipulation of both
a classical understanding of melancholy (its association
with the colour black, the idea that fresh air might prove
curative to it) and the sophisticated poetical language that
would suggest that the melancholy afflicting him is an
Aristotelian 'malady of great minds'.[44] His blind reliance
on humoral terminology betrays a failure to grasp the
refined, early modern understanding of the concept and
what it implies in the specific context of Navarre's court.
The play draws on the prevalent ethnological division of
foreign and English melancholy by positioning Armado as
the figure of ridicule. When Armado makes his entrance in
the next scene, his discussion on the nature of melancholy
with his Page Mote further highlights his misapplication of
genial melancholy:

ARMADO: Boy, what sign is it when a man of great spirit
 grows melancholy?
MOTE: A great sign, sir, that he will look sad.
ARMADO: Why, sadness is one and the selfsame thing,
 dear imp.
MOTE: No, no, O lord, sir, no.
ARMADO: How canst thou part sadness and melancholy,
 my tender juvenal?
MOTE: By a familiar demonstration of the working, my
 tough señor.
ARMADO: Why 'tough señor'? Why 'tough señor'?
MOTE: Why 'tender juvenal'? Why 'tender juvenal'?
            (I, ii, 1–12)

Douglas Trevor remarks that his inquiry to his page 'alerts sophisticates in Shakespeare's audience to the Spaniard's unfamiliarity with recent developments in theories of the passions'.[45] Though the exchange rapidly devolves into Moth entrapping Armado into his verbal jesting, the Spaniard's opening question offers a distant echo to the one that begins Aristotle's *Problem XXX*. In not knowing that a melancholy disposition is the very *ethos* of men of great spirits, Armado betrays his inadequate knowledge of the sophisticate English affect. His inability to differentiate between sadness and melancholy further cements him as a comic foil. The parallel is pushed further throughout the scene by his admission that his 'spirit grows heavy in love' for Jaquenetta (I, ii, 118). Even the blundering foreigner abandons aristocratic rhetoric for the throes of love-melancholy. In this sense, his reliance on melancholic clichés is no different from the gentlemen's bumbling attempts at courtship, since both approaches are excessive and fundamentally ill-suited to the intended goal. Yet the young lords' melancholy is legitimised through its contrast with Armado's postured affectation.

When they encounter the Princess and her attending ladies (Rosaline, Katherine and Maria), each lord immediately becomes infatuated with one of them. Berowne's brief exchange with Rosaline highlights the play's treatment of lovesickness:

> BEROWNE: Lady, I will commend you to mine own heart.
> ROSALINE: Pray you, do my commendations. I would be glad to see it.
> BEROWNE: I would you heard it groan.
> ROSALINE: Is the fool sick?
> BEROWNE: Sick at the heart.
> ROSALINE: Alack, let it blood.
> BEROWNE: Would that do it good?
> ROSALINE: My physic says 'ay.'

BEROWNE: Will you prick't with your eye?
ROSALINE: *Non point*, with my knife.

(II, i, 179–90)

Despite cautioning others against immoderate behaviour
early on, Berowne adopts the language of the stereotypical
love-melancholic, intimating that his sick heart can only be
cured with Rosaline's affection. In professing his affection
for Rosaline, Berowne recalls the classical understanding of
love-melancholy, identifying his heart as the seat of his affliction and asking her to prick it with her eye.[46] The exchange,
couched in humoral language, embodies the larger power
dynamic in the comedy by which the women hold the upper
hand throughout the back-and-forth wooing games that
the lovers engage in, easily thwarting the suitors' advances.
Rosaline, who earlier in the scene described Berowne as a
man of mirth whose 'fair tongue . . . Delivers in such apt and
gracious words . . . So sweet and voluble is his discourse' (II, i,
72–3; 76), has no problem refusing him. She advises bleeding
to cure his ailing heart and suggests that she prick it with her
knife rather than her eye. Rosaline shows the superior wit of
female characters in the play by manipulating the language
Berowne throws at her and negating its humoral connotations. The comedy stems from the courtship games that such
a process engenders as the play draws on audiences' familiarity with ideas of lovesickness. The interaction between
men and women also relies on the comic symmetry it offers
(four lords, four ladies) to set up the expectation of eventual
romantic pairings. Much like the melancholic identity crises
in *Errors*, the comedy builds towards a union between the
lovers which will sensibly purge the men of their lovesickness. Yet as the play progresses it gradually shifts away from
such an idea. The women weary of the affect. A discussion
between Katherine and Rosaline relating to Navarre's prior

involvement with Katherine's sister showcases the inherent dangers of female melancholy:

> ROSALINE: You'll ne'er be friends with him. 'A killed
>   your sister.
> KATHERINE: He made her melancholy, sad, and heavy,
> And so she died. Had she been light, like you,
> Of such a merry, nimble, stirring spirit,
> She might ha'been a grandam ere she died.
> And so may you, for a light heart lives long.
>
> (V, ii, 13–18)

Early modern medical writings generally held that female melancholy was a dangerous condition. Ferrand writes that although men prove love-melancholic more often, 'women experience more violently this brutal desire'.[47] Going back to Hippocrates, female love-melancholy was one of several ailments that were thought to originate in the 'mysterious, hidden source of both power and sickness' that was the uterus.[48] The focus on female sexual organs as the site of the illness, as opposed to the heart and brain in men, helped to create a gender hierarchy distinction between 'a predominantly masculine, intellectual (and positively valorised) melancholia and a predominantly feminine, bodily (and negatively valorised) opposite'.[49] While masculine love-melancholy was still a medical condition to be treated and cured, it did not incur the types of dangers and symptoms that female melancholy did. This distinction was commonly upheld onstage as well. Bridget Gellert Lyons notes how 'the male-melancholic on the stage was almost always . . . a figure of fun. Only women were invested with genuine pathos in that role'.[50] The mention of a female strand of melancholy in the passage above, one that develops *outside* the play but bears implication *within* it problematises the build towards a comic conclusion. The account of the death of Katherine's sister somewhat taints Navarre's character as the story drastically shifts the comedy's tone, if only momentarily. It suggests a potentially similar fate for the Princess and her attending ladies should they yield to the men's courting. Though the play makes use of the traditional understanding of lovesickness as a diseases of the young, noble and articulate, it makes a point of addressing the more serious (and less comical) feminine counterpart. Yet it somewhat amends the lower status of their ailment by having them outwit the men throughout their games of courtship.

Such serious concerns are momentarily forgotten as the final scene bears witness to three consecutive performances by several of the characters meant to elicit laughter both on and off the stage. In the first instance, (V, ii, 157–265), the men come to court the women disguised as Muscovites, and their female counterparts scorn them mercilessly. Navarre and his lords subsequently return (V, ii, 311–454) and are mocked once again for the absurdity of the oaths they have pledged to their beloved. Finally, the lovers gather to watch a pageant of the Nine Worthies (V, ii, 485–711) put on by Armado and his fellow tributary characters. Here, male and female lovers join in ridiculing each 'actor' taking the stage, until the pageant comes to a halt when Costard informs Armado of Jaquenetta's pregnancy (V, i, 669–74), and the professional clown and the braggart confront each other.

As the four pairs of would-be lovers are gathered onstage, delighting in the ridicule of the performance, the comedy seems poised to fulfil its inherent promise of symmetrical coupling (and the comic purging of love-melancholy thought to accompany it). The entrance of Marcade bearing news of the French king's death irreparably shatters such a possibility:

PRINCESS: Welcome, Marcade,
But that thou interruptest our merriment.
MARCADE: I am sorry, madam, for the news I bring
   Is heavy in my tongue. The King your father –

PRINCESS: Dead, for my life!
MARCADE: Even so. My tale is told.

(V, ii, 713–17)

The news echoes Berowne's early description of the French king as 'decrepit, sick, and bedrid' (I, i, 137), suggesting that the potential for tragedy lurked around the comedy but, like other small incursions of more serious concerns, was kept at bay until now by the naïve, unadulterated merriment of the young lovers. The announcement effectively negates the possibility of a romantic resolution and puts an end to the pageant and to the comedy more generally. Likewise, the love-melancholy developed throughout the play comes into harsh contrast with more tangible grief of mortality. In haste to return to their homeland, the Princess and her attendants no longer have the inclination to pursue the wooing games they had engaged in. Not satisfied with the oaths that the suitors proclaimed, the Princess demands that Navarre

> Go with speed
> To some forlorn and naked hermitage,
> Remote from all the pleasures of the world;
> There stay until the twelve celestial signs
> Have brought about the annual reckoning.
> If this austere insociable life
> Change not your offer made in heat of blood;
> If frosts and fasts, hard lodging, and thin weeds
> Nip not the gaudy blossoms of your love,
> But that it bear this trial, and last love;
> Then at the expiration of the year,
> Come challenge me, challenge me by these deserts,
> And, by this virgin palm now kissing thine,
> I will be thine.   (V, ii, 790–803)

In requiring Navarre to take a new oath, the Princess brings the play full circle; what began with intellectual vows ends with emotional ones tied to the sobering news of her father's passing. Her request that Navarre undergo a year of austerity in a hermitage before resuming the courtship betrays more general anxieties about the excessive behaviours that male characters have displayed while wooing them 'in heat of blood'. The delay also functions as a curative practice for the lords' lovesickness. Ferrand explains that 'Galen recognises the importance of time and its passage in the healing of our passions, describing it as a remedy for erotic melancholy. Time', he adds, 'achieves the desired ends by allowing all manner of new thoughts and activities to preoccupy our minds, unravelling and fading the formerly frenzied and enraged imagination, no matter how strong it was'.[51] The female characters have doubted the authenticity of their suitor's courtship throughout the play, and this last demand indicates their continued suspicions. The speech also outlines the dramatic problem that the French monarch's death creates, denying the audience the expected comic conclusion and heterosexual couplings and asking whether the feelings presented in the play can survive a prolonged exposure to the 'frosts and fasts, hard lodging and thin weeds' that extend well beyond the realm of the comedy. Rosalind's similarly arduous request to Berowne poses a similar interrogation:

> You shall this twelvemonth term from day to day
> Visit the speechless sick and still converse
> With groaning wretches, and your task shall be
> With all the fierce endeavour of your wit
> To enforce the painèd impotent to smile.   (V, ii, 840–4)

Berowne's impassioned reply stresses the tonal quagmire that the play has reached: 'to move wild laughter in the throat of death? / It cannot be. It is impossible. / Mirth cannot move a soul in agony' (V, ii, 845–7). It interrogates the play's own conflation of romantic courtships with death, questioning the sustainability of the laughter that animated most of the play in the wake of a tangible source of emotional trauma. Given the king's death and the abrupt end of courtship and derision, wild laughter is simply not possible. Once again, the play brings attention to the precarious conflation of comedy and melancholy and the seeming incompatibility of their traditional definitions.

The play ends with dual songs of spring and winter which offers the final contrast between life and death, love and sorrow, mirth and melancholy (V, ii, 884–917). The spring's ballad, heralded by the cuckoo, is surprisingly bitter, structured around the image of 'the cuckoo then on every tree [which] mocks married men' (V, ii, 888–9). Conversely, the staring owl's winter song provides 'a merry note, / While greasy Joan doth keel the pot' (V, ii, 908–9), channelling the conviviality called forth by a cold winter's night. As John Pendergast writes, the play inverses 'the usual conventional metaphor of winter as death or melancholy and spring as life'.[52] In its final moments, the play furthers the precarious coexistence of comedy and melancholy through the dual (and duelling) songs as a way to maintain the ambiguity surrounding its conclusion. For Pendergast, the songs 'allow the play to avoid a choice between an artificial happy or sad ending . . . They are complex yet simple, traditional while surprising, pleasing and harsh, and beautiful while sincere'.[53] In his *Preface to Shakespeare*, Harley Granville-Baker famously rejected the notion that the ending of the play was to be perceived as melancholy, since merrier elements, according to him, supplanted the darker undertones of its ending.[54] While the play possesses its share of delightful elements, the abrupt turn the comedy undertakes in Act

5 cannot be overlooked. Undeniably, the play frustrates its own set up, echoing Berowne's dejected exclamation that 'our wooing doth not end like an old play; / Jack hath not Jill. These ladies' courtesy / Might well have made our sport a comedy' (V, ii, 864–6). The songs, soothing as they may be, do not erase the death of the king, nor do they compensate for the shattered symmetry of the play's initial premise. This haunting ambiguity concerning the play's closing hints at the apparent incompatibility of traditional definitions of melancholy within the comic genre.

Love's Labour's Lost's treatment of melancholy offers similar evidence to that of *The Comedy of Errors* regarding Shakespearean comedy's problematic engagement with humour. Melancholy is not the focal point of these works, but the paradoxical role it holds, facilitating the anglicising of foreign settings and sources, as well as putting pressure on conventional comic depictions, suggests a burgeoning pattern in Shakespearean comedy. Moreover, the contrast of melancholic male characters relying on humour as a mode of self-expression with more emotionally resourceful female characters such as Adriana and Rosaline marks a gendered distinction of comic melancholy that grows more prevalent in later plays. Shakespeare's early comedies are of their time, scientifically, ethnologically and dramatically, but the marked ambiguity at the end of each play, and the failure to purge away their melancholic pangs, suggests that classical definitions of melancholy do not serve Shakespearean comedy adequately. It is ultimately telling that an early comedy such as *Love's Labor's Lost* denies Jack his Jill but allows the pangs of sable-coloured melancholy to roam the stage. It is not quite the *comique féroce* that Baudelaire assigns to England a few centuries later, but it speaks volumes as to Shakespeare's subsequent development of comic melancholy.

Notes

1. Baudelaire, *Curiosités Esthétiques*, 256–7.
2. Bodin, *Six Bookes of the Commonwealth*, 149.
3. Harrison, *The Description of England*, 445–6.
4. Floyd-Wilson, *English Ethnicity and Race in Early Modern Drama*, 7.
5. Floyd-Wilson 12.
6. Levin, *Playboys and Killjoys*, 24.
7. Frye, *Natural Perspective*, 47.
8. Bevington, 'The Comedy of Errors', 2.
9. Miola, 'The Plays and the Critics', 38.
10. Segal, 'The MENAECHMI: Roman Comedy of Errors', 121.
11. 'The Two Menaechmuses', *Plautus*, 363–487.
12. McCarthy, *Slaves, Masters and the Art of Authority in Plautine Comedy*, 47.
13. Freedman, *Staging the Gaze*. See also Mentz, *At the Bottom of Shakespeare's Ocean*, 35–49; Withworth, 'Rectifying Shakespeare's Errors', 227–60; and Janet Adelman, 'Male Bonding in Shakespeare's Comedies', 73–103.
14. Cooper, *English Romance in Time*, 5.
15. Freedman 262.
16. Enterline, *Tears of Narcissus*, 191–2.
17. Klibansky et al., *Saturn and Melancholy*, 130–1.
18. Foucault, *History of Madness*, 12.
19. Foucault 12.
20. Enterline 198.
21. Plato, *The Laws* 4: 6, 159.
22. Plato 160.
23. Burton writes that there is 'no better physic for a melancholy man than change of air and variety of places, to travel abroad and see fashions', *Anatomy of Melancholy*, II, 67.
24. Bacon, 'Of Travel', 135.
25. Babb, *Elizabethan Malady*, 74.
26. Babb 75–6.
27. Paster, *Humoring the Body*, 209.

28. Enterline 200–3.
29. Tempera '"Now I play a merchant's part"', 155.
30. Enterline 218–19.
31. Tofte, 'From Alba', 41.
32. Bristol, 'Shakespeare's Sonnets and the Publication of Melancholy', 208.
33. Several critics have claimed that the play makes reference to famous debates or attacks between the likes of Gabriel Harvey and Thomas Nash or George Chapman and Walter Raleigh. See John S. Pendergast, *Love's Labor's Lost*, 33–5.
34. Mazzio, 'The Melancholy of Print', 188.
35. Mazzio 191.
36. Daniel, *Melancholy Assemblage*, 91.
37. Ferrand, *Treatise on Lovesickness*, 238.
38. Burton 49.
39. Ferrand 326.
40. Ferrand 261. Ferrand is referring to Hippocrates' *Of Airs, Waters and Places*.
41. Ibid.
42. Burton 56.
43. Lynne Magnusson identifies a connection between the character and Antonio Perez (1534–1611), the secretary of state for Philipp II, who fled Spain and persecution, published an account of his life, and was eventually arrested for murder, '"To gaze so much at the fine stranger,"' 56–7.
44. Babb 74.
45. Trevor, *Poetics of Melancholy*, 15.
46. Ferrand draws on Aristotle in thinking of 'erotic passions as disease', Beecher and Ciavolella write, situating 'the case of love more firmly in the body, assigning to the heart and reproductive organs more central roles in the generation of erotic appetites', in 'Introduction', Jacques Ferrand, *Treatise on Lovesickness*, 44–5. Likewise, his treatise concurs with the common belief that the eyes represent the gateway to the body and the soul, Ferrand 269.
47. Ferrand 312. Burton concurs that the ailment is worse for women, 56.

48. Wells, *The Secret Wound*, 221–2.
49. Wells 224.
50. Lyons, *Voices of Melancholy*, 25.
51. Ferrand 354.
52. Pendergast 95.
53. Pendergast 77–8.
54. Granville-Baker, *Preface to Shakespeare*, 14.

CHAPTER 3

MELANCHOLIC DISSONANCE AND THE LIMITS OF PSYCHO-HUMORALISM

'I'd never join a club that would allow a person like me to become a member.'

Groucho Marx's resignation joke, allegedly included in a letter informing the Friars' Club of his withdrawal from membership, provides an arresting parallel to the melancholic figures I discuss in this chapter. It has been attributed over the years to dignitaries such as Sigmund Freud and Woody Allen (whose *Annie Hall* character Alvy Singer, an iconic comic melancholic himself, actually opens the film with this quote, acknowledging both Freud and Marx). To use Marx's terms, the melancholy of *Much Ado about Nothing* and *The Merchant of Venice* strikes an altogether dissonant comedic note that proves at once integral to and inherently at odds with the plays that contain it. If *The Comedy of Errors* and *Love's Labour's Lost* underscored the impracticality of galenic and Aristotelian philosophies of melancholy within Shakespearean comedy, the plays examined in this chapter bring such understandings to their point of collapse. They achieve such a rupture by exacerbating the negative traits associated with each of them as to render them utterly incompatible with the comic genre. The plays transform the galenic tenet of fear and sadness without cause into an overwhelming despondency that thwarts any attempt to turn melancholy into a comic foil. Concomitantly, the idea of genial melancholy morphs into a stubborn claim for interiority that rejects any potential for tempering or alleviating efforts. These dramatic manoeuvres highlight the growing disconnect between traditional definitions of melancholy and Shakespeare's comic re-envisioning of the concept. Conversely, they attest to the gradual transformation of comedy that Shakespeare's development of the melancomic provokes.

As this chapter suggests, both Don John and Antonio obstinately self-identify as melancholics, a characteristic that bespeaks their general lack of dramatic involvement. Contrary to Antipholus of Syracuse or the lovers of Navarre's Academe, comic action develops *around* them rather than through them. While the potential for their remediation exists in each play, their inertia ultimately leads to their failure to fully integrate with the play-worlds they inhabit. The ambivalent closing tableau of each play signals the breakdown of psycho-humoral representations of melancholy in Shakespearean comedy. Don John's brief participation in *Much Ado* provides a blueprint for such a process, since his nebulous claims of villainy in opposing the festive spirit that otherwise infuses Messina always proves subsidiary to his melancholic countenance. Shakespeare fully develops this pattern in The *Merchant of Venice* through Antonio. As the dramatic fulcrum for the comedy's various plotlines, the melancholic merchant embodies the inherent incompatibility of traditional philosophies of melancholy within Shakespeare's comic dramaturgy, resisting the play's final pull towards the underpinnings of romance and festivity by clinging to a melancholic disposition that is no longer proper to Belmont.

Overall, the melancholy of Don John and Antonio yields surprisingly little mockery or amusement in itself. This phenomenon proves a stark contrast to the popular humour comedy genre, which relies on satirical depictions of humours as its central source of laughter. Jonson's *Every Man* plays offer an unabashed assault on humours that pokes fun at the totalising effects individuals ascribe to their humours and the foregoing of responsibilities that generally accompanies such an attitude. In *Every Man in His Humour*, the merchant Kitely, struggling to describe the jealousy that afflicts him, remarks that

> it may well be call'd poor mortals' plague;
> For, like a pestilence, it doth infect
> The houses of the brain. First, it begins
> Solely to work upon the phantasy,
> Filling her seat with such pestiferous air,
> As soon corrupts the judgement; and from thence
> Sends like contagion to the memory:
> Still each to other giving the infection.
> Which as a subtle vapour spreads itself
> Confusedly through every sensive part,
> Till not a thought or motion in the mind
> Be free from the black poison of suspect.   (II, i, 222–39)

Jonson relies on the audience's built-in understanding of the bubonic plague to convey his critique, using the trope of infection to explain how a humour would conceivably take hold of a body's governing functions. Jonson's criticism, as Paster writes, also takes aim at the 'socially performative uses of humours in order to flaunt eccentricity'.[1] Jonsonian characters seek to validate their identities through their humours, while the comedies work to undo this process through public derision. Dramatic mockery acts as a corrective measure seeking to deconstruct the 'agreed-upon social fiction by which [characters] describe and claim individuality' both on and off the stage.[2] Jonson's critique of melancholy centres mainly on the disingenuousness of its proponents, who flaunt it as a feigned marker of sophistication. A brief exchange between the town gull Mathew and the fool Stephen in *Every Man In* shows the eager absurdity with which characters will affect melancholy:

> STEPHEN: Ay, truly sir, I am mightily given to melancholy.
> MATHEW: Oh, it's your only fine humour, sir; your true melancholy breeds your perfect fine wit, sir. I am melancholy myself, divers times, Sir and then do I no more but take pen and paper, presently, and overflow you half a score, or a dozen of sonnets at a sitting. . . .
> STEPHEN: I thank you, sir. I shall be bold, I warrant you; have you a stool, there to be melanch'ly upon?
>
> (III, i, 80–4; 90–1)

Jonson is not so much critiquing the humour itself as he is its misappropriation in order to 'reflect hierarchical social values'.[3] In a misguided attempt to elevate their social status, the characters project the idea of melancholy onto material objects, from a pen and paper to a stool, in a flagrantly artificial bid for individuality clearly meant to elicit derision. Jonson stresses the point by having Stephen contract the word melancholy (melanch'ly), bringing further attention to their unrefined bid for status. In a similar deriding of feigned nobility, Puntarvolo's assertion of his complexion while courting a gentlewoman in *Every Man Out* – 'Mine is melancholy' – is met with Carlo Buffone's swift retort: 'so is the dog' (II, i, 233–4). Jonson once again draws laughter by ascribing melancholy to a nonhuman target, undercutting Puntarvolo's claim for sophistication. Jonsonian satire focuses on human behaviours rather than actual humoral makeup, placing his humour comedies in a direct lineage with the comedy of manners tradition that later informs Henri Bergson's comic theory. For Bergson, laughter neutralises the threat to social cohesion that an individual's 'inelasticity' of character poses. As he explains,

> the comic is that side of a person which reveals his likeness
> to a thing, that aspect of human events which, through its
> peculiar inelasticity, conveys the impression of pure mech-
> anism, of automatism, of movement without life. Conse-
> quently it expresses an individual or collective imperfection
> which calls for an immediate corrective. This corrective is
> laughter, a social gesture that singles out and represses a
> special kind of absentmindedness in men and in events.[4]

The process Bergson defines here strongly echoes Jonson's
model of humour comedy, where the intention of laughter is
always to engender social change and improve behaviour.[5]
Mocking such abhorrent humoral displays (on and off the
stage) becomes akin to a civic duty.

This stylistic link between Jonsonian characterisation
and Bergson's comic theory broadly echoes the unyielding
professions of melancholy to which Don John and Antonio
adamantly cling. Yet, it falls short of delineating their chief
dramatic function in the larger context of Shakespeare's
ongoing revision of comic melancholy. Their melancholic
utterances, problematic as they may be, are not ridiculed, nor
is their legitimacy ever truly questioned. Rather, Don John
and Antonio frustrate the comedies' efforts to understand,
naturalise and eventually purge them of their melancholy.
This resistance likewise dislocates their characters from the
traditional binary of social integration heralded by Frye and
Barber. The dynamics of Shakespearean comedy exceed this
model by emancipating melancholic characters from comic
expectations. If anything, their despondency seemingly prevents them from capitalising on their otherwise ripe comic
potential. In doing so, Shakespearean comedy draws attention to how vestigial classical representations of melancholy
are in the wake of a rapidly evolving dramatic genre.

The failure to resolve Don John and Antonio's stories in
favour of allowing them to become background characters

in an attempt to resolve a generic conundrum by suppressing their melancholy rather than curbing or purging it obfuscates celebratory acts of comic closure and is problematic for the genre. Accordingly, the exclusionary practices found at the end of *Much Ado about Nothing* and *The Merchant of Venice* should not be interpreted as a victimisation effort, as is often argued, but as the logical dramatic outcome prompted by the characters' incessant refusal to purge their melancholy. The ambiguity of their final status formulates a rejection of conventional melancholic philosophies in Shakespearean comedy. Don John's punishment is delayed until the next morning, and while Antonio is not overtly rejected from Belmont, he does not seem to fit in as deftly as other characters. In highlighting their necessary removal from the comic resolution yet drawing attention to the generic complications of such a manoeuvre, the plays underscore the limits of psycho-humoral characterisations of melancholy.

Maskless in Messina: The Melancholic Remainder in Much Ado about Nothing

Don John's critical afterlife mirrors that of the play he hails from. Despite recent efforts to account for its darker, more complex undertones, *Much Ado about Nothing* often struggles to unshackle itself from its romantic comedy label. Conversely, its resident melancholic figure usually suffers a hasty dismissal, as when Bridget Lyons sums up his involvement as failing 'to turn *Much Ado about Nothing* into a tragedy'.[6] My contention is that Don John's brief participation in *Much Ado* provides succinct dramatic evidence of the way in which Shakespearean comedy applies pressure on staged melancholy. His oddly pointed sense of sadness parodies the galenic predication on physical excess and the purported influence of natural phenomena on human anatomy. Don John's articulation of his melancholy rests on a paradoxical insistence on his lack of control over the variability of his disposition and his adamant refusal to partake in most of the play's proceedings. Unlike the treatment Jonson's characters' humours receive, Don John's humour is not met with much scorn or social derision (at least not overtly). The character is granted multiple opportunities for redemption, which he continually rejects. His problematic status in the play's closing moments provides the final emblem of his comic incongruity. *Much Ado about Nothing* depicts a contested theatrical space in which mirth and melancholy repeatedly overlap, but one in which the drive towards festivity inevitably triumphs.

The play opens on a conversation between Leonato, the Governor of Messina, and a messenger detailing the return of Don Pedro from a successful military campaign. When the bravery of young Claudio is broached, Leonato inquires as to the reaction of Claudio's uncle upon hearing the news:

LEONATO: Did he break out into tears?
MESSENGER: In great measure.
LEONATO: A kind of overflow of kindness. There are no
    faces truer than those that are so washed. How much
    better it is to weep at joy than to joy at weeping!

(I, i, 24–8)

Claudio's uncle is commended for shedding an inordinate number of joyful tears. The inherently galenic comments, with the imagery of flowing humoral displays, echo the precarious coalescence of affects that characterises the play. *Much Ado* unfolds in the aftermath of war, amidst a pressing communal desire for the merriment and budding romantic courtships to hold more sorrowful matters at bay. Messina is an unstable emotional arena in which humours constantly crash into one another, where excess passes as the norm and in which mirth ultimately trumps melancholy. From its onset, the play's interest in disproportionate masculine emotional displays frames Don John's melancholy as antagonistic. Thus, the image of

Claudio's uncle weeping of joy 'in great measure' is quickly contrasted with Don John being described by Conrade two scenes later as being 'out of measure sad' (I, iii, 2). To Conrade's query as to why he should be so melancholic and not seek remedy for it, Don John replies,

> I wonder that thou, being, as thou sayst
> thou art, born under Saturn, goest about to apply a
> moral medicine to a mortifying mischief. I cannot hide
> what I am: I must be sad when I have cause and smile
> at no man's jests, eat when I have stomach and wait
> for no man's leisure, sleep when I am drowsy and
> tend on no man's business, laugh when I am merry
> and claw no man in his humour.   (I, iii, 10–17)

Don John's answer implies an understanding of melancholy rooted in its implacable nature, yet integrated within a diversified and well-regulated range of affects and needs. He first identifies Conrade as a fellow melancholic (having been born under the sign of Saturn) before chiding him for suggesting the existence of a cure for what he perceives to be his irremediable condition. In his insistence on individualising his sorrow, Don John ultimately validates the traditional tenets of melancholy his character exacerbates. The allusion to astrological influences on human behaviour dovetails with the classical consideration of nature as a binding agent for all living organisms, in which features of the natural world such as planets were thought to influence – if not dictate – an individual's humoral makeup and behaviour.[7] Writing about 'celestial' influences of melancholy, Ficino explains that Saturn imparts melancholy from birth in certain individuals, which suggests that for some life as a melancholic is predetermined.[8] Don John's affirmation that he cannot hide who he is implies a belief that a melancholic person born under Saturn essentially lacks any responsibility towards the ailment. The character's opening speech firmly positions him within a classically oriented philosophical understanding of melancholy as an external force bearing internal influence.

The remainder of Don John's speech provides a surprising rejection of the same galenic tradition, most notably the belief that excess fosters melancholy. Galen's notion that humours existed in constant mingling, as a 'complex alteration of substances' necessitating balance, expanded in the Renaissance to cover an impressive matrix of natural factors which, if certain factors were present in excess, could cause melancholy.[9] 'There is not so much harm proceeding from the substance itself', Robert Burton writes,

> as there is from the quantity, disorder of time and place, unseasonable use of it, intemperance, overmuch or overlittle taking of it . . . as a lamp is choked with a multitude of oil, or a little fire with overmuch wood quite extinguished.[10]

The idea does not narrow melancholic causes as much as it alters their categorisation, now being associated with an excess of food, drink, sleep, idleness and a slew of other potential triggers. Don John's profession to be 'sad when I have cause' rejects the galenic dichotomy of excess and balance by suggesting that his disposition, melancholic or otherwise, cannot be modified, even when 'out of measure'. His reply to Conrade includes melancholy within a range of emotional states and fundamental needs requiring instantaneous and unmitigated satiation. Unlike the flux of humours, Don John hints at a capacity to experience states *sequentially*, in a logical orchestration that suggests rigid moderation rather than outlandish excess. This last idea stresses the character's self-purported inability to modify his melancholic behaviour. Don John is not a melancholic, but is melancholic *at this particular moment*, as if his current situation requires it. In questioning his melancholy, Conrade warns Don John (and the audience) that such behaviour will create ripples in a festivity-inclined city such as Messina.

The seldom recognised fact that the scene presents two melancholic characters yet surreptitiously singles out Don John as the one thwarting social conventions further stresses the idea that the character's opening speech makes for a problematic entry into a comedy strongly invested in merriment and romantic celebrations. Conrade advises him to keep his humours in check, reminding him of his recent and tenuous reconciliation with his brother Don Pedro. He preaches that Don John 'should take true root but by the fair weather that / you make yourself. It is needful that you frame the / season for your own harvest' (I, iii, 22–4). As a fellow melancholic, he does not condemn Don John's disposition, but he seeks to curb it towards a socially acceptable stance. For Conrade, the safer play is to moderate melancholic tendencies so as not to appear out of tune with the otherwise festive atmosphere in Messina. Don John has no intention to cater to his brother's good graces, unequivocally professing that he would

> Rather be a canker in a hedge than a
> rose in his grace, and it better fits my blood to be
> disdained of all than to fashion a carriage to rob love
> from any.
> . . .
> It must not be denied but I am
> a plain-dealing villain. I am trusted with a muzzle and
> enfranchised with a clog;
> . . .
> Let me be that I am, and seek not to alter me.
>   (I, iii, 25–8; 29–31; 34)

Don John once again selects a deliberately melancholic stance over one brought on by excess, claiming that he prefers to stick out unfavourably since his blood is better suited for such a position. Don John once again selects a deliberately melancholic stance over one brought on by excess, claiming that he prefers to stick out unfavourably since his blood is better suited for such a position. Though he does not deny the possibility that his humour could be curbed, he asks Conrade to refrain from attempts to change him. The speech also introduces Don John's purported villainy, depicting him as a dangerous yet subdued beast, muzzled and clogged. The captive imagery accords with the notion that Don John cannot alter the state he is in, yet his insistence that Conrade should not try to 'alter' him (recalling the galenic principle of *alloiousthai* – the idea that matter could transform itself) clearly demonstrates the hierarchal dynamics at play between his villainy and his melancholy.[11]

Critics usually short-change Don John's melancholy by identifying it as dramatic signpost of his role as a 'plain-dealing' villain. This interpretative strategy opens the way to the kind of dismissive criticism alluded to earlier, epitomised in statements such as George Bernard Shaw's assertion that Don John is 'a true natural villain . . . having no motive in this world except sheer love of evil'.[12] Don John's initial despondency in the wake of impending festivities links him with the widely popular tradition of the malcontent, a dramatic figure whose reputation for 'seditious activity' led early modern audiences to associate it with criminality.[13] In this sense, Don John's initial avowal of melancholy anticipates the haste with which he turns his attention to plotting against Hero and Claudio. Though he professes a desire to ruin Claudio's union, Don John proves arrestingly passive following his initial machinations. The melancholy he so vehemently defends in the first act remains his primary contribution to the play and frustrates any anticipation of criminal behaviour that his character type might foster. Don John takes on the role of villain within the festive atmosphere of

Messina because he would prefer to be despised rather than be coerced into modifying his behaviour. This subtle shift suggests that Don John's persistent self-identification as melancholic forces him into an antagonistic relationship with the play's championing of festivity and self-mitigation. When Borachio subsequently enters and informs him of Claudio and Hero's upcoming nuptials, Don John turns his attention to more villainous endeavours, hoping that ruining their wedding 'may prove / food to my displeasure' (I, iii, 61–2). This hatred of Claudio, displayed on the heels of his elaborate defence of a melancholic demeanour, betokens galenic humoralism more than comic villainy. Mention of Claudio's wedding places Don John at a dramatic crossroads between the generic expectations that his melancholy creates and his refusal to be anything other than melancholic. In this sense, his discontent can be understood as complementary yet subservient to his initial melancholic state.

Don John's insistence on his unequivocal but measured sense of sadness further contrasts the play's larger commentary on excess, in which eventual temperance regarding food, drink and festive behaviour leads to romantic (and comic) fulfilment. Indulgence was a common – if not normative – early modern behaviour and, in *Much Ado*, the disproportionate celebratory indulgences of male characters come to be replaced by socially sanctioned acts of romantic couplings. This shift is epitomised by the contentious relationship between Beatrice and Benedick.

From early on, Benedick is associated with the consumption of food, as Beatrice, mockingly commenting on his military prowess, describes him as 'a very valiant trencherman [with] an excellent stomach' (I, i, 48–9), equating notions of masculine bravura with a lack of control over one's appetites. As the figurehead of excessive masculine indulgence, it is through Benedick that the play introduces the idea that extreme behaviour of any kind, what Timothy Bright refers to as 'disorderly behaviour of our own parts, in such actions as belong to the government of our health', could breed melancholy.[14] Beatrice, whose ability to assess other characters is extolled throughout the comedy, takes great pleasure in berating him on the subject. As she dances with him during the masque scene, she deplores the fact that 'Signor Benedick' will

> But break a comparison or two
> on me, which peradventure not marked or not laughed
> at strikes him into melancholy; and then there's a partridge
> wing saved, for the fool will eat no supper that
> night.   (II, i, 140–4)

Beatrice notes that the mere failure on her part to laugh at Benedick's witty remarks will plunge him into melancholy and actually deprive him of his appetite, which she previously identified as one of his chief attributes. The two passages present him not only as excessive but also as inconstant, swaying from being a man with a voracious stomach to one with no stomach at all. Beatrice's comments also offer another contrasting melancholy to that of Don John's. The comparison further segregates Don John, who only eats when he feels hungry and feels sad when he ought to, within the play's male population and their inclinations towards excess. In Messina, it seems that an unrestricted display of melancholy would be better received than a measured and uncompromising one.

Don John's adamant refusal to placate society by abandoning his melancholic countenance disturbs other characters. Early on, Beatrice remarks to Hero that

> He were an excellent man that were made
> just in the midway between him and Benedick. The
> one is too like an image and says nothing, and the
> other too like my lady's eldest son, evermore tattling.
>   (II, i, 6–9)

Beatrice positions the men on opposite ends of a binary of modulated behaviour, one being too withdrawn into melancholy, the other is childishly loquacious. Her conflation also implies a hypothetical middle ground between the two men, 'half Signor Benedick's tongue in / Count John's mouth', as Leonato subsequently suggests, 'and half Count John's melancholy / in Signor Benedick's face' (II, i, 10–12), that once again stresses temperance. For Beatrice, an 'excellent man' is neither melancholic nor merry in abundance but one who presents a balance of both dispositions.

It is Don John's unwillingness to change that truly sets him aside from Benedick, Claudio and the play's other male characters, all of whom ultimately temper or repent unruly behaviours. This contrast is most evident in the masque put on in the second act (II, i, 80–147). The scene pits the perfunctory, clumsy nature of masculine demeanour with the cleverer attitudes of their female counterparts, as the women have no difficulty identifying their disguised dance partners. More importantly, the masque provides a visual example of Don John's resistance to adopting a different role from that which he perceives to be his (even within the pretence of the masque). Though the masque allows him and his acolytes to put their machinations in place, Don John essentially relinquishes his role as comic villain in the following scene, as Borachio and Conrade carry out the plot against Hero and Claudio from then on. The shift is dramatically apparent in the gradual reduction of Don John's lines throughout the scene to expository queries – 'show me briefly how?' (II, ii, 11), 'What proof shall I make of that?' (II, ii, 26) – so as to backlight Borachio's longer, more detailed speeches. The character's subsequent disappearance from the play confirms his expandability. His relevance to the play's central plot (as Don Pedro's disgruntled brother) is severely problematised by the irrelevance of his involvement following his initial scheme. The addition of two villainous characters in Conrade

and Borachio undoes the comic symmetry that the play seemingly sets up in its first act.

This paradoxical characterisation attests to the difficulties tied to comic stagings of melancholy that go beyond
ridicule. Don John's excessive melancholy simply does not
create opportunities for laughter, and the eventual news of
his capture complicates the play's ending more than it offers
any sense of closure for the character, comic or otherwise.
In the wake of Hero's persecution and Beatrice's admon-
ishment to Benedick to 'kill Claudio' (IV, i, 288), the play's
urgent turn towards festivity in the last scene clatters against
the need for justice to be carried out once the news of Don
John's capture reaches the stage. The comedy cannot concern
itself with a proper punishment in its final moments. Upon
being informed that Don John has been 'tak'n in flight, [and]
brought with armèd men back to Messina' (V, iv, 123–4),
Benedick all but dismisses the character's fate in the play's
closing lines: 'Think not on him till tomorrow. I'll devise /
thee brave punishments for him. Strike up, pipers!' (V, iv,
125–6). The precise nature of the punishments in question
remains indeterminate (even inconsequential), as characters prove more eager to celebrate upcoming marriages and
musicians are instructed to drown out any concerns that the
mention of Don John might elicit. While we can potentially
understand this situation as a Girardian scapegoating of
Don John for the egregious discriminations committed by
Borachio and Conrade, as well as the harsh treatment of Hero
by Claudio, Leontes and Don Pedro once they learn of her
alleged infidelity, the very mention of the character attests to
the impossibility of integrating or completely excluding him
from the comedy.

In his exhaustive performance history of the play, John
Cox explains how 'the messenger's announcement of Don
John's capture and Benedick's references to punishments

were deleted in most Victorian and Edwardian productions [so as to make] the ending appear more harmonious than the full text. Some late twentieth-century productions', he adds, 'have foregrounded the passage as a dissonant element in the play's conclusion'.[15] Don John does not undermine the end of *Much Ado about Nothing* as forcefully as other melancholic characters in Shakespeare do their plays (as will be discussed shortly), but his incongruity lingers on stage, even with Benedick's advice not to think of him. The final scene repositions him as the muzzled, cankerous melancholic who remains an unresolved disruption to harmony, despite ongoing festivities. In pointing out the inherent unsuitability of humoral melancholy within the realm of comedy, *Much Ado about Nothing* comes close to representing the way in which melancholy would affect a comedic plot in its actuality. Don John's melancholy, unabashed and unchecked, saddles the play with a barely perceptible yet persistent knot at its close. Perhaps the success of such a dramatic undertaking can account for the widespread critical dismissal the character generally incurs. In a play where characters wear masks, mask their feelings and participate in elaborate masquerades of courtship and gossip, the motto 'I cannot hide what I am' deserves a certain amount of commendation for the individuality it promulgates. Unfortunately for Don John, this stance, as far as Shakespearean comedy is concerned, can only lead to exclusion. It seems the worst situation one can find oneself in in *Much Ado*, is to be maskless in Messina.

The Idle Business of Humour in The Merchant of Venice

In sooth, I know not why I am so sad.
It wearies me, you say it wearies you;
But how I caught it, found it, or came by it,
What stuff 'tis made of, whereof it is born,

I am to learn;
And such a want-wit sadness makes of me
That I have much ado to know myself.   (I, i, 1–7)

Even for a play as tonally ambiguous as *The Merchant Venice*,
Antonio's proclamation remains a striking beginning to
a comedy, a fact reinforced by the plethora of criticism
that the merchant's enigmatic sadness has sparked. Virtu-
ally every argument has been expounded in an attempt to
ascribe cogent meaning to Antonio's mystifying sorrow. A
regrettable side effect of this large-scale investigation is that
his melancholy has morphed gradually into an argumenta-
tive stepping stone, an obligatory roadblock that needs to be
addressed in a general sense but which need not loom large
in subsequent analysis. Thus, in trying to define it properly,
scholars often fail to account for the function of Antonio's
melancholy *within* the play, treating it instead, as Drew
Daniel suggests, 'as a discursive switch point that allows it
to "carry" any and/or all of the multiple, overdetermining
explanations his behaviour solicits: merchant capitalist anxiety, Christian heroism, unrequited homoerotic desire [and]
moral masochism'.[16] Daniel's argument outlines the critical
pitfall that the merchant's sadness represents as a *discourse*,
one whose 'daunting curriculum . . . mocks his exhaustion'.[17]
In other words, the source of Antonio's melancholy, despite
plentiful and sometimes illuminating critical commentary,
does not underscore its salient comic feature. Eschewing the
nature of his condition in favour of its dramatic impact, I
want to bypass the notion of 'root cause' to argue that Antonio embodies the point of collapse for traditional definitions
of melancholy in Shakespearean comedy. The melancholy
in *Merchant* unfolds at the forefront of dramatic development, shaping Antonio's involvement in both the wooing of
Portia by Bassanio and the bond he agrees to with Shylock.
By developing around a comic protagonist crippled by an

unyielding melancholy (and eventually abandoning him), the play highlights the irremediable dissonance between classical philosophies and Shakespeare's comic revision of melancholy. What makes Antonio sad, ultimately, does not matter as much as the fact that he remains so at the end of the play, bringing an underhanded damper to its closing festivities. The merchant's figurative exclusion in Act 5 suggests that comic depictions of melancholy in their classical sense have reached a dead end on the Shakespearean stage.

Though a case can be made – and certainly has been – that the entirety of Shakespeare's comic canon deviates from the genre's commonly accepted conventions, echoing Frye's idea that 'a comedy is not a play which ends happily [but one] in which a certain structure is present and works through to its own logical end', the question of whether *The Merchant of Venice* can actually be considered a comedy is one that has punctuated scholarly discourses rather incessantly over the last four centuries.[18] In a sense, as Graham Holderness remarks, the play became a comedy by deduction; it was classified as such in the 1623 folio, being neither a re-enactment of English history nor containing the death and destruction usually akin to Shakespearean tragedy.[19] Criticism to this day struggles to ascribe to the play a definitive genre beyond this initial classification. Mariangela Tempera declares it to be the 'bitterest of Shakespeare's comedies'.[20] Linda Woodbridge defines the play as a 'revenge comedy', an inventive term that partially captures its skewed tonal ambiguity.[21] If certain aspects of the play call for a comedic tone (Bassanio's wooing of Portia and the ethereal atmosphere of Belmont, reminiscent of Arden and Illyria), more serious elements offset this precariously romantic construction, validating James Bulman's contention that *The Merchant of Venice* manages to be 'various things at once – allegory and folk tale, romantic comedy and problem play', a versatility that became increasingly troublesome in modern interpretations of the play.[22]

The plot closely mirrors that of Giovanni Fiorentino's 1598 novella *Il Pecorone*, in which a young man (Giannetto) undertakes a lengthy sea voyage, financed by his merchant godfather, Ansaldo, in order to woo a rich widow. A number of failed attempts leave an indebted Ansaldo at the mercy of an unnamed Jewish usurer who demands a pound of flesh as restitution. The merchant is eventually spared, the moneylender punished and Giannetto ultimately wins the lady's hand.[23] Yet the melancholy that epitomises Antonio's character finds no equivalent in the Italian story. Nor do we find any evidence of it in Christopher Marlowe's *The Jew of Malta*, where the focus remains wholly on the villainous antics of Barabas. It stands as a Shakespearean addition that complicates the play's comic and romantic underpinnings more insistently than Don John's antagonistic demeanour in *Much Ado*.

The first act weaves an insistent depiction of melancholy through its otherwise comedic fabric. What renders it problematic from the onset is Antonio's inability to explain the overwhelming sense of sadness afflicting him. Unlike Don John's confident claim that he must feel sad when inclined to, Antonio's opening lines offer an interesting modulation of the seminal principle that melancholy is best defined as the elicitation of fear and sorrow without cause; Antonio worries about the causeless sadness he experiences. As he questions whether he 'caught it, found it, or came by it' (I, i, 3), each verb substantially decreases his sense of agency until he appears altogether passive vis-à-vis the ailment. Despite the anxieties it creates, Antonio proves eager to consider publicly the particularities of his melancholy. His inquiry as to the 'stuff' that comprises it, beyond its galenic connotations, presents melancholy as a commodity. Antonio perceives it as his personal possession, which he hopes to sell to his friends as a topic of interest. From the onset, Antonio seeks to cultivate interest in his melancholy by ascribing it a social value that could render it (and him) desirable within Venice's mercantile community. His concluding statement that he has 'much ado to know [himself]' further stresses the correlation between melancholy, identity and public expression that the merchant strives for. Indeed, the play's first words ('in sooth') imply the synthesis of a longer conversation that audiences will never be privy to, one that may occur repeatedly for Antonio and his friends.

His friends' first inclination is to identify a source so as to possibly enact a cure. The comedy's mystifying opening utterance of sadness thus leans towards a galenic model of causation that leads other characters (and audiences alike) to indulge in Antonio's desire to locate his melancholy at the core of the play's focus. The success of such an endeavour rests on the merchant's insistence on the enigmatic quality of his sadness. He rapidly denies claims that his sorrow stems from mercantile or even romantic complications. To Salerio's assertion that his 'mind is tossing on the ocean' along with his ships (I, i, 8–9), he merely replies: 'my merchandise makes me not sad' (I, i, 45), refuting his occupation as a possible cause for his melancholy without associating it with mirth in return. Accordingly, Solanio's suggestion that Antonio is 'in love' is cast aside in an even more dismissive fashion: 'Fie, fie!' (I, i, 46). By implying in his professions of sadness that fortune and the pursuit of a suitable mate would not affect his disposition, Antonio negates the possibility that in the play two attributes commonly associated with comic premises (money and love) will offer tangible and potentially remediable dramatic obstacles. His repudiation of these possibilities marks a stark departure from the melancholic merchant characters of *The Comedy of Errors*, whose identities are vested ultimately in marital and financial bliss. Likewise, Antonio's silence as to a plausible hypothesis highlights the incapacitating effect of his melancholy. What persists beyond his refutations, the only piece of information that Antonio willingly supplies, is the persistence of melancholy.

This behaviour troubles his friends, whose perceived eagerness to do away with his sadness and move on to the comedy at hand suggests a dramatic landscape in which mirth and melancholy cannot co-exist within the same individual. Solanio promptly abandons the guessing game and declares,

> Then let us say you are sad
> Because you are not merry; and 'twere as easy
> For you to laugh and leap, and say you are merry
> Because you are not sad.   (I, i, 47–50)

Solanio's ensuing conclusion that 'nature hath framed strange fellows in her time . . . of such vinegar aspect / That they'll not show their teeth in way of smile' (I, i, 51; 54–5) suggests a polarised dichotomy of mirth and sadness, where an individual feels emotions sequentially rather than concurrently. This perception is severely problematised by Antonio's prominent status within the Venetian social setting. Other characters not only wish he would recover, they actually need him to abandon his melancholic demeanour since they cannot dismiss him in the same way that their counterparts in *Much Ado* could Don John. In trying to root out its cause, Salerio and Solanio spend a considerable amount of time attempting to visualise the totalising effect of Antonio's melancholy, an exercise which signals to audiences the merchant's hopeless lassitude. Salerio shares his suspicions that his friend's mind is

> Tossing on the ocean,
> There where your argosies with portly sail,
> Like signors and rich burghers on the flood,
> Or as it were the pageants of the sea,
> Do overpeer the petty traffickers
> That curtsy to them, do them reverence
> As they fly by them with their woven wings.   (I, i, 8–14)

The vision imposes a Venetian social structure onto the maritime landscape, anthropomorphising Antonio's ships as rich signors that 'fly by [other ships] with their woven wings' (I, i, 14). The speech underscores the elevated status Antonio enjoys in Venice, both in wealth and in standing, and in making it, Salerio explicitly conflates merchant with merchandise, a manoeuvre that feeds into Antonio's notion that he exerts no control over his ailment, as though he is tossed around by the ocean's powerful swells. Believing Antonio to be worried about the status of his argosies, Salerio momentarily puts himself in Antonio's situation and imagines how he would react to his goods being so far away from him:

> My wind cooling my broth
> Would blow me to an ague when I thought
> What harm a wind too great might do at sea.
> I should not see the sandy hourglass run
> But I should think of shallows and of flats,
> And see my wealthy *Andrew* docked in sand,
> Vailing her high-top lower than her ribs
> To kiss her burial. Should I go to church
> And see the holy edifice of stone
> And not bethink me straight of dangerous rocks
> Which, touching my gentle vessel's side,
> Would scatter all her spices on the stream,
> Enrobe the roaring waters with my silks,
> And, in a word, but even now worth this,
> And now worth nothing? (I, i, 22–36)

The extensive metaphor depicts Antonio at the mercy of the elements, an image reminiscent of Galen's depiction of man as subjected to overwhelming natural phenomena.[24] In it, as his ships sail the globe, Antonio remains idly in Venice, connected with them solely through the harshness of the natural landscape: his own breath cooling his soup reminds Antonio of the winds threatening his ventures at sea; the sand of the hourglass evokes the danger of shipwreck on distant shores, where the reefs, the liminal point of convergence between land and ocean, ruthlessly slit his ships' sides and cause them to bleed out silks and spices. The paradigm of excess and loss it establishes firmly situates Antonio's melancholy within the boundaries of its classical definitions. Yet the sense of powerlessness that emerges from the metaphor also depicts Antonio as idle. It is the fear of drifting away aimlessly at sea that Salerio's speech primarily highlights. In such a scenario, melancholy stems from the idea that, as his livelihood floats adrift, scattered on the ocean and out of his control, Antonio remains passively on land, caught in its throes.

This first scene goes to great lengths to establish an oceanic parallel with Antonio's melancholy and his mercantile lifestyle. Understood as a space beyond the reach of human knowledge, the ocean – and the mystique it generated – was entrenched in the early modern psyche; the unknowability of the very thing with which he is intimately associated underscores the precarious status that Antonio occupies within the play, melancholically drifting on through the bustling Venetian microcosm.[25] In Burton's *Anatomy* the idea that melancholy increases a character's sense of loss is further linked to the noxious effects that idleness can foster. He writes of melancholics that

> whilst they are anyways employed in action, discourse, about any business, sport, or recreation, or in company to their liking, they are very well; but if alone or idle, tormented instantly again; one day's solitariness, one hour's sometimes, doth them more harm than a week's physic, labour, and company can do good . . . as fern grows in untilled grounds, and all manner of weeds, so do gross humours in an idle body.[26]

Burton does not reference oceans, but the passage draws particular attention to the fact that any amount of solitude, even when dwarfed by time spent in intense labour, can prove a breeding ground for melancholy. The image of the fern growing on desolate soil and being overtaken by weeds suggests that the body finds itself at the mercy of 'gross humours' when left socially unstimulated. The crisis mirrors that of the melancholic merchant, whose lifestyle offers little in the way of a grounded sense of belonging, being constantly tossed between the solitude of the open ocean and the mercantile Venetian community. For Lynn Enterline, this sense of loss that accompanies melancholy points to the 'consolidation of masculine identity' in the play, in which Antonio represents 'a self whose contours appear, in fact, only in contrast to self-loss' as the play's opening yokes together identity and property.[27] For Enterline, such passivity implies the transfer of Antonio's identity onto his merchandise. Despite inviting connotations, the merchant partly resists such a classification since he is not at sea with his wares; he essentially suffers from the expected affliction of oceanic travels without actively participating in such activities. Therein lies the primary difference between him and Antipholus of Syracuse, who does travel and proves willing to 'loose himself' (I, ii, 40) rather than remain inactive. Though Antonio is uncertain of why that is, he remains convinced that he *must* be melancholic. 'I hold the world but as the world', he informs Gratiano later on, 'a stage where every man must play a part, / And mine a sad one' (I, i, 77–9). This feeble sense of resignation frames his problematic relationship with melancholy. Though questioning its significance earlier on, Antonio sees no reason to challenge it (unlike everyone else). Comically, Antonio's melancholy sets up a slew of dramatic anxieties ripe with comedic potential that are never directly addressed afterwards. Gratiano chastises him to that effect, deploring the fact that he has 'too much respect upon the world', advising him to 'fish not with this melancholy bait / for this fool gudgeon, this opinion' (I, i, 74; 101–2). Gratiano expresses

a clear distaste for such posturing. In response to the merchant's assertion that his is the sad role, he replies:

> Let me play the fool.
> With mirth and laughter let old wrinkles come,
> And let my liver rather heat with wine
> Than my heart cool with mortifying groans.
> Why should a man whose blood is warm within
> Sit like his grandsire cut in alabaster?
> Sleep when he wakes, and creep into the jaundice
> By being peevish?   (I, ii, 79–86)

The binary of hot and cold Gratiano introduces immediately recalls the galenic tradition, painting Antonio's excessive melancholy as not only unnatural but detrimental to
the individual. For Gratiano, to be melancholic is to ignore
human instincts, which dictate mirth and vitality. Though
he first channels galenic philosophy, Gratiano's real disdain
seems aimed at Aristotelian melancholy. He rejects the idea
that such a countenance implies wisdom, depth of character
and *gravitas*:

> There are a sort of men whose visages
> Do cream and mantle like a standing pond,
> And do a willful stillness entertain
> With purpose to be dressed in an opinion
> Of wisdom, gravity, profound conceit,
> And who should say, 'I am Sir Oracle,
> And when I ope my lips let no dog bark!'
> O my Antonio, I do know of these
> That therefore only are reputed wise
> For saying nothing, when, I am very sure,
> If they should speak, would almost damn those ears
> Which, hearing them, would call their brothers fools.
>   (I, i, 88–99)

Gratiano's attack on feigned melancholic posturing is reminiscent of Jonson, but his critique is also implicitly relevant to the play's Venetian setting, in which the business of life hinges on social interactions. Gratiano suggests that pretences of wisdom under melancholic guises can be highly damaging to one's reputation and identity. Yet, as Daniel remarks, Gratiano's

> caricature of the somber melancholic is so humourous and distracting one almost does not notice that in fact Antonio's own melancholy strives to achieve precisely the opposite effect . . . not to deepen the level of discourse progressively but to hold stubbornly at the surface.[28]

The logical divide between Gratiano's critique and Antonio's self-perception illustrates the incompatibility of classical understandings of melancholy with the comic development found in the play. Gratiano's warning, misdirected as it may be, nevertheless points to a general unease throughout the play with regard to Antonio's sadness and the fact that it resists comic integration at every turn. Comically, the exchange marks another potential outlet for Antonio's sadness (an unacceptable behaviour to be corrected) that the play subsequently frustrates. The opening scene thus never pinpoints a cause for Antonio's sadness. In an endless vacillation between the two, it is attributed either to a physical, galenic, or to an intellectual, Aristotelian, cause. Rather than revealing such a key piece of information, Antonio seems more invested in acquiring, in Freudian terms, 'satisfaction from self-exposure'.[29] As Freud writes, it is not 'crucially important whether the melancholic is being accurate in his painful disparagement . . . it is more a question of him providing an accurate description of his situation'.[30]

Antonio does anything but provide an accurate description of his situation beyond clinging to his melancholy as a surrogate identity marker. The merchant seeks to keep the conversation focused on what ails him as a way of refraining from actively participating in the unfolding social dynamics. As the first scene comes to a close, the origins of Antonio's enigmatic sadness remain a mystery. 'I would have stayed till I had made you merry,' Salerio declares as he departs, 'If worthier friends had not prevented me' (I, i, 60–1), emphasising once more the widespread desire to rid Antonio of the unnatural state of unhappiness that plagues him. Antonio's melancholy is never explicitly addressed following this opening dialogue, yet the remainder of the play develops a careful critique of it through multiple contrasts with Bassanio, Portia and Shylock. The first scene instils the vague sense that Antonio will not grow merrier as the play develops.

The following scene opens with Portia informing her waiting-gentlewoman Nerissa that her 'little body is *aweary / of this great world*' (I, ii, 1–2, my emphasis), immediately forming a contrast with Antonio's weariness. Portia's melancholy proves more concrete than the merchant's elusive lethargy since her stasis is literal: she is physically confined to Belmont by the devise of her late father until she is won by a suitor who correctly solves a riddle. Her predicament is thus more clearly defined than the vague melancholic drifting that Antonio expressed earlier. Unlike the dichotomy of mirth and melancholy that Salerio, Solanio and Gratiano elaborate in response to Antonio's dejected state, Nerissa preaches temperance and balance to her mistress:

> You would be [weary], sweet madam, if your miseries
> were in the same abundance as your good fortunes
> are; and yet, for aught I see, they are as sick that surfeit
> with too much as they are that starve with nothing. It is
> no mean happiness, therefore, to be seated in the
> mean. Superfluity comes sooner by white hairs, but
> competency lives longer.   (I, ii, 3–9)

The implication is that any excessive display of emotion is not beneficial, no matter the affect, and that a measured countenance will provide an individual with optimal health. Portia rapidly accepts Nerissa's suggestion and moves on to more pressing concerns.

Rather than succumb to languishing introspective qualms, Portia proceeds to lambast a list of suitors read out by Nerissa, taking issue in each case with a dominant personality trait she deems abhorrent. One of those critiques concerns the County Palatine, a suitor who, Portia declares

> Doth nothing but frown, as who would say,
> 'An you will have me, choose.' He hears merry
> tales and smiles not. I fear he will prove the weeping
> philosopher when he grows old, being so full of
> unmannerly sadness in his youth. I had rather be
> married to a death's-head with a bone in his mouth.
>
> (I, ii, 45–50)

Portia's rejection of Palatine for his 'unmannerly' melancholy recalls the same condition in Antonio. Her concern that he will eventually become a weeping philosopher suggests her disdain for the self-invested, introspective scholarly melancholy explored by Aristotle, Burton and Ficino. The criticism fits neatly with Gratiano's previous attack of melancholic posturing. While Nerissa's advocacy for temperance echoes with classical humoral doctrines, the scene departs from early modern understandings of female melancholy by highlighting Portia's capacity for self-regulation. As Gail Kern Paster remarks, early modern representations of the female body, drawing on the galenic classification of fluids, tended to express a 'particular kind of [bodily] uncontrol as a function of gender [and] display that body as beyond the control of the female subject, and thus as threatening the acquisitive goals of the family and its maintenance of status and power'.[31]

Thus, Portia's capacity for self-regulation or, more simply put, her ability to move on after expressing her sorrows, contrasts with Antonio's passive and pessimistic attitude. The two characters are, as Paster puts it, 'diacritically related', not only in their relation to blood, as she suggests, but in their dialogical relationship to comic melancholy.[32] The two scenes set up a gender binary between Antonio and Portia vested in their opposing enactment of melancholy, one that pits action against passivity, self-control against abandonment and flexibility against stubbornness.

The actual cause of Portia's sadness does not matter as much as her response to it, which distinguishes her from Antonio in her willingness to change. While Portia's situation fits the classical humoral understanding of the condition in terms of greensickness (or virgin melancholy), it defies the early modern axiom that 'women's condition relative to men's was passive rather than active'.[33] Indeed, humoral wisdom postulated that, being cold and dry, melancholy usually brought the masculine body closer to its female counterpart.[34] The first two scenes in *The Merchant of Venice* effectively reverse this concept by depicting an overly passive melancholic character and immediately contrasting him with a much more temperate (and active) female character. The swiftness of her transformation here highlights the fact that, by accomplishing in this scene what Antonio seems incapable of achieving (regulating his affect to an acceptable mean), Portia begins the systematic undercutting of his melancholy. If *Merchant* is to be understood as a play concerned with the risks and rewards of venturing into the unknown, the heiress of Belmont gains a clear edge over the lethargic Venetian merchant.

The idea that the play is built partly on a contrast between Antonio and Portia is a common critical reading, one that usually ascribes ulterior motives to Antonio's willingness to help Bassanio reach Belmont.[35] Such interpretative strategies usually frame the potential loss of Bassanio as the trigger for Antonio's melancholy, making the precarious claim that the play's opening lines pre-emptively attest to the merchant's distress over the eventual departure of his friend. Without questioning at length the validity of such readings, I think that the contrast between Antonio and Portia is best understood as one revolving around comic melancholy, where Bassanio represents a potent site of friction between competing models. While Portia's situation concords with dramatic (Shakespearean) representations of greensickness in the period, particularly in the process by which her 'initial sadness is discarded for love', it more importantly offers an alternative (and more suitable) depiction of comic melancholy.[36] Portia's weariness is rapidly discarded by Bassanio's courtship, while Antonio's inability to temper his own melancholy increasingly disconnects him from the rest of the comedy.

Although Antonio agrees to finance Bassanio's wooing of Portia after he is appealed to as the one to whom Bassanio 'owe[s] the most, in money and in love' (I, i, 131), his involvement remains utterly lethargic.[37] He proves willing to help but reluctant to act. 'All my fortunes are at sea' (I, i, 177), he initially informs his friend before urging him to 'go forth [and] / Try what my credit can in Venice do; / That shall be racked even to the utmost' (I, i, 179–81). The advice underscores a pattern by which the melancholic Antonio strives to remain at the centre of the play's concerns without any active involvement; we find ourselves staring once again at the creamy surface of a standing pond. Bassanio must go and verify for himself what his friend's reputation will procure him, stretching Antonio's name across Venice. Likewise, in order to secure the bond from Shylock, Bassanio must dangle Antonio as bait:

SHYLOCK: Three thousand ducats, well.

BASSANIO: Ay, sir, for three months.

SHYLOCK: For three months, well.

BASSANIO: For the which, as I told you, Antonio shall be bound.

SHYLOCK: Antonio shall become bound, well.

BASSANIO: May you stead me? Will you pleasure me? Shall I know your answer?

SHYLOCK: Three thousand ducats for three months and Antonio bound

(I, iii, 1–10)

The intermediary role held by Antonio throughout the exchange is striking. In a masterful inversion, the scene opens with Shylock repeating a sentence previously uttered by Bassanio ('three thousand ducats'), implying that Shylock directs the conversation while, in reality, he merely reiterates Bassanio's assertions (which came from Antonio). In an ominous echoing of Gratiano's earlier advice to him not to 'fish with this melancholy bait', Bassanio offers Antonio as prey for Shylock to seize upon. Though it feeds the 'ancient grudge' (I, iii, 44) he bears against Antonio, Shylock's bond highlights the merchant's paradoxical involvement in the play; Antonio will place his own safety at risk, but he will do so on a theoretical plane. The arrangement is of no concrete value for the Jewish usurer initially, and he admits as much when he asks Antonio and Bassanio:

> What should I gain
> By the exaction of the forfeiture?
> A pound of man's flesh taken from a man
> Is not so estimable, profitable neither,
> As flesh of muttons, beefs, or goats.   (I, iii, 162–6)

The passage draws attention once again to Antonio's lack of value by suggesting that he is less profitable than livestock.

In other words, the bond is established on Shylock's awareness of the absurd, detrimental behaviour of Venetians such as Antonio. Shylock's hatred of Antonio also suggests his larger aversion to what he perceives to be behaviour ruled by overwhelming and unregulated humours. When asked at the trial why he would prefer a pound of Antonio's flesh rather than the money he is owed, Shylock retorts:

> You'll ask me why I rather choose to have
> A weight of carrion flesh than to receive
> Three thousand ducats. I'll not answer that,
> But say it is my humour. Is it answer'd?
> . . .
> Some men there are love not a gaping pig,
> Some that are mad if they behold a cat,
> And others, when the bagpipe sings i'the nose,
> Cannot contain their urine; for affection,
> Mistress of passion, sways it to the mood
> Of what it likes or loathes.   (IV, i, 40–3; 47–52)

The absurdity of Shylock's examples, focusing on a loss or lack of control over specific behaviours, recalls Jonson's characterisation in humour comedy, but it also echoes Antonio's stubborn melancholic state. Shylock mocks the humoral system he perceives to be operating rampantly in Venice, by which individuals can hide behind the overwhelming influence of their humours, and the refusal on the individual's part to alter his temperament ('it is my humour'). Comically, Antonio's melancholy embodies such a phenomenon as his posturing – catering to public exposure without active participation – grows increasingly problematic once the play's romantic plot moves to the forefront.

Antonio disturbs Portia and Bassanio's nuptials from afar once he defaults on the bond, as a letter reaches the lovers in Belmont: 'the paper as the body of my friend,' Bassanio informs his beloved, 'And every word in it a gaping wound / Issuing lifeblood' (III, ii, 264–6).[38] The merchant, it seems, is determined to play the sad part to the end, even from a distance. Pragmatically, the comedy cannot allow its titular character to surrender his life for the benefit of other characters. For the comedy (and the marriage) to be successful, Antonio must be saved. Bassanio, feeling the pangs of culpability, must venture back to Venice to assist his friend. Portia must remind her soon-to-be husband to 'first go with me to church and call me a wife' (III, ii, 303) before he can set out to rescue Antonio. Portia embodies the collective dramatic pressure that mounts against the merchant's melancholic fancies. By interposing himself in between Bassanio and Portia's union and its presumed sexual consummation later that night, Antonio's melancholy becomes an opposing force to comic resolution.

Much as Don John distances himself from villainous undertakings in *Much Ado*, Antonio barely participates in the trial to decide his fate. Even with his life on the line, he remains intent on not actively participating, as the scene rapidly becomes a showdown between Portia (cheered on primarily by Gratiano) and Shylock. More than a death wish or a manipulative ploy to obtain Bassanio's affection, Antonio's resignation to 'suffer with a quietness of spirit' (IV, i, 12) furthers his efforts to remain the focus of attention without actually integrating himself in the play's proceedings. His self-description near the beginning of the trial suggests as much:

> I am a tainted-wether of the flock,
> Meetest for death, the weakest kind of fruit
> Drops earliest to the ground, and so let me.
> You cannot better be employed, Bassanio,
> Than to live still and write mine epitaph.   (IV, i, 114–18)

The two metaphors – the neutered ram and the overripe fruit – simultaneously position him as part of a larger community while singling him out as somewhat marginalised owing to an irremediable affliction. His request to Bassanio similarly suggests a desire to have his life story revolve around his melancholy. When it initially appears that Shylock will triumph, Antonio reiterates the request:

> Commend me to your honorable wife.
> Tell her the process of Antonio's end,
> Say how I loved you, speak me fair in death;
> And, when the tale is told, bid her judge
> Whether Bassanio had not once a love.   (IV, i, 271–5)

Antonio's use of third person pronouns underscore his attempt to become his own story, a proposition that the comedy cannot allow, if only because his professed love for Bassanio poses a clear hindrance to Portia just as his letter did earlier in Belmont. Sparing Antonio ensures that her husband will not be assailed with guilt over his friend's demise. More importantly, the trial scene pushes Antonio's melancholy to its comic breaking point. Once Shylock is dealt with, the play turns to Belmont and the multiple marriages it will celebrate. The merchant's ambiguous status in the last act offers a final representation of the rupture of Shakespearean comedy with classical stagings of melancholy. If Antonio is not explicitly cast aside at the end of the play, he unmistakably hovers on its fringes since the system of mercantile male friendship he relies on is of no value in Belmont.

The final act opens with Lorenzo and Jessica relating tragic love stories to one another (V, i, 1–24). The scene channels pangs of melancholy yet directs them away from Antonio's nebulous sorrow, grounding them in the more comprehensible tragedy of couples such as Troilus and Cressida or Pyramus and Thisbe. The exchange suggests that there may be a suitable place for melancholy in a comedy (indeed, Lorenzo and Jessica's exchange can be played for laughs), but Antonio's humour is out of place. When Jessica remarks, 'I am never merry when I hear sweet music' (V, i, 69), Lorenzo launches into a praise of its power to overtake the mind and overwhelm the body:

> The reason is, your spirits are attentive.
> For do but note a wild and wanton herd,
> Or race of youthful and unhandled colts,
> Fetching mad bounds, bellowing and neighing loud,
> Which is the hot condition of their blood;
> If they but hear perchance a trumpet sound,
> Or any air of music touch their ears,
> You shall perceive them make a mutual stand,
> Their savage eyes turned to a modest gaze
> By the sweet power of music.
> . . .
> The man that hath no music in himself,
> Nor is not moved with concord of sweet sounds,
> Is fit for treasons, stratagems, and spoils;
> The motions of his spirits are dull as night
> And his affections dark as Erebus.
> Let no such man be trusted. Mark the music.
>
> (V, i, 70–9; 83–8)

Lorenzo's detailed description of wild horses being tamed by the sweet sounds of music offers a parallel to the three male characters (Bassanio, Gratiano and himself) being drawn away from the bustling Venetian world (where the hot condition of their blood runs amuck) and towards the ethereal world of Belmont where the 'savage eyes' of their youth will transform into the 'modest gaze' of marital life. It also suggests that the type of melancholic self-examinations with which Antonio opened the play, keeping everyone's spirits

attentive to his mysterious melancholy, is no longer wel-
comed. As David Hoeniger writes, the idea that music could
mitigate humours harks back to the galenic principle of balance or harmony. 'The harmonies of music', he explains,
'can purge and purify the passions, or at least mitigate the
causes of the perturbation of mind [while] inner disharmony
. . . is cured by the affect of harmony'[39] The focus on music's
powers to calm and enchant, signals that the merchant's
unyielding melancholy will not be well received. The second
half of Lorenzo's speech, which warns against men with no
music, drives home the point that, as the comedy moves on
to its romantic conclusion, the sad merchant threatens to
spoil the mood.

This critique is reiterated once Portia enters and comments on the music being played in her own house: 'Nothing is good, I see, without respect. / Methinks it sounds much
sweeter than by day . . . / How many things by season, sea-
soned are / To their right praise and true perfection!' (V, i,
99–100; 107–8). By emphasising the idea that things such
as music are best enjoyed in their optimal context, Portia once
again underscores Antonio's comic infelicity. If even in comedy (or especially in comedy) there is a proper time and place
for melancholy, it seems to have been in the play's Venetian
opening act. This last scene revolves primarily around Portia's
subjugation of Bassanio (and Gratiano) through the ring trick,
as the final step in her guiding of male characters into proper
married behaviour. The scene is ripe with comic potential to
that effect, and Antonio's attempt to bring back the dramatic
focus onto his melancholic demeanor are rapidly nipped by
Portia:

ANTONIO: I am th'unhappy subject of these quarrels.
PORTIA: Sir, grieve you not; you are welcome notwith-
    standing.

(V, i, 238–9)

Portia's reply is both an invitation to remain in Belmont and a rejection of the merchant's grief. His final efforts to 'be bound again, / My soul upon the forfeit', (V, i, 251–2) for Bassanio's sake are all but ignored by Portia who produces the ring, reveals her stratagem and scores a final comic victory through the miraculous return of Antonio's ships:

> ANTONIO: Sweet Lady, you have given me life and living;
> For here, I read certain that my ships
> Are safely come to road.
> PORTIA: How now, Lorenzo?
> My clerk hath some good comforts too for you
>
> (V, i, 285–9)

By not addressing the merchant, Portia signals the play's lack of interest in Antonio as it turns towards its climatic nuptial celebrations.

Antonio's exclusion, as I see it, is not a literal one, as Portia does indeed prove quite welcoming to him. His very presence onstage in Belmont (as opposed to Shylock's absence) denotes inclusion, yet the glaring asymmetry found onstage – the melancholic merchant surrounded by three newlywed couples – supersedes any claim of integration. In most stagings of the play, this is visually flagrant at the very least: as characters exit to celebrate the nuptials, logic dictates that each couple do so together, leaving Antonio to depart alone.[40] By defining him through an unyielding sadness that precedes most of the occurrences critics usually point to as sources (the loss of his ships, the departure of his friend Bassanio for Belmont), the play suggests that in this last act, once spared from Shylock's blade, Antonio is returned to his initial state of 'want-wit sadness'. In this sense, his exclusion is considerably more understated than Don John's, but it nevertheless points to the same

dramatic failure to upend his melancholy and fully integrate the character by the end of the comedy. Antonio's
humour is never directly addressed following his opening
speech, leaving characters and critics alike to assume that
his melancholy has subsided by Act 5. This failure is even
more apparent when considering the potential symmetry
laid out by the play's initial premise (and its main source
text), where one could expect both Antonio *and* Bassanio to
find love in Belmont. Fiorentino's *Il Pecorone* sees the older
merchant character (Ansaldo) marry the rich widow's lady-
in-waiting, completing the heterosexual symmetry that is
conspicuously absent in Shakespeare's version.[41] Instead,
it is Gratiano who gains access to the newly created social
sphere alongside Bassanio and Lorenzo (and speaks the
play's closing lines). This shift recalls his initial condemnation of Antonio's sadness. In Shakespearean comedy, it
appears that playing the fool will ultimately trump fish-
ing with a melancholy bait. Antonio is not expelled from
Belmont, but the final scene somewhat bends under the
weight of his incongruous presence amidst three married
couples, as one would not expect the titular merchant of
Venice to end up sticking out like a sore thumb.

Don John and Antonio do not fundamentally undercut
the plays they occupy. *Much Ado about Nothing* and *The
Merchant of Venice* remain comic plays where revelry and
romanticism ultimately triumph. Nevertheless, the plays'
failure to properly do away with their melancholy suggests
that classical models cannot develop within the evolving
genre of Shakespearean comedy. The symmetrical models
operating in *The Comedy of Errors* and *Love's Labour's
Lost*, which sought to rehabilitate melancholic characters
in order to usher in a satisfying climax, erodes sharply
here. The plays underscore the growing incompatibility of
galenic and Aristotelian philosophies of melancholy within

Shakespearean comedy through dissonant characters who ultimately engineer their own exclusions. In actuality, characters such as Don John and Antonio represent the point of collapse for traditional philosophies of melancholy as far as Shakespearean comedy is concerned. The two characters offer purported interiority without the required self-awareness (and comic awareness) needed to legitimise it. Thinking back to Groucho Marx' s words, it is not so much that Don John and Antonio would never want to belong to a club that would accept them as members, but that they are so busy languishing in their own melancholy that they fail to notice that the party has moved on and left them behind.

Notes

1. Paster, *Humouring the Body*, 24.
2. Paster, *Humouring the Body*, 197.
3. Paster, *Humouring the Body*, 214.
4. Bergson, 'Laughter', 117.
5. Bergson 211.
6. Lyons, *Voices of Melancholy*, 35.
7. See also Galen, 'On the Natural Faculties', 85.
8. Ficino, *Book of Life*, 89.
9. Galen, 'On the Natural Faculties', 11.
10. Burton, *Anatomy of Melancholy*, 227–8.
11. Timothy Hampton, 'Strange Alteration', 277.
12. Shaw, *Shaw on Shakespeare*, 157.
13. Babb, *Elizabethan Malady*, 86.
14. Bright, *Treatise of Melancholy*, 36.
15. Cox, *Much Ado About Nothing*, 234.
16. Daniel, *Melancholy Assemblage*, 102.
17. Daniel 92.
18. Frye, *Natural Perspective*, 46.
19. Holderness, 'Comedy and *The Merchant of Venice*', 24.

20. Tempera, '"Now I play a merchant's part"', 159.
21. Woodbridge, 'Payback Time', 29.
22. Bulman, *The Merchant of Venice*, 6.
23. Giovanni Fiorentino, 'Il Pecorone', 84–99.
24. See Galen, *On Antecedent Causes* and 'On the Natural Faculties'.
25. Brayton, 'Shakespeare and the Global Ocean', 178.
26. Burton 243.
27. Enterline, *Tears of Narcissus*, 22; 190.
28. Daniel 97.
29. Freud, 'Of Mourning and Melancholia', 207.
30. Ibid.
31. Paster, *The Body Embarrassed*, 25.
32. Paster, *The Body Embarrassed*, 92.
33. Paster, *Humouring the Body*, 99. See 95–101 for Paster's summary of Burton's discourse on virgin melancholy relating to these matters.
34. Paster, *Humouring the Body*, 77.
35. Chief among these are Cynthia Lewis's, which links Antonio to feigned Christian ideas of saintly martyrdom, and Steve Patterson's, which perceives Antonio's acceptance of the bond's terms and subsequent wish for death as manipulative, homoerotic gestures to retain Bassanio's love, *Particular Saints*, 21. See also Steve Patterson, 'Bankruptcy of Homoerotic Amity', 9–32.
36. Paster, *Humouring the Body*, 105.
37. Note the reiteration of the two attributes Antonio so vehemently refuted as causes for his melancholy in the first scene (love and money).
38. Drawing from the connection between ink and black bile (gall), W. G. Sebald notes the sixteenth-century belief that writing creatively with gall ink could potential induce melancholy in the writer, 'Constructs of Melancholy', 210. Bassanio's metaphor echoes such an idea, Bristol, 'Shakespeare's Sonnets', 204.
39. Hoeniger, 'Musical Cures of Melancholy and Mania in Shakespeare', 58.

40. Bulman recalls a production by Henry Irving in which, as she is about to exit the stage, Portia 'suddenly remembers Antonio and conveys in pantomime how selfish it was of them to have forgotten him. She turns around, graciously smiles, extends her hand', 51.
41. Fiorentino 98.

CHAPTER 4

MELANCHOLIC AMBIENCE AT THE COMIC CLOSE

In trying to establish a comprehensive chronology of Shakespearean drama, eighteenth-century critic Edmond Malone reached the editorial conclusion that *Twelfth Night* was Shakespeare's final play, explaining that the comedy 'bears evident marks of having been composed at leisure, as most of the characters that it contains are finished to a higher degree of dramatic perfection than is discoverable in some of our author's earlier comic performances'.[1] Erroneous as it is, Malone's argument echoes a widespread perception of the play as the apogee of Shakespearean comedy. Generically speaking, Shakespeare's last comedies are *As You Like It* and *Twelfth Night*, written at the cusp of the seventeenth century, ahead of his major tragic works. As this chapter suggests, the two plays also represent his most overt and paradoxical treatments of melancholy. They can be understood as completing the shift towards a novel understanding of the concept that exceeds characterisation. Though replete with melancholic characters, the comedies foster a sense of comic melancholy tied to ideas of setting and landscape that legitimises it as valid comic emotion.

The idea that a landscape could prove melancholic is generally held as a modern one, whereas, through literature, 'the word melancholy lost the sense of a quality and acquired instead that of a mood that could be transferred to inanimate objects'.[2] This understanding, in turn, resonates with medical considerations of the relationship between melancholy and landscapes. As Jennifer Radden explains, the potential transference of an inner state of melancholy onto a natural phenomenon results from our innate capacity (and desire) to attach our affective states onto our visual environment. 'We attribute melancholy to landscapes', she writes, 'by some alchemy derived from the associative attachment between visual and affective aspects of our conception of melancholy. Aspects of the landscape make us think of, not (or not merely) feel melancholy.'[3] The landscape becomes an extension of more than a reminder of an individual's melancholy, we *read* it more than experience it as melancholic. As I argue in this chapter, a similar pattern operates in *As You Like It* and *Twelfth Night*, which transpose their melancholy onto their respective dramatic landscapes. Arden Forest and Illyria are remote playworlds whose insular wistfulness exudes frivolity and leisure. They are also settings in which melancholy proliferates without impinging too harshly on social or comic structures as it does in Messina, Ephesus or Venice. The notion of a physical space as melancholic also suggests a significant shift in comic depictions of melancholy in Shakespeare, from an inner state to an externalised mood, which can ultimately go beyond the stage and into the audience.

The idea of melancholic comic settings channels Timothy Morton's notion of 'ambience' as a philosophical blend of ecocriticism and aesthetic theory. Morton describes ambience as 'a sense of circumambient, or surrounding, *world*. It suggests something material and physical though somewhat intangible, as if space itself had a material aspect'.[4] For Morton, poetics of ambience recall Derrida's idea of the re-mark, 'a kind of echo [or] a special mark (or a series of them) that makes us aware that we are in the presence of (significant) marks

[and] differentiates between *space* and *place*'.[5] According to him, environmental ambience is quintessentially melancholic since it always looks to our past in tracking 'the inevitable too-lateness of the way in which things arise'.[6]

The concept of a melancholy mood attaching itself to a particular setting and being tied to the passage of time reso-nates sharply with the two plays discussed in this chapter. Beyond the ridiculous emoting of characters such as Jaques and Orsino, the ephemeral nature of the Arden and Illyria they inhabit (as temporary sites of revelry which comic char-acters must eventually abandon) generates their melancomic quality. This ethereal sense of affect is thus tied to the plays' commentary on the unrelenting passage of time, on the inevi-table end of festivity and on the bittersweet angst that accom-panies these ideas. It echoes Walter Benjamin's idea that, in discussing the formal language of the *Trauerspiel*, of crucial importance to the Baroque life is 'the transposition of the originally temporal into a figurative spatial simultaneity'.[7] In the pastoral, Benjamin suggests, this attitude becomes repre-sentative of the process by which 'chronological movement is grasped and analysed in a spatial image', a phenomenon indicative of 'the experience of the destructive effects of time [and] inevitable transience'.[8] This juxtaposition of time and space is both created by and sustains a strong sense of mel-ancholy. As Judith Butler remarks,

> the internal topography by which melancholy is partially explained is itself the effect of that melancholia. Walter Benjamin remarks that melancholia spatializes, and that its effort to reverse or suspend time produces 'landscapes' as its signature effect. One might profitably read the Freudian topography that melancholy occasions as precisely such a spatialized landscape of the mind.[9]

Setting aside Butler's psychoanalytic focus (which we will come back to in the last chapter), a similar topography is created in *As You Like It* and *Twelfth Night*, one that yokes time, setting and melancholy through the figure of the comic fool and imbues each ending with a subtle yet distinct melancholic tint. While plays such as *The Comedy of Errors* relied on principles of climatology to legitimise the melancholy they depicted, melancholy itself is the underlying climate of the plays discussed here. No longer a nemesis to comic resolution, it becomes its logical end point, a sobering dramatic ambience that curtails the plays' exuberant mirth. *As You Like It* and *Twelfth Night* not only mark the final Shakespearean efforts in 'pure' comedy but also signal the transformation of Shakespearean melancholy into a comic mood.

'Either a fool or cypher': The Melancholic Underside of Arden Forest

I usually resist Harold Bloom's prodigious bardolatry, but I want to begin my analysis of *As You Like It* by drawing attention to one of his observations about Arden Forest that connects with my vision of it as a dramatic repository for melancholy. In *Shakespeare and the Invention of the Human*, Bloom discusses characters such as the Bastard in *King John*, whom he feels 'deserves a better play than the one in which he finds himself . . . being a hopeless Romantic'; he goes on to write, 'I would also like Falstaff at the end of *Henry IV, Part Two*, to forget the ungrateful Prince Hal and go off cheerfully to the Forest of Arden in *As You Like It*'.[10] Setting aside Bloom's infatuation with Falstaff, the comment is significant because it attests to the transformative and redemptive qualities of the play's setting. Bloom's fantasy depicts Arden as an ideal comic locale which can shield characters from otherwise sobering realities. Most critics understand it as a temporary regenerative space preparing characters for an eventual return to courtly life. Arden likewise offers a space in which characters can indulge their melancholic fancies to their fullest before undergoing social reintegration. As I argue, it is also a setting that fosters and thrives on melancholy. If, as Joseph Alulius maintains, the play explores the binary of 'nature and convention, the former understood as both standard and native impulse, the latter understood as a society's accepted ideas of right and wrong and the mechanisms by which such ideas are made to govern our lives',[11] Arden's capacity as a repository for melancholy materialises in its embracing of the quality as a natural impulse – whereas the court would condemn its affectation, thereby legitimising its comic potential. Yet, this state of acceptance remains temporary. The characters' experiences in Arden transform them ahead of a return to court, with the underlying caveat that undesirable traits such as excessive melancholy should be abandoned prior to reintegrating into society. In situating the play almost exclusively in Arden (and in not staging the aforementioned return to court), Shakespeare brings attention to its inherent comic melancholy. The play's closing tableau, even in the midst of romantic triumph, is one of bittersweet celebration and idyllic revelry in its final paroxysms.

As You Like It borrows profusely from Thomas Lodge's prose romance *Rosalynd*, closely mirroring its initial premise in which a pair of lovers-to-be meet up in the forest, where the heroine, in male disguise, wins her beloved's affection. Shakespeare's comedy undertakes a stark departure from Lodge in terms of its emphasis on setting and on its melancholic tenor. While nearly half of *Rosalynd* takes place before its protagonist enters the forest, it takes all but three scenes for Shakespeare's characters to do the same, as the play proves anxious to begin their comic transformations. The drama opens with a criss-cross of scenes showcasing how the play's two protagonists, Rosalind and Orlando, each abandon a deplorable courtly existence. After falling in love following a chance meeting at a wrestling bout, they separately

flee for Arden. The first act quickly establishes their respective melancholies (the lovesick Orlando is 'overthrown' by
Rosalind's beauty, and the grief-stricken Rosalind deplores
her father's banishment). In this way, the pair are made to
underscore the play's contrast between the worlds of court
and forest. They bring into Arden necessary elements to validate the comic premise (the lovesick, immature young male;
the clever, cross-dressed heroine; concealed, noble identities
and so on) and the ideal dispositions to undergo transformation, from individual quality to ambient dramatic emotion.
From its onset, *As You Like It* envelops Arden in pastoral
mysticism. When Oliver asks the wrestler Charles about
Duke Senior's whereabouts, he replies,

> They say he is already in the Forest of Arden,
> and a many merry men with him; and there they live
> like the old Robin Hood of England. They say many
> young gentlemen flock to him every day, and fleet the
> time carelessly as they did in the golden world.
>
> (I, i, 110–14)

The description of the Duke's makeshift court, reminiscent
of the fabled golden world, underlines Arden's idyllic potential as an alternative site of dwelling away from social codes
and sanctions. The allusion to Robin Hood, likewise, underscores its perceived lawlessness or perhaps more accurately,
the sense of escapism it offers to those who enter it. Arden
loosens the binds of social realities, allowing maidens to
become boys, court jesters to congregate with shepherds and
banished dukes to set up a Utopian society where one finds
'tongues in trees, books in the running brooks, / Sermons in
stones, and good in everything' (II, i, 16–17). More importantly, as Charles mentions, Arden grants an opportunity to
escape the grasp of time itself, if only momentarily, and fleet
it away carelessly, where the dual inference of fleeting (as

passing away but doing so rapidly and imperceptibly) reinforces the connection between Arden Forest and the comic
mood that accompanies the end of festivities.

Dating back to Barber and Frye, the setting of Arden has
been much discussed, yet critics have often overlooked the
preponderance of melancholy that characterises it. Certainly,
a great deal has been written about melancholy in the play,
most of it concerning its epitomic character, the melancholy
Jaques, but seldom has the play and its setting been conceived of as melancholic. As I argue, *As You Like It* presents
dovetailing depictions of melancholy, parodying traditional
definitions of it through comic characterisation while suggesting a more liminal sense of it by depicting Arden as a
'desert inaccessible [where] under the shade of melancholy
boughs, [one can] / Lose and neglect the creeping hours of
time;' (II, vii, 109–11). These representations intersect in
Jaques, Shakespeare's most overt characterisation of the
humour. Jaques essentially acts as a siphon, draining other
characters of their melancholy (and thus readying them for
an eventual return to court) and subsequently transferring it
onto the dramatic landscape.

At the onset of the second act, Duke Senior entreats a
few of his lords to go deer hunting. One of them answers by
relating a peculiar spectacle he beheld moments prior:

> The melancholy Jaques grieves at that,
> And in that kind swears that you do more usurp
> Than doth your brother that hath banished you.
> Today my lord Amiens and myself
> Did steal behind him as he lay along
> Under an oak, whose antic root peeps out
> Upon the brook that brawls along this wood,
> To the which place a poor sequestered stag
> That from the hunter's aim had ta'en hurt
> Did come to languish. And indeed, my lord,

The wretched animal heaved forth such groans
That their discharge did stretch his leathern coat
Almost to bursting, and the big round tears
Coursed one another down his innocent nose
In piteous chase. And thus the hairy fool,
Much markèd of the melancholy Jaques,
Stood on th'extremest verge of the swift brook,
Augmenting it with tears.   (II, i, 26–43)

The passage, reminiscent of Don Armado's introduction in *Love's Labour's Lost*, positions Jaques as a melancholic object of ridicule before he even sets foot on the stage. While the masculine characters introduced so far are men of action (hunting, wrestling and actively looking to change their fates), Jaques is first described as lying by the water in melancholic contemplations. He validates the stereotypical characterisation of the affect as socially counterintuitive. Yet the scene the lords relate to Duke Senior also exemplifies my claim that Jaques operates as a siphon within Arden. As the animal lies dying, its sorrowful demeanour (languishing on the ground, filling the air with groans and augmenting the brook with its own tears) conflates the stag with the environment it occupies. As the site of its final moments, the brook and Arden much like it, are themselves melancholic, and Jaques is said to be profoundly affected by such a spectacle. The lords describe how they left him at the scene, 'weeping and commenting / Upon the sobbing deer' (II, i, 65–6). As several critics point out, the image of the crying stag mirrors that of the sobbing Jaques, likening him to the wounded animal.[12] In addition to offering a 'striking moment of poetic ekphrasis', the scene stresses the interconnectedness of character and setting within the play's ambient comic melancholy.[13] Winfried Schleiner points out that early moderns believed that the deer possessed both the coldness and dryness generally associated with melancholic dispositions. For that reason, he writes,

'medical authorities of the Renaissance strictly and consistently forbid melancholics to eat of the stag'.[14] The image of
Jaques adding his tears to the animal's in the nearby brook
underscores the pervasiveness of melancholy within Arden.

Jaques' power as critic (and as melancholic) is under-
mined by the fact that the stag episode is related at second
hand. The scene positions him as a source of entertainment
in Arden more than an actual voice that warrants serious
consideration. Duke Senior is fascinated rather than moved
by the story: 'But what said Jaques? / Did he not moralise
this spectacle? . . . Show me the place. / I love to cope him
in these sullen fits, / For then he's full of matter' (II, ii, 43–4;
66–8). Given this association with entertainment, Jaques
takes on the jester's role within the Duke's makeshift court,
a notion that recalls Babb's definition of the (melancholic)
malcontent character type, individuals, he writes, 'disap-
pointed and disgruntled by their countrymen's failure to rec-
ognise and reward the talents and acquirements which they
believed they had, [who] were given to railing satirically at
their unappreciative contemporaries'.[15] Comic representations often included such cynical characters, Babb explains,
who were 'regarded with tolerant amusement [and] granted
. . . privileges like those of a court jester', allowed to speak
their minds without ever being taken too seriously.[16] The
play underscores such an idea, as every character Jaques
interacts with (Rosalind, Orlando, the Duke or Touchstone) invariably gets the best of him. Yet the melancholy
association between the character and the dramatic landscape he occupies persistently meshes with this traditional
comic characterisation. Audiences are invited to laugh at
Jaques' exaggerated affect, but they are also to contemplate
his capacity (and need) to draw in melancholy from various
sources.

When Jaques does appear on stage, he relies on animal
imagery once again to affirm his connection to melancholy

as he encourages Amiens to continue singing to him: 'More, I prithee, more. I can suck melancholy / out of a song as a weasel sucks eggs. More, I / prithee, more' (II, v, 11–13). The implication of Jaques' request seems clear enough: he is proud of the ease with which he can extract melancholy from a ballad. The simile he uses highlights both his comic dependence on melancholy, as a figurative sustenance, and his pride in his ability to draw it from a given situation.[17] The image echoes Maynard Mack's definition of the character as a 'type of comic vampire feeding curiosity on the acts and feelings of those more vital than himself'.[18] The idea that weasels could empty an egg without damaging its shell appears to be an early modern one, since classical works of zoology by Aristotle (*De Generationae Animalium*), Pliny the Elder (*Natural History*) or Ambroise Paré (*Des Monstres et de prodiges*) never articulate such a claim. It possibly emerges out of loose translations of Latin texts, such as Albertus Magnus' *De Animalibus* (printed 1489) or, more importantly, Conrad Gesner's *Historiæ Animalium* (c. 1551–8).[19] Gesner's lengthy entry on weasels notes how the animal devours chicken eggs by swallowing them whole (thus latently suggesting that the shells go untouched).[20] Shakespeare does not coin the idiomatic expression – it appears as early as 1580 in Austin Sacker's *Narbonus*, which compares the inherent symbioses of the natural world with the way in which the weasel 'sucketh up the yolkes, but leaveth the shelles' – but *As You Like It* is the only one of his plays to use it explicitly.[21] The passage relies on the early modern myth to stress Jaques' synecdoche of the play's larger development of comic melancholy.[22] Jaques not only feels melancholic, he is melancholy, and he seeks it out at every turn. He is both the comic foil displaying exacerbated traits and the bridge between melancholy and the play's setting. Jaques both validates and resists the stereotypes of traditional melancholy. He declares to Rosalind later on,

I have neither the scholar's melancholy, which
is emulation, nor the musician's, which is fantastical,
nor the courtier's, which is proud, nor the soldier's,
which is ambitious, nor the lawyer's, which is politic,
nor the lady's, which is nice, nor the lover's, which is
all these; but it is a melancholy of mine own, compounded
of many simples, extracted from many
objects, and indeed the sundry contemplation of my
travels, in which my often rumination wraps me in a
Most humourous sadness.   (IV, i, 10–19)

Jaques defines his melancholy by enumerating what it is not in a bid for genuineness. Going through its seemingly endless subcategories, the passage draws attention to the inherent inauthenticity of melancholy on the comic stage. His use of the pseudo-scientific vernacular of compounds and extracts, coupled with his allusion to the travel melancholy (one of its most popular comic forms) negate his attempt to legitimise his humour. Yet his ongoing conflation with the landscape of Arden renders him an integral component of Rosalind and Orlando's eventual self-transformation. Both characters enter Arden under the pangs of melancholy, and their encounters with Jaques effectively drain them of their unwarranted humours.

The lovesick Orlando gets the better of him as they trade barbs about love and poetry. He ridicules Jaques' overall attitude by rebutting his every statement and mocking his cadence:

JAQUES: *I thank you for your company,*
but, good faith, I have as lief have been myself alone.
ORLANDO: And so had I; but yet, for fashion's sake,
   I thank you too for your society.
JAQUES: God b'wi'you. Let's meet as little as we can.
ORLANDO: I do desire we can be better strangers.
JAQUES: *I pray you, mar no more trees with writing* love-
   songs in their barks.

ORLANDO; *I pray you, mar no more of my verses with reading* them ill-favouredly.

> (III, ii, 250–9, my emphasis)

The passage underscores the inauthenticity of Jaques' persona, exposing his feigned misanthropic requests to be left alone by having him pursue a dialogue with Orlando. When Jaques advises him not to carve love poems into the forest's trees (providing one more instance of melancholy being impressed upon Arden's landscape) Orlando's reply dismisses him altogether:

JAQUES: Rosalind is your love's name?
ORLANDO: Yes, just.
JAQUES: I do not like her name.
ORLANDO: There was no thought of pleasing you when she was christened.

> (III, ii, 260–4)

The comment represents Orlando's defence of his beloved, as well as an acknowledgement of Jaques' lack of influence on such matters, even within his self-appointed role as Arden's social critic. In dismissing him, Orlando also rejects a putative version of himself: an overly melancholic fellow unable to function socially beyond his affect. Mocking Jaques' behaviour, in a sense, incites him to modify his own:

JAQUES: The worst fault you have is to be in love.
ORLANDO: 'Tis a fault I would not change for your best virtue. I am weary of you.
JAQUES: By my troth, I was seeking for a fool when I found you.
ORLANDO: He is drowned in the brook. Look but in, and you shall see him.
JAQUES: There shall I see mine own figure.
ORLANDO: Which I take to be either a fool or a cipher.

> (III, ii, 278–86)

Jaques' matter-of-fact reply to Orlando's allusion to him being drowned ('There shall I see mine own figure') not only shows him being rhetorically overthrown by his opponent, it more importantly recalls the character's emblematic introduction, fusing his tears with the stag's into the brook. In impressing his melancholy into Arden, Jaques seemingly becomes part of it, siphoning the humour away from other characters as it inevitably traps him there. Jaques is both the comic fool *and* the melancholy cypher, vital to other characters' comic transformation yet incapable of undergoing one himself. His excessive display of melancholy serves as a warning to Orlando not to yield to his own melancholic preoccupations.

Rosalind's exchange with Jaques develops along a similar ridiculing of his highly formulaic affect:

> ROSALIND: They say you are a melancholy fellow.
> JAQUES: I am so. I do love it better than laughing.
> ROSALIND: Those that are in extremity of either are abominable fellows and betray themselves to every modern censure worse than drunkards.
> JAQUES: Why, 'tis good to be sad and say nothing.
> ROSALIND: Why then, 'tis good to be a post.
>
> (IV, i, 3–9)

Like other comic heroines discussed so far, Rosalind displays considerable agency in discarding her own state of weariness and seeking to improve her situation. She advocates for a temperance of affects (mirth and melancholy) that takes aim at Jaques' refusal to be anything but melancholy. Like Orlando's, her final jab ('Why then, 'tis good to be a post') mocks his cadence and compares him to a nonhuman, inanimate (and insignificant) object. She reserves a particular degree of scorn for Jaques' cultivation of his image as a melancholy traveller, underscoring the stereotypical idioms and images associated with the concept. When Jaques points out the life experience that his many travels have procured, she retorts,

> Your experience makes you sad. I had
> rather have a fool to make me merry than experience
> To make me sad – and to travel for it too!
> . . .
> Farewell, Monsieur Traveler. Look you lisp,
> and wear strange suits, disable all the benefits of your
> own country, be out of love with your nativity, and
> almost chide God for making you the countenance
> you are, or I will scarce think you have swam in a
> gondola.   (IV, i, 25–7; 31–6)

As the play's primary comic agent, Rosalind evidently favours the fool over the cynic. In drawing further attention to the distinctive and generic features of the travelling melancholic, she not only undercuts Jaques' bid to have his affect recognised as original and unique to him but, by stressing the artificiality of his behaviour, also suggests his uselessness to the play's larger comic concerns. The melancholy man becomes a mere afterthought. More so even than Orlando's, her interaction with Jaques signals the growing incompatibility (rather than legitimate opposition) of individual characterisations of humour within Shakespearean comedy. The courtship between Orlando and Rosalind rests on several comic elements (reaching Arden, the 'education' of the young de Boys by the cross-dressed Ganymede, the eventual restoration of social order, parentage and heterosexual identities) but it seemingly necessitates them coming into contact with Arden's melancholy weasel as well. Each scene examined above is followed by a lengthy exchange between the lovers (III, ii, 293–422, IV, i, 36–192) that solidifies their romantic entanglement; each character needs to consciously reject melancholy in favour of mirth and romance.

The idea that traditional comic characterisations of melancholy grow increasingly irrelevant and subordinate to a broader and ethereal sense of the affect onstage comes across most sharply through Jaques' interaction with the fool Touchstone. More than a strict opposition of comedy and melancholy, the two figures represent dovetailing poles of Arden's emotional charge that bring about the eventual melancomic mood described at the outset of this chapter. Their conflation does not render the play 'tonally even', as Anne Barton writes, or necessarily indicative of 'a stillness at the centre [of the play] which no turn of the plot, apparently, can affect', but rather, it infuses it with a hybrid dose of melancholy and merriment, one that brings to mind the sobering effects of the passage of time in the wake of dwindling festivities.[23]

Jaques appears profoundly marked by his first encounter with Touchstone. As he relates to the Duke:

When I did hear
The motley fool thus moral on the time,
My lungs began to crow like Chanticleer,
That fools should be so deep-contemplative,
And I did laugh sans intermission
An hour by his dial.   (II, vii, 28–33)

Touchstone is not only a gifted orator, being 'so deep-contemplative', but does so 'in good terms', managing to make the melancholic Jaques laugh out loud. Simply put, the melancholic fool is no match for the professional one. Touchstone represents a stark departure from previous fool characters in Shakespearean comedy such as Lancelot Gobbo or the Dromios, acting as an acerbic commentator rather than a bumbling clown. While this characterial shift can be attributed partially to Will Kemp's departure from Shakespeare's acting company in 1599 and the subsequent addition of Robert Armin, it also points to a larger shift in the treatment of melancholy within Shakespearean comedy.[24]

For the most part Touchstone's foolery revolves around the relativity with which he 'moral[s] on the time', as Jaques puts it, particularly as it relates to its unrelenting progression. 'And so from hour to hour we ripe and ripe,' he professes to Jaques, 'And then from hour to hour we rot and rot, / And thereby hangs a tale' (II, vii, 26–8). This mind-set somewhat dovetails with Jaques' 'Seven Ages of Man' speech (II, vii, 138–65), which details the bitter progress of human life, with its unavoidable descent into debilitation that leaves the individual in 'second childishness and mere oblivion, / Sans teeth, sans eyes, sans taste, sans everything' (II, vii, 164–5), yet betrays a more nihilistic temporal awareness, one that sees things as cyclical rather than dialogical. For Touchstone,

> To have is to have.
> For it is rhetoric that drink, being poured
> Out of a cup into a glass, by filling the one doth empty
> The other.   (V, i, 39–42)

The relativity with which Touchstone understands the worlds of court and of Arden offers a comedic counterweight to Jaques' idle melancholic languishing that recuperates the affect comically. The fool mocks Jaques, certainly, but the pragmatism with which he suggests that everything not only has its place but proves ultimately equally insignificant (emptying one cup into another) suggests that the fool and the melancholic enjoy identical comic claims.

As You Like It's final act fully embraces Arden's potency in staging a ludicrous number of resolutions and reveals through four weddings, two *in extremis* conversions and a divine visitation from Hymen. The celebrations are punctuated by the announcement of Duke Frederick's sudden departure from court and his vow to live as a hermit (V, iv, 153–64). The stage is set for Duke Senior to reclaim his power and lead everyone in a triumphant return to court, and the effervescent revelry of these final moments also implies that the time in Arden is coming to an end. Under these terms, Jaques' departure from the play (or more importantly, his refusal to leave the forest) consolidates his association with the melancomic ambiance the play develops in its final act. Though he appears initially content to sit by and comment on the revelry that transpires before him, the arrival of the third de Boys brother – also named Jaques – offers a physical representation of his comic irrelevance. The doubling, which critics tend to read as either a vestigial remnant of an earlier draft in which both characters are in fact the same person or a continuation of the play's broader concern with doublings (two Olivers, cross-dressing characters, to name a few) confirms Jaques' symbiotic association with the melancholy that dwells in Arden.[25] While Jaques enjoyed an acceptable – albeit derided – role in Arden, the arrival of the third de Boys brother suggests that there is no such position for him back in the 'real' world of court. One cup empties into another and characters can leave Arden with a suitable Jaques while leaving the melancholic one behind. Jaques does not undergo the transformation that characters such as Orlando and Rosalind do, because that version of himself already exists in Jaques de Boys.

The announcement that Fredrick will now live as a hermit (delivered by Jaques de Boys) gives Jaques the cue to eclipse himself. 'To him will I,' he declares, 'Out of these convertities / There is much to be heard and learned' (V, iii, 183–4). Despite a faint request from Duke Senior to remain, Jaques leaves the stage:

> So, to your pleasures.
> I am for other than dancing measures.
>   . . .

To see no pastime I. What you would have
I'll stay to know at your abandoned cave.

(V, iii, 191–2; 194–5)

Jaques' apparent disinterest is both for revelry itself (to see no
pastime) and for the life he left behind in coming to Arden (to
see no past time). His final act is to claim the Duke's former
cave as his own, laying claim to Duke Senior's golden world
in the process. Whether Jaques could ultimately fit in does
not matter as much as the fact that he deliberately chooses
to remain in Arden. Unlike the departures of Don John or
Antonio, there is nothing forced or ambiguous about Jaques'
final comedic status. The Duke's response to his departure,
'Proceed, proceed. We'll begin these rites, / As we trust they'll
end, in true delights' (V, iv, 196–7), confirms the play's lack
of regard for individual characterisations such as he offers.
Understatedly, it also suggests that melancholy will never
leave Arden, that its flora, fauna and bodies of water will
remain tainted with its affective powers and that, through
them, Jaques will continue to symbiotically feed off it and
disseminate it back into the landscape.

The fact that the play ends while still in Arden and that
the touted return to court remains a potentiality rather than
a fait accompli strikes a final sobering note that clouds the
otherwise festive atmosphere. The play's careful oscillation
between mirth and melancholy, between Touchstone and
Jaques and between Arden's idyllic, transformative powers
and its unavoidable desertion, goes on relentlessly. With its
celebration of multiple marriages and of Duke Senior's return
to power, the comedy achieves political, romantic and affective normalcy, but the overall pragmatism with which the play
comments on the cyclical nature of time remains all-too-pow-
erful. 'Maids are May when they are maids,' Rosalind informs
Orlando, 'but / the sky changes when they are wives' (IV, i,
141–2). The apparent triumph of mirth does not preclude an

eventual recoiling into melancholy. The play ending in Arden signifies that the melancholy ambience remains on the stage after all. It persists in the unresolved fate of Old Adam, out of Amiens' songs and Jaques' haunting absence. *As You Like It* offers Shakespeare's last, traditional characterisation of melancholy and manages both to show its obsolescence and to recuperate it within its newly fashioned comic ambience. In doing so, it suggests that Shakespearean comic melancholy increasingly shifts away from 'dancing measures'.

Twelfth Night's *Melancholic Revenges*

At its core, *Twelfth Night* is comedic recycling. The play is built on the romantic entanglements of a cross-dressing heroine, on the crisis that she and her twin brother cause and on the 'stranger in a strange land' trope that occurs following their shipwreck on the mysterious country of Illyria. Thinking back to Edmond Malone's ironically accurate mistake, *Twelfth Night* reads and feels like the culmination of Shakespeare's comic writing, an apogee of characterisation, festivity and emotional aesthetics. Not surprisingly, it recuperates several of the melancholic elements found in other plays discussed so far (it even has a merchant named Antonio).

Much like *As You Like It*, the play is rampant with melancholy. Shakespeare floods the stage with examples of lovesickness and mourning. Like Jaques, these characterisations are meant to be ridiculed. Concurrently, they underscore their own shortcomings in the face of an increasingly present melancomic mood. *Twelfth Night* fleshes out the idea of melancholy as a cyclical comic emotion tied to the inevitable passage of time. What Joel Fineman describes as the play's 'vaguely inappropriate melancholy'[26] eventually overtakes the festive atmosphere, mixing in a considerable amount of bitterness within the play's climactic celebrations. It is embodied in the subplot's revellers and their attack on Malvolio and, while

Toby, Maria and Andrew epitomise the comedy's hailing of saturnalian indulgence, they also offer its most pointed criticism. This shift defines the transformation of Shakespearean comedy through its sustained engagement with melancholy. *Twelfth Night* portrays revelry at its tipping point, and the tricking of Malvolio nudges the comedy forward. The ordeal comes across as a futile effort to delay the inevitable end of festivities, a desire to end on a high note, as it were, and bid comedy farewell in a blaze of glory. The play is undoubtedly comical, but in itself, in its reference to the end of the Christmas festival, in its closing song and in its status as the last 'Comedy' that Shakespeare ever writes, *Twelfth Night*'s final ambience is that of a sobering disillusionment in the face of the unrelenting passage of time. This barely perceptible sorrow amidst ecstatic celebrations strikes at the very essence of comic melancholy in Shakespeare. Though several critics point to Malvolio as the play's resident melancholic, the shift from characterisation to mood discussed above lies primarily with Feste, the aging court jester embittered against the world he inhabits.[27] Feste's undoing of language, the songs he performs and his allusions to the unrelenting passage of time, all suggest that *Twelfth Night* represents Shakespearean comedy's last stand against an ever-present melancholic ambience. The so-called problem comedies that follow (*All's Well that Ends Well*, *Measure for Measure* and *Troilus and Cressida*) show little concern for comic melancholy, and their considerable tonal and stylistic differences distance them further from the comic tropes examined so far. *Twelfth Night*'s melancomic mood looks beyond these works towards the later phase of Shakespeare's writing career.

As David Schalkwyk notes, *Twelfth Night* opens with three consecutive melancholic iterations, 'a triple blow of separation, mourning, and loss', in which Orsino, Viola and Olivia each express an overwhelming sense of sadness.[28] The play opens on Duke Orsino begging for more music:

If music be the food of love, play on;
Give me excess of it, that, surfeiting,
The appetite may sicken, and so die.
That strain again! It had a dying fall;
O, it came o'er my ear like the sweet sound
That breathes upon a bank of violets,
Stealing and giving odour.   (I, i, 1–7)

In galenic fashion, Orsino wishes to purge himself of an over-whelming lovesickness by gorging himself on music. From its outset the play hints at the strong connection between music and melancholy (a fact Shakespeare reinforces in using the name Viola, a name also denoting a small musical instrument). Orsino's mention of a 'dying fall' (I, i, 4), as Stevie Davies points out, offers an interesting parallel with the play's overall tonal arc. As she explains, the dying fall

> was a quite specific technical device, vital to ayres, ballets and madrigals of the Elizabethan collections, in which the melodic curve moves characteristically upward to a grace-ful peak, in order to descend conclusively to the lowest or one of the lowest notes in the range.[29]

Similarly, the play gradually climbs towards the ultimate spheres of romantic comedy before descending into pro-found melancholy in its final moments. Orsino's opening speech validates traditional comic depictions of love-mel-ancholy, in which the male sufferer embraces his lack of control over the humour while asserting it as an identity marker. He is the prototypical love-melancholic, fluctuat-ing between total surrender to and an adamant rejection of his affect. 'Enough, no more,' Orsino suddenly orders the musicians, ''Tis not so sweet now as it was before' (I, i, 7–8), showcasing an inconstancy expected on the comic stage. His discourse on Olivia continues along the same humoural lines:

Why, so I do, the noblest that I have.
O, when mine eyes did see Olivia first,
Methought she purged the air of pestilence.
That instant was I turned into a hart,
And my desires, like fell and cruel hounds,
E'er since pursue me.   (I, i, 17–22)

In praising the passion that afflicts him, Orsino draws upon
familiar metaphors associated with lovesickness (disease,
water and animals), underlining once again the predictability
of his melancholy by depicting himself as defenceless against
cruel desires. This point of view also shapes the way in which,
he imagines, passions would affect Olivia:

How will she love, when the rich golden shaft
Hath killed the flock of all affections else
That live in her; when liver, brain, and heart,
These sovereign thrones, are all supplied, and filled
Her sweet perfections, with one self king!   (I, i, 34–8)

Female love in his envisioning is framed by a similar sense
of implacability. He imagines love as a force that physically
overtakes Olivia's body; while he feeds his humour with
music, hers assails her organs. The passage accentuates the
male conceit of love as conqueror ('one self king') but it also
sets up the romantic entanglement that will follow as exem-
plarily comedic in terms of humoral masculinity.

   This opening scene also provides insight as to Olivia's own
melancholic dependency, brought on by the deaths of her
father and brother. As one of Orsino's attendants explains,

The element itself, till seven years' heat,
Shall not behold her face at ample view;
But like a cloisteress she will veilèd walk,
And water once a day her chamber round
With eye-offering brine – all this to season

A brother's dead love, which she would keep fresh
And lasting in her sad remembrance.   (I, i, 25–31)

The mourning rituals described depict Olivia as similarly ridiculous to Orsino in his love-melancholy. In vowing to cloister herself in her house for the next seven years and weep for her brother 'in lasting sad remembrance', Olivia is also seen as yielding to an all-encompassing affect. Since they serve as the play's dual authority figures, the behaviour of Orsino and Olivia sanctions the widespread presence of overbearing passions and abnormal conduct that erupt across the play.

In the following scene, Viola washes up on the Illyrian shoreline after a shipwreck:

VIOLA: What country, friends, is this?
CAPTAIN: This is Illyria, lady.
VIOLA: And what should I do in Illyria?
    My brother he is in Elysium.   (I, ii, 1–4)

Viola's mourning of her brother provides an immediate contrast to Olivia's grief, but it also furthers the association of Illyria with melancholy. Viola imagines her brother in Elysium, the paradise of Greek mythology where heroes are granted eternal rest. By situating her brother in an ethereal place of perfect happiness, she conversely locates herself in an antithetical setting. If Sebastian lies in the blissful Elysian Fields, Viola dwells elsewhere, on the shores of melancholic Illyria. The seashore, what Steve Mentz describes as the 'no man's-land [which] characterises the swirling mix of sentimentality, cynicism, and ale-soaked mirth' of the play itself, becomes the liminal meeting point of melancholy and comedy.[30]

In a manner reminiscent of Rosalind on the threshold of Arden Forest, Viola turns to cross-dressing as a safety measure in the wake of extraordinary hardship. She decides to seek refuge in Orsino's court by posing as a eunuch, Cesario. 'I can sing / And speak to him in many sorts of music', she tells the captain, (I, ii, 57–8). This decision will grant her the freedom to spark a chain reaction in Illyria that ultimately brings about profound transformations in other characters. Her intention to speak music to Orsino echoes his earlier desire to consume it, a parallel that suggests Viola's ability to cater to the Duke's melancholy. The relationship that develops between them positions Viola as the ideal conduit for both heterosexual and homosocial desires. As Cesario, she brings Orsino to confess his somewhat unstable temperament in the face of romantic endeavours. Her male persona allows her to bring him closer to a more sensible understanding of love, paving the way for their eventual union. The persona also brings Olivia, who falls in love with Cesario following their initial meeting, away from the pangs of mourning in which she has enveloped herself at the beginning of the play:

> Even so quickly may one catch the plague?
> Methinks I feel this youth's perfections
> With an invisible and subtle stealth
> To creep in at mine eyes. Well, let it be.   (I, v, 290–3)

The speech, which reveals the suddenness of her enamouration with Cesario, likening it to the speed at which one can catch the plague, provides a contrast with her intentions for lasting sad remembrances of her brother. Viola emulates other Shakespearean comic heroines in showcasing activism and adaptability in the face of an overwhelming melancholy. Yet, as she woos Olivia on Orsino's behalf, she becomes enamoured with the Duke herself, and the melancholy that her brother's loss engendered is thus supplanted by the fever of romance running amuck in Illyria. As Cesario, she relates to the Duke the story of her 'sister', which offers a glimpse of the turmoil she endures:

> She never told her love,
> But let concealment, like a worm i' the bud,
> Feed on her damask cheek. She pined in thought,
> And with a green and yellow melancholy,
> She sat like Patience on a monument,
> Smiling at grief.   (II, iv, 110–15)

Through the layered narrative of a fictional sibling, Viola manages to express the confines of the lovesickness that afflicts her. This conversion emphasises the potency of the melancholy that infuses *Twelfth Night* and its power to affect even the comedy's heroine through the traditional rhetoric of female greensickness. Despite a farcical degree of convolution, the melancholy that stems from this love triangle is typical of romantic comedies; once Sebastian appears, the quandary progresses towards a familiar comic outcome. By depicting both of Illyria's authority figures (as well as their go-between) as melancholic, the first act firmly implants the notion that the setting itself is indeed one where you might be 'boiled to death with melancholy' (II, v, 3). The melancholic mood that eventually takes over comes in surreptitiously through secondary characters.

The play's dual time scheme reinforces the idea that the immediacy of the comic plot is contrasted by a less regulated sense of time predicated on the melancholy longing for the past. Thus, Orsino can mention Feste's singing at his house the night before (II, iv, 42) and Cesario can go straight from Olivia's house to the Duke's, yet Valentine expresses astonishment at Cesario's quick ascension within Orsino's court, marvelling at the fact that the Duke 'hath known you but three days, and already you are / no stranger' (I, iv, 3–4). Likewise, when Antonio is captured and brought before Orsino, he relates how he has known Sebastian 'three months before [today]' (V, i, 91). It is not uncommon for Shakespeare to play with time onstage, but here the disjointing reinforces the idea that the unrelenting passage of time brings about a profound melancholy on the play itself. *Twelfth Night* is where time, melancholy and comedy effectively crash into each other the way the ocean's waves lap the Illyrian shores. The play's melancholic mood recalls the speaker of 'Sonnet 12':

> When I do count the clock that tells the time,
> And see the brave day sunk in hideous night;
> When I behold the violet past prime,
> And sable curls all silver'd o'er with white;
> When lofty trees I see barren of leaves
> Which erst from heat did canopy the herd,
> And summer's green all girded up in sheaves,
> Borne on the bier with white and briskly beard.   (1–8)

The references to sable curls and violet (colours generally associated with melancholy) invite the reader to think of melancholy from the beginning.[31] In imploring his interlocutor to have children as a defence against 'Time's scythe' (13), the sonnet's speaker concomitantly hints at the profound melancholy stemming from the passage of time and the changing of the landscape from lush summer to barren winter. While a solution is brought forth in the sonnet's closing line (insuring a legacy through procreation), the poem also suggests that romantic concerns are no match for the implacable longing for times gone by. The multiple references to elapsing time in the play, to life suspended in idyllic carousing while the pendulum inexorably oscillates, infuse characters' actions with a sense of anxious, and ultimately futile, urgency.

The tendency to unruly melancholy in the socially superior characters finds its counterpart in a penchant for excessive revelry on the part of the characters of the subplot. In keeping with his mistress' vows of mourning, Malvolio attempts to quell the merriment in which members of her household (the cantankerous Sir Toby and Sir Andrew; the lady-in-waiting, Maria, and the fool Feste) have been indulging. They, in turn, join together to take revenge on him in a plan which culminates in his utter humiliation. As the play progresses, the revellers gradually reveal their moroseness, symptomatic of the fact that beyond their amusement lies a desperate attempt to retain a rapidly fading sense of mirth and careless gratification. This melancholic reaction foreshadows the sobering reality that ultimately descends on the final act in which, Barton writes, 'a world of revelry, of comic festivity, fights a kind of desperate rearguard action against the cold light of day'.[32] According to her, the play puts forth dual conceptions of time that 'run parallel throughout the comedy, diverging only at its end. One is the time of holiday and of fiction, measureless and essentially beneficent . . . The other is remorseless and strictly counted'.[33] Thus, the correlation between time and melancholy, briefly perceptible in As You Like It, crystallises within the confines of Illyria, overshadowing its characterisations of excessive and irrational behaviour. What Yu Jin Ko terms the play's 'progress from pleasure to decay' can also be understood as its fostering, to borrow from Gabriele Taylor, of a melancholic mood state.[34] Taylor explains that

> moods are objectless in the sense that there is no specific thing, situation, or event which can be picked out and described independently of the mood itself and which the state is 'about' . . . It is a constitutive feature of moods that they involve a way of seeing the world . . . The difference between emotions and moods is reflected also, of course, in the person's actions and reactions. When in a mood-state, her tendency to behave in certain ways will not have a specific focus but will manifest itself more generally in an increased or decreased interest in the world around her, a greater readiness to be provoked, discouraged, or encouraged.[35]

Taylor's understanding of a mood as not so much tied to a particular context but bespeaking a more general perception of the world comes close to the melancholic underpinnings found in Shakespeare's Illyria. It echoes Leo Spizer's definition of the French word *ambiance* as 'a spiritual climate or atmosphere, emanating from, hovering over a *milieu* . . . a word offering not a definition but an escape into the poetry of the vague and the imponderable: the antithesis of the deterministic *milieu* (*ambiant*)'.[36] This mood creeps up throughout *Twelfth Night* and gradually overtakes the more traditional comic melancholy, defeating the revellers' desperate 'rearguard actions', as Barton puts it.

In his first appearance onstage, Toby deplores the sternness that reigns in Olivia's household. His drunken carousing with Sir Andrew offers a stark contrast to the romantic extolments of the first act:

> ANDREW: Shall we set about some revels?
> TOBY: What shall we do else? Were we not born under Taurus?
> ANDREW: Taurus? That's sides and heart.
> TOBY: No, sir, it is legs and thighs. Let me see thee caper.
>   (I, iii, 132–8)

Their rhetoric proves much more literal than their romantic counterparts'; while the lovers are concerned with the heart and the eyes (potential sites of infection by lovesickness), Toby and Andrew praise the lower body stratum, (the 'legs and thighs'). While Orsino seeks the food of love, Toby and Andrew delight in actual sustenance and libations:

> TOBY: Does not our lives consist of the four elements?
> ANDREW: Faith, so they say, but I think it rather consists of eating and drinking.
> TOBY: Thou'rt a scholar; let us therefore eat and drink.
>   (II, iii, 9–14)

The exchange favours consumption over dominance by the humors. Although they similarly champion excess as a dominant code of conduct, they prove impervious to the galenic logic that affects other characters, exhibiting an even greater relinquishing of control over their appetites. More importantly, the commitment to festivity that these characters demonstrate comes in direct opposition to the austerity of Olivia's steward, who seeks to lead the household into replicating his mistress' mournful demeanour.

Critics look to Malvolio's grim temperament and dark garments as evidence of his melancholy. However, the character offers very little evidence of possessing any melancholic undertones, especially not the more complex ones that develop in the play. At his core, Malvolio is opportunistic more than humorous, and the penchant for melancholy he seemingly entertains evolves out of social aspirations. Maria implies as much with her description of the steward:

> A time-pleaser; an affectioned ass, that cons
> state without book and utters it by great swarths; the
> best persuaded of himself; so crammed, as he thinks,
> with excellencies that it is his grounds of faith that all
> that look on him love him; and on that vice in him
> will my revenge find notable cause to work.
>
> (II, iii, 147–52)

Serving a mistress who proves, in her words, 'addicted' to melancholy (II, v, 198), Maria suggests that Olivia's mourning affords Malvolio the perfect opportunity to exert control in a household that favours melancholy. His longing for social mobility appears most tangible when he daydreams about gaining prominence within Olivia's household and becoming 'Count Malvolio' (II, v, 34). The scene in which the revellers enact revenge upon him (III, iv) is crucial to an understanding of the character as socially opportunistic

rather than melancholic. With the assistance of a forged letter intimating Olivia's love for him, the characters coerce
Malvolio into acting foolishly in front of his mistress, so much
so that she orders him locked up on suspicions of insanity.
Malvolio is a Bergsonian comic figure. The trick exposes his
overly mechanical demeanour and exacerbates a sycophancy
he already possessed. This attribute, however, relates to narcissism more than it does to melancholy. Malvolio's subsequent imprisonment underscores this notion even further. In
its degrading treatment of the steward for the amusement of
everyone on and offstage, the punishment parallels Jonsonian
humour comedies – particularly the bitterness of *Everyman
Out of His Humour* – more than it does any treatment of
overly melancholy characters in Shakespearean comedy. This
idea is substantiated by the refusal of the last act to provide
any reconciliatory amendment to this process. Malvolio is
not 'cured' so that he can join in the final celebrations, nor is
he expelled because he endangers comic progression. Essentially, the character is forgotten, cast aside in a dark cell as the
comedy moves on to the mistaken identity crisis ushered in by
Sebastian's arrival. The closest Malvolio comes to belonging
within the sense of melancholy the play fosters is in his opposition to its emblematic figurehead, Feste.

Disgruntled by his position as an aging jester, Feste embodies the melancholic passage of time. The opening of the play
sees his return to Olivia's household after a prolonged absence,
which angered the countess. Feste's absence has also shifted
the household's balance of power towards Malvolio. These
characters are vying for the status of a tolerable nuisance,
as it were, within her household, gaining precedence one
over the other according to her prevalent mood; one pushes
towards melancholy and mourning while the other draws her
into foolery and indulgences. Feste navigates the Illyrian landscape with ease, blurring the boundaries between romance

and revelry, as well as between comedy and melancholy. He appears nearly ubiquitous – cavorting with Toby and Andrew in one scene (II, iii) before arriving at Orsino's house in the very next (II, iv). Viola actually provides the best assessment of his remarkable aptitude to curry favour wherever he may be when she remarks that

> He must observe their mood on whom he jests,
> The quality of persons, and the time,
> And, like the haggard, check at every feather
> That comes before his eye.   (III, i, 62–5)

Feste excels at reading other characters and, as a result, manoeuvres to his best advantage by offering them what they seek. He can assuage Olivia's grief by pointing out that her brother's soul is in heaven just as easily as he can drink and rejoice alongside Toby and Andrew. Likewise, he provides Orsino with what he craves the most: sustenance for his love-sickness. The scene where he sings for the duke begins with Orsino, in a mood reminiscent of the first scene, clamouring,

> Give me some music
> . . .
> That old and antic song we heard last night.
> Methought it did relieve my passion much,
> More than light airs and recollected terms
> Of these most brisk and giddy-pacèd times.   (II, iv, 1; 3–6)

Feste is merely obliging Orsino, who appears eager to feed on the pangs of melancholy, but the piece 'Come away, death' (II, iv, 51–66) provides a sharp contrast to the festive mood that otherwise dominates the early portion of the play. Its emotional charge actually supplants the one Orsino sought out. The fool's parting words to Orsino reveal his awareness of the Duke's inconstant temperament:

> Now, the melancholy god protect thee, and the
> tailor make thy doublet of changeable taffeta, for thy
> mind is a very opal. I would have men of such constancy
> put to sea, that their business might be everything
> and their intent everywhere, for that's it that
> always makes a good voyage of nothing.   (II, iv, 73–8)

In referencing taffeta and opals (objects known for their fluctuating features) Feste harps on the volatility of Orsino's melancholy as much as he comments on its near ubiquity in Illyria. Feste is a melancholy peddler, seeking to disseminate it so that 'its business might be everything [and its] intent everywhere'. His musical prowess acts as a conduit for the melancholy he releases onto the play, disrupting other characters and momentarily unhinging them from their unyielding emotional frames. Masquerading as trivial ballads, Feste's songs carry with them the harshness of old age and an awareness of the deterioration that accompanies it. The love song he performs for Toby and Andrew halts their boisterous debauchery (if only temporarily) with its bleak outlook on love and mocking commentary of old age:

> What is love? 'tis not hereafter;
> Present mirth hath present laughter;
> What's to come is still unsure.
> In delay there lies no plenty.
> Then come kiss me, sweet and twenty;
> Youth's a stuff will not endure.   (II, iii, 47–52)

The allusion to the fleeting nature of youth, communicated to a pair of aging buffoons, provides a moment of clarity that the two men hastily suppress by redirecting the conversation. After admitting that the fool possesses 'a contagious breath' (II, iii, 54) Toby seems eager to move on from the performance: 'shall we make the welkin dance indeed? Shall we / rouse the night owl in a catch that will draw three / souls out of one weaver? Shall we do that?' (II, iii, 57–9). Toby's insistent repeating of the question 'shall we?' betrays his uneasiness towards Feste's song and his anxious desire to move on from it. Much like the one he sang to Orsino, Feste's song signposts the shift away from revelry and toward more disconcerting matters. Feste offers the quintessential mixture of mirth and melancholy, stemming from utter disappointment in his status, a veiled contempt for the patrons he serves and an inescapable feeling that time has passed him by. By the time the play reaches its climax, Feste's contagious breath has brought *Twelfth Night* to its tipping point.

Viola's reunion with her brother transpires with a surprising degree of emotional restraint. Her refusal to embrace her brother, echoed in her refusal to celebrate her union with Orsino until she has changed back into her feminine guise, throws an additional wrench into the intended celebrations the final act would foster. 'Do not embrace me', she hastily informs Sebastian,

> Till each circumstance
> Of place, time, fortune, do cohere and jump
> That I am Viola – which to confirm
> I'll bring you to a captain in this town
> Where lie my maiden weeds.   (V, i, 251–5)

That Shakespeare would further complicate this final scene by keeping Viola's clothing out of her reach indicates the uneasiness about comic resolution that *Twelfth Night* reaches. This delay undermines the expected sense of festivity that dual nuptial celebrations would engender, offering a stark contrast to the multiple weddings that punctuate *As You Like It*. The scene is an inseparable mix of frustration and catharsis.

The reappearance of Malvolio further suggests the shift towards melancomic. Feste's final attack on the steward casts it explicitly under such a frame:

> But do you remember? 'Madam, why laugh
> you at such a barren rascal? An you smile not, he's
> gagged?' And thus the whirligig of time brings in his
> revenges.   (V, i, 374–7)

In flinging Malvolio's own words from their earlier exchange back at him (I, v, 80–6), Feste reveals a vindictiveness that, once again, casts his carefree fooling under a suspicious light. More importantly, the image of the whirligig he conjures up, a spinning top that runs its course before inevitably toppling over, offers an ideal metaphor through which to consider *Twelfth Night*. Much like a whirligig, the revellers are cast aside when the time for merriment draws to a close. Despite a brief appearance onstage, the participation of Maria, Toby and Andrew in the final act proves inconsequential. The play has moved beyond their desperate attempts to prolong merriment, and their opposition is swiftly quelled. Antonio, who assists Sebastian in his journey to Illyria, suffers a similar fate, as he proves suspiciously silent in the play's final moments.

Only a vague promise of future celebrations remains. Too many discordant notes have been emitted for the play to offer harmony in its resolution. Left alone on the stage, Feste performs a final song, singing directly at the audience, his contagious breath conveying the play's powerful melancomic tone one final time:

> When that I was and a little tiny boy,
> With hey, ho, the wind and the rain,
> A foolish thing was but a toy,
> For the rain it raineth every day.

But when I came to man's estate,
With hey, ho, the wind and the rain,
'Gainst knaves and thieves men shut their gate,
For the rain it raineth every day.

But when I came, alas, to wive,
With hey, ho, the wind and the rain,
By swaggering could I never thrive,
For the rain it raineth every day.

But when I came unto my beds,
With hey, ho, the wind and the rain,
With tosspots still had drunken heads,
For the rain it raineth every day.

A great while ago the world begun,
With hey, ho, the wind and the rain,
But that's all one, our play is done,
And we'll strive to please you every day.   (V, i, 389–408)

Though it strongly echoes *King Lear*'s fool and the song he sings during the storm (III, ii), it also brings us back to *As You Like It*. Much like Jaques' 'Seven Ages of Man' speech, the song narrates episodes from its speaker's life, ranging from the infancy of a 'tiny boy' to that of older debilitated 'tosspots'. It also harks back to a song performed by Amiens, which highlights the cyclical nature of emotional and temporal hardships:

Blow, blow, thou winter wind.
Thou art not so unkind
As man's ingratitude.
Thy tooth is not so keen,
Because thou art not seen,
Although thy breath be rude.
Heigh-ho, Sing heigh-ho, unto the green holly.

Most friendship is feigning, most loving mere
folly.
Then heigh-ho, the holly!
This life is most jolly.   (II, vii, 174–83)

In Amiens' song, the roughness of winter weather is contrasted
with human behaviour, and the closing lines advocate for the
acceptance of less desirable parts of life. The nostalgic undertones in Feste's refrain and the notion that rain inevitably falls
down cradle every verse in a similarly melancholic embrace.
Time hurries past from couplet to couplet, encompassing an
entire life in the span of minutes, and while it celebrates the
merriment of the play that has taken place, the song provides
an equally fitting end to a comedy that has consistently frus-
trated its revelry with more sombre concerns. It hails a newly
fashioned comic perspective of melancholy as an essential
component of the cyclical understanding of human nature.
For Barbara Everett, the importance of the song lies not in

> what Feste says, but what, with greater detachment, he
> leaves unsaid . . . The theme of the song is, after all, sim-
> ply growing up, accepting the principle that nights before
> have morning after; that life consists in passing time, and in
> *knowing* it.[37]

Its chorus urges its listeners to accept the idea that melancholy,
the wind and rain in an otherwise healthy disposition, will
manifest itself regardless and should be considered as an everyday impediment rather than a grave threat. Feste thus provides
the ideal ending to a play after which Shakespeare was to sever
ties with traditionally understood comic structures. Like the
fool himself, the existence of this sense of melancholy is liminal; it lives on the outskirts of the comedy. Yet beyond the
celebrations of the final act, its nostalgic tone urges tolerance
rather than upheaval in the face of melancholy. Feste's song

suggests that coming to terms with melancholy trumps the futile desire for its eradication.

The argument that *Twelfth Night* represents the last Shakespearean comedy does not hold much critical value in itself, but the fact remains that, at the dawn of the seventeenth century, Shakespeare seemingly abandons romantic comedy, if not comedy altogether. In ending on such a distinctively melancomic note, *Twelfth Night* gestures towards the darker, more tonally complex works that follow it. *As You Like It* and *Twelfth Night* navigate the precarious dramatic territory that lies between celebrating the apogee of romantic comedy and highlighting its inevitable breakdown. A more elusive, cyclical conception of melancholy replaces the humoral characterisations of earlier comedies. Time, and the emotions it elicits both on and off the stage, takes on a considerably larger role in Shakespeare's late melancomic writing.

Notes

1. Malone, 'Attempt to Ascertain the Order', 344.
2. Radden, 'Melancholy, Mood and Landscape', 183.
3. Radden, 'Melancholy, Mood and Landscape', 186.
4. Morton, *Ecology without Nature*, 33.
5. Morton 48–9.
6. Morton 76.
7. Benjamin, *Origin of German Tragic Drama*, 81.
8. Benjamin, *Origin of German Tragic Drama*, 92.
9. Butler, *Psychic Life of Power*, 174.
10. Bloom, *Shakespeare and the Invention of the Human*, 51.
11. Alulius, 'Fathers and Children', 38.
12. See Michael Bath, 'Weeping Stags and Melancholy Lovers' 13–52, for an account of how the scene 'is probably the closest approximation we have in Shakespeare to an actual emblem

....all the details of [the] description are iconographically heavily loaded in terms of the visual arts of Shakespeare's time', 14.

13. Sullivan, *Beyond Melancholy*, 116.

14. Schleiner, 'Jaques and the Melancholy Stag', 176.

15. Babb, *Elizabethan Malady*, 75.

16. Babb 91–2.

17. In early modern zoology, it was believed that the weasel could suck 'an egg through a very small orifice at one end, leaving the shell itself entire', Knowles, *New Variorum*, 101.

18. Mack, 'Engagement and Detachment in Shakespeare's Plays', 112–13.

19. The selected English translation of Gesner's work by Edward Topsell in 1607 acknowledges that weasels devour eggs but does not refer to the sucking of their content, Topsell, *Historie of foure-footed beastes*, 728.

20. Topsell, 755.

21. Sacker, *Narbonus*, 79.

22. The expression only appears in one other play, *Henry V*: 'For once the eagle England being in prey, / To her unguarded nest the weasel Scot / Comes sneaking, and so sucks her princely eggs' (I, ii, 169–71).

23. Barton, *Essays*, 98–9.

24. Armin starred as both Touchstone and Feste when each play was first performed. His musical abilities and penchant for minimalist acting are thought to have influenced the composition of both roles. See James Shapiro, *Year in the Life*, 221–3.

25. See Cynthia Marshall, 'Double Jaques', 376, and Tatyana Hramova, 'Mystery of Two Jacques', 122–5.

26. Fineman, 'Fratricide and Cuckoldry', 85.

27. Winfried Schleiner, for example, sees in Malvolio, and his ultimate humiliation at the hands of the revellers, 'the nexus of madness, melancholy and possession', *Melancholy, Genius and Utopia*, 263.

28. Schalkwyk, *Shakespeare, Love and Service*, 130.

29. Davies, *Shakespeare: Twelfth Night*, 38.

30. Mentz, *At the Bottom of Shakespeare's Ocean*, 5.

31. Violets were also commonly thought to be an ingredient for curing melancholy. Winfried Schleiner argues that Viola's name in the play (Latin form of violet) implies such a connotation in relation to Orsino's name (meaning 'little bear', an animal often connected with melancholy), 'Orsino and Viola', 135–6.

32. Barton 109.

33. Barton 110.

34. Ko, 'Comic Close of *Twelfth Night*', 396.

35. Taylor, 'Deadly Vices?', 165.

36. Spizer, *Essays in Historical Semantics*, 219.

37. Everett, 'Or What You Will', 207. According to Paul Edmondson, Feste's song stresses 'the silence between the songs of the Owl and the Cuckoo at the end of *Love's Labour's Lost* – caught in the tension between seasonal change and seasonal decline', 'Melancholy and Desire', 146–7.

CHAPTER 5

MELANCOMIC TIME IN LATE SHAKESPEARE

'Your stuff's been pretty peculiar. What was *The Winter's Tale* about? I ask to be polite.'

(Ben Jonson to Shakespeare,
Peter Whelan's *The Herbal Bed*)

In *The Future of Nostalgia*, Svetlana Boym discusses the work of early twentieth-century photographer Jacques-Henri Lartigue, 'who used still images to capture motion'. Lartigue, she explains,

> worked against the media; instead of making his photographic subjects freeze in a perfect still, he captured them in motion, letting them evade his frame, leaving blurry, over-exposed shadows in the dark background. Fascinated by the potential of modern technology, Lartigue wanted photography to do what it cannot do, namely, capture motion. Intentional technical failure makes the image at once nostalgic and poetic.[1]

In this chapter, I suggest that a similar 'intentional technical failure' is at play in Shakespeare's late works and their sustained engagement with melancholy. A great deal has already been written about these plays in terms of their problematic taxonomy. According to Anne Barton, 'the last plays as a group flaunt their own impossibilities and theatrical contrivance . . . Only the emotions generated are, miraculously, real'.[2] Shakespeare's late plays are generic quagmires in themselves, and the ongoing critical debate as to what to call these works – romances, tragicomedies or the more straightforward 'late plays' put forth most convincingly by Gordon McMullan – testifies to their oddly successful blend of tragic and comic elements.[3] Here, I look at *The Winter's Tale* and *Pericles* (and briefly, to *The Two Noble Kinsmen*) to examine the notion that late Shakespearean works question the recuperative powers of humour in the face of significant temporal and traumatic gaps. In their first halves, the plays stage instances of deep familial loss, displacement and mourning that endure over lengthy periods of time within each dramatic narrative. Each play then shifts to self-contained humorous scenes (as momentary interludes) before moving on to the kind of joyous and restorative conclusions expected of comedy. Yet the profound melancholy created by the tragic events in each play (purported losses of time, identity and familial bonds) is never fully dissipated from the stage. It looms over the lighter concerns of later scenes and seriously undermines the attempts at celebratory reconciliation found in each work.

In examining such a phenomenon, my chapter underscores two lines of inquiry. First, in questioning its validity following lengthy temporal intervals, the plays suggest that comedy is most (if not only) viable in the immediate; the wistful looking back on tragic events incapacitates attempts at comic relief. The ending of each play is tinged with a mix of nostalgic longing and unresolved trauma. Second, *The Winter's Tale* and *Pericles* offer evidence that the long-standing dramatic binary of comedy and tragedy is no longer de rigueur in Shakespeare's late works (or in the seventeenth-century dramatic landscape more generally). Late plays are best understood as profoundly melancomic works which

never yield completely to one side of the affective spectrum
but carefully oscillate between them, the way a laser franti-
cally reverberating between two mirrors eventually appears
to stand still. Such a potent state of stagnation is found in
Shakespeare's melancomic late plays and in their engagement with melancholy at the nexus of emotional trauma and
theatrical contrivance. To echo Lartigue's work once again,
they showcase the intentional failure of comic resolution to
fully alleviate melancholy. Plays such as *Pericles* and *The
Winter's Tale* develop tragic situations for their characters,
compounded by lengthy temporal intervals, before undergoing tonal and thematic shifts in their later halves. Yet, in
their miraculous resolution scenes, the plays consciously fail
to dispel the sorrows they have put forth. The endings are
comic, but hastily so. Melancholy clings to the plays themselves as a reminder of the tragic downfalls that cannot be
undone. Families are reunited in *Pericles* and *The Winter's
Tale* but never restored (or reset) to their pre-traumatic
states. The audience is thus meant to appreciate the resolution being staged without ever forgetting the troubles that
marred the characters throughout. In this sense, melancholy
in late Shakespeare can be understood as a dramatic early
modern precursor to nostalgia.

The medical use of the term 'nostalgia', from the Greek
(*Nostos-* / *-algia*), to describe a set of physical symptoms
induced by longing for home did not occur until the latter
half of the seventeenth century.[4] Channelling melancholia and
hypochondria, nostalgia morphed primarily into a psychological affliction symptomatic of our complex relationship
to 'the irreversibility of time that plagues the human condition'.[5] While the plays appear antithetical to nostalgia, as
self-contained time units that can be repeatedly performed,
Shakespeare's late works consciously undercut these facets
by spanning lengthy periods of time, a dramatic manoeuvre
that brings characters and audiences alike to reflect on past

events while the plays progress towards resolution. The sorrow found at the core of *Pericles* and *The Winter's Tale* approximates to what Boym terms reflective nostalgia, a longing 'oriented towards an individual narrative that savors details and memorial signs, perpetually deferring homecoming itself'.[6] Though Pericles rediscovers Marina and Thaisa and Leontes is ultimately reunited with Hermione and Perdita, actual homecoming (as a return to past relationships) is perpetually delayed, even suggested to be impossible. More importantly, the putative homecoming is meant to transpire offstage, never to be witnessed. The lingering sense of melancholy that characterises these plays resides in their liminal affective and narrative crevices, in the non-said and the unstaged. The plays give us the potential for a redemptive homecoming rather than its actuality. In essence, the families reconstituted at the end of both plays are not the ones we encountered at their onsets. The trauma suffered has negated the possibility of a dramatic homecoming and the melancholy that clings on to both plays suggests that such a homecoming was never possible to begin with. To paraphrase Boym, neither *Pericles* nor *The Winter's Tale* are nostalgic for the past, but for what the past could have been.[7]

The melancholy of late Shakespearean works, like the nostalgic longing itself, similarly echoes Walter Benjamin's Angel of History, a figure '"looking as though he is about to move away from something he is fixedly contemplating" . . . We might confront this angel of history', Boym writes,

> just as Benjamin describes him: on the threshold of past and future . . . he looks toward us but not at us; diverting our gaze from the stormy vision of progress, yet not allowing us to turn back. The angel can neither make whole the past nor embrace the future.[8]

For Benjamin, remembering the past is always part of a futile hope for redemption; it is never actual recollection, but 'the

seizing of a memory as it flashes up at the moment of danger
. . . a process of empathy whose origin is the indolence of
the heart, *acedia*'.[9] The intentional emotional and generic
failure of Shakespeare's late works is predicated on a similar
illusory relationship to the past and to powerful moments of
danger (shipwrecks, death, jealousy and so on). Characters
never really recall past events but rather, their redemptive
potential. The emotional ambiguity that surrounds eventual
reunions with long-lost family members attests to the lingering melancholy of these plays, whose brief climactic scenes
cannot alleviate the sense of lost opportunity conveyed by the
lengthy temporal gaps that divide the plays. Like Benjamin's
angel, the plays' final acts, miraculous as they may be, cannot make whole the past, nor can they decisively speak to
the futures of the characters onstage. In doing so, the plays
create melancomic tableaux that precariously juxtapose the
immediate bliss of crisis resolution with the persisting after-
taste of wasted potentials.

Past Trauma and the 'storm perpetual'

Both plays are deeply concerned with the emotional and narrative impacts of temporality. *Pericles*' Prologue, spoken by
Old Gower, underscores the power that ancient stories seemingly hold over audiences:

> From ashes ancient Gower is come,
> Assuming man's infirmities
> To glad your ear and please your eyes.
> It hath been sung at festivals,
> On ember eves and holly-ales;
> And lords and ladies in their lives
> Have read it for restorative.
> The purchase is to make men glorious,
> *Et bonum quo antiquius eo melius.*
>
> (Prologue, 2–10)

The opening positions histories as highly valuable, suggesting their inherent appeal to early modern audiences. While this can be understood as gesturing towards the play's classical setting (as does the reference to England's literary past in the person of John Gower), the idea also alludes to the temporal liberties that *Pericles* will indulge in, a dramatic elasticity designed to accentuate the immateriality of the melancholy that the play soon develops. The Latin maxim *et bonum quo antiquius eo melius* ('and the older a good thing is, the better'), coupled with the intimation that such stories hold restorative capabilities, implicitly suggests that remembering the past is vital. From the beginning, the play hints at Time's ability to intensify passions, heal wounds and impress emotions onto certain events or memories. The play's repetitive structure, in which characters must relate their mishaps time and again as an identity marker, points to the importance not only of the past but also of its memorialising process. Gower's praise of a regenerative return to the old similarly foreshadows the culmination of Pericles' trials and the eventual reunion with his family, yet his very presence onstage speaking the prologue concomitantly points to the impossibility of such a return.

A similar concern with time pervades *The Winter's Tale*, a play, as Ruth Nevo describes it, 'fissured by oppositions of time, place, tempo [and] mood', and in which 'tragedy will not absorb or synthesise comedy, nor comedy tragedy'.[10] Such a focus echoes that of its primary source text, Robert Greene's *Pandosto: The Triumph of Time*, as the plot structures mirror each other: a jealous king (Pandosto) imprisons and banishes his infant daughter (Fawnia) only to encounter her as a young maiden years later. Greene's prose romance is much more harrowing than Shakespeare's tale (Pandosto's wife actually dies, the king initially woos his daughter prior to recognising her and although they are both initially made happy by the discovery of their true identities, he ultimately kills himself when overcome with shame and guilt). *Pandosto*'s narrative core creates a lasting tragic impression in which no possible redemption exists. *The Winter's Tale* does not venture into such tragic depths, but it similarly suggests the redemptive impossibility that its lengthy time gap creates. The play opens with insistent praising of the bonds of amity that unite Leontes and Polixenes Polixenes' request to depart at the onset of the second scene betrays his fears that his extended welcome in Sicily has created political uncertainty in Bohemia:

> I am questioned by my fears of what may chance
> Or breed upon our absence, that may blow
> No sneaping winds at home to make us say
> 'This is put forth too truly.' Besides, I have stayed
> To tire your royalty.   (I, ii, 11–15)

Moreover, anxieties about what may 'breed' back home during Polixenes' absence foreshadow Leontes' apprehensions of cuckoldry and progeny later in the scene (an idea also suggested by the mention that the visit has lasted nine months) but also allude to a more general concern with the passage of time and the fact that the Bohemian sovereign might have exhausted his host's generosity. For Michael Bristol, the scene characterises the play's overall contrast of temporal perceptions. As he explains,

> the action of *The Winter's Tale* unfolds within a temporality both classical and contemporary in its semantic and social content. Viewed as a whole, moreover, the play seems equivocally situated between the narrative space-times of 'here and now' and of 'once upon a time' . . . The spatiotemporal heterogeneity of this play is now most often understood as a question of genre.[11]

Bristol's analysis of the play's duelling time schemes is crucial to an understanding of its development of melancholy given its connections to the play's elastic yet fleeting temporalities. By oscillating between Bristol's classical and contemporary poles, the play predicates itself on a longing for the past that can never be satiated. The exchange between Leontes and Polixenes embodies the clash of folkloric and actual time since the former's vague sense of dread concerning the extensiveness of his stay is contrasted with the precision of Leontes' insistence that he remain for one more day. Time-wise, the play opens at the juncture where the two temporal models reach a breaking point; the lengthy stay in Sicily seemingly overexerts the play's purported comic stock and the additional day requested by Leontes proves one too many. Essentially, *The Winter's Tale* begins at its comic collapse, and the breakdown manifests itself through Leontes's inexplicable and sudden jealousy. The competing temporal perceptions thus usher in the crisis that will entrench the play in melancomic longing.

Both plays develop their conflation of time and melancholy through the emotional instability of their male protagonists. Leaving Antioch behind in the first act, Pericles is rapidly struck by a 'sad companion, dull-eyed melancholy' (I, ii, 3) that he cannot seem to shake off:

> Then it is thus: the passions of the mind,
> That have their first conception by misdread,
> Have after-nourishment and life by care;
> And what was first but fear what might be done
> Grows elder now, and cares it be not done. (I, ii, 12–16)

His weariness evolves into a more liminal sense of longing as fear 'grows elder' into melancholy. While Pericles' general malaise can be partly explained by his uncovering of an incestuous relationship between King Antiochus and his daughter, it also marks a pattern in the play whereby he looks back on hardships he endured and lets himself be traumatised anew by what John Gillies describes as his 'tendency to reflective melancholy [which proves] morbid, hypochondrial and excessive to dramatic needs'.[12] Within the play's episodic first half, Pericles' growing melancholy acts as an emotional tether for the otherwise disparate settings he travels to and from. His desires to reflect constantly on his sorrows continues the play's engagement with temporality and nostalgic longing. The pattern repeats itself when he washes up on the shores of Pentapolis and later when he loses his wife and daughter during a storm at sea.

Leontes' volatility, expressed mainly through the emotional and linguistic breakdowns that his sudden fit of jealousy incurs, also conflates melancholy with reflective and ultimately self-destructive tendencies. The play's failure to produce a satisfying cause for Leontes' jealous rage has generated a substantial number of critical interrogations. Of these, David Houston Wood and Barbara Mowat's interpretations come closest to the one proposed in this chapter in terms of connecting it to melancholic longing. Both critics point out that the scene (and Leontes' breakdown) follows the tenets of early modern humoral psychology in order to convey the characters' emotional distress but that the resulting melancholy extends far beyond them. Houston Wood explains that the narration of Leontes' 'subjective bodily transformation from one humoral state into another can be seen to carry with it a commensurate psychological transformation [which] itself conveys an analogous shift in the subject's impression of time'.[13] The transformation, he argues, is anchored in a melancholy produced 'through emotions of nostalgic loss that stem from a troubled moment of intense self-reflection'.[14] The intense moment of self-reflection Leontes undergoes as he looks upon his son Mamilius, leads him to 'recoil / Twenty-three years' in the past and imagine himself as a boy, 'unbreeched, / In my green velvet coat, my dagger muzzled' (I, ii, 154–6).

The image conveys the power of memory to dictate current emotional states. His recalling of himself as a boy forms a distorted mingling of innocence, impotence and longing which precipitates his descent into jealous fury. What differs here, as Mowat points out, is that the play prevents any sense of tragic empathy towards the character by depicting him in a state of emotional crisis so early on. 'We see too little of Leontes in his normal state', she writes, 'to be able to judge his true character . . . it is significant that not once in the "Leontes-story" does a character refer to [his] goodness or single out any of his virtues for praise.'[15] In an interesting reversal from *Pandosto*, in which 'a certain melancholy passion entering the mind' of the king eventually drives him into a jealous rage, Shakespeare inverts the afflictions, subjugating his jealousy to the more elusive sense of nostalgic melancholy that pervades the play. The haste with which the play brings about the crisis renders Leontes' jealousy, like Pericles' reflective tendencies and the melancholic longing it creates, his natural or 'true' character. Both plays build towards a massive tragic event, but they establish their protagonists' instability from the beginning.

The plays compound this sense of emotional volatility through scenes of loss that effectively isolate each protagonist and catalyse the traumatic memory going forward. In *Pericles*, a storm provokes Thaisa into an early labour that claims her life. After throwing her body overboard at the urging of superstitious sailors (III, i, 47–9), Pericles decides to leave his infant daughter, Marina, 'all that is left living of [his] queen' (III, i, 20), in tutelage in Tarsus (III, iii, 15–18). As a paradoxical embodiment of the purity of life and the horrors of death, Marina's birth represents the dramatic nexus of Pericles' past and present, the convergence of tragedy and comedy that eventually subjugates Pericles' physical, grief-induced melancholy to the more elusive temporally driven one. Even though Pericles' situation (witnessing the destruction of his family during a storm at sea) echoes the melancholic travails of Egeon in *Errors*, the play negates its impact by depicting Thaisa's 'resurrection' at the hands of Lord Cerimon in the following scene (III, ii).[16] Her miraculous awakening sets up the eventual reunion in the fifth act; however, it also indicates that the real trauma endured is not the tragic loss of the family in the moment of danger but the fourteen years they will spend apart, stressing once again the play's conflation of memory, time and melancholy. The prologue of the fourth act reinforces the shift away from Pericles and towards Marina as the play undertakes its most significant temporal displacement. The jump, dramatically necessary to render Marina of marriageable age, suggests a wistful sense of lost opportunity that interrogates Pericles' failure to seek out his daughter and, conversely, Thaisa's decision not to return to her husband. The substantial break compounds their moment of traumatic loss to the point where a joyful reunion at the play's close cannot amend it.

The Winter's Tale follows a similar pattern but ascribes all the blame to Leontes. While Pericles can be said to have reacted poorly to extraordinary circumstances, Leontes' jealousy singlehandedly brings about the destruction of his family. Ignoring his wife, Hermione, her attendant, Paulina, and even the oracle's verdict, the breakdown that the king experiences at the beginning of the play irreparably splinters his family. He imprisons his wife and tasks Antigonus with the disposal of his infant daughter, Perdita (II, iii, 170–83). On the heels of Hermione's captivity and the news of his son's sudden illness, the casting away of his daughter severs Leontes' final bonds of kinship. The oracle's verdict succinctly resolves the issue:

> Hermione is chaste, Polixenes blameless,
> . . . Leontes a jealous tyrant,
> his innocent babe truly begotten, and the King shall

live without an heir if what is lost be not
found.   (III, ii, 132–6)

The concluding idea places further importance on notions
of recollection, on finding what is lost, a process which
becomes unbearably futile once the king is informed of
his wife and son's deaths. Grief stricken, Leontes asks
Paulina to

> Bring me
> To the dead bodies of my queen and son.
> One grave shall for both. Upon them shall
> The causes of their death appear, unto
> Our shame perpetual. Once a day I'll visit
> The chapel where they lie, and tears shed there
> Shall be my recreation. So long as nature
> Will bear up with this exercise, so long
> I daily vow to use it.   (III, ii, 234–42)

Leontes' oath to visit the chapel daily and weep recalls Olivia's
somewhat excessive vows of mourning in *Twelfth Night,* but
it also stresses his intention to commit to memory the causes
of their death and frame them as his 'shame perpetual'. The
memory of his loss becomes a place of worship, where what
is lost cannot be found but only longed for. Pericles suffers a
similar fate once news of his daughter's alleged death reaches
him. Gower explains that he,

> In sorrow all devoured,
> With sights shot through and biggest tears o'ershowered,
> . . .
> [swears] Never to wash his face nor cut his hairs;
> He puts on sackcloth, and to sea. He bears
> A tempest, which His mortal vessel tears,
> And yet he rides it out.   (IV, iv, 25–31)

In shutting himself up in his grief, refusing to alter his physical appearance and remaining in a perpetual storm, Pericles, much like Leontes, encases himself in the memory of his loss. While Leontes will prostrate himself daily at the physical monument of his sin, Pericles, will ride out tempests on the site of his own failings. Both of their lives now revolve solely around their reflective melancholy.

Antigonus' arrival on the shores of Bohemia with the infant in Act 3 marks the culmination of the tragic spiral the play undergoes in its first half. Much like the birth of Marina at sea during a storm, *The Winter's Tale*'s transition from tragedy to comedy, from grief to nostalgic longing, hinges on the figure of the daughter. The scene represents an almost palpable tonal shift, away from the tragedy of Leontes' jealousy and towards Perdita. The utter tragedy of Antigonus abandoning the infant is pushed to a grotesque extreme when he is devoured by a bear as the ongoing storm sinks his ship. Yet the horror of that moment is simultaneously contrasted with Perdita's rescue by a passing shepherd. For Bristol, the appearance of the bear offers a vivid dramatisation of the play's duelling temporal perceptions. According to him, the scene conjures 'the symbolic identification of the bear with the winter season', suggesting a turn towards a cyclical understanding of time, an eventual return to what was thought to be lost. The animal, Bristol writes, can be perceived as 'a figure of boundaries and of transformation, marking both the moment of ending or death and the moment of her beginnings or birth'.[17] The animal is the linchpin on which the play manages to shift away from Leontes and towards his daughter. Hence, the events transpiring on the Bohemian shore act as a tragicomic device, eliciting in turn pity and fear (the bear) as well as surprise and relief (Perdita's rescue). The recollection by the shepherd's son of the shipwreck and of the bear's attack attests to the careful oscillation of tragic and comic concerns that the scene puts in place:

> O, the most piteous cry, of the poor souls!
> sometimes to see 'em, and not to see 'em; now the ship
> boring the moon with her mainmast, and anon swallowed
> with yeast and froth, as you'd thrust a cork into
> a hogstead. And then for the land-service, to see how
> the bear tore out his shoulder bone; how he cried to
> me for help and said his name was Antigonus, a nobleman.
> But to make an end of the ship: to see how
> the sea flapdragoned it! But first, how the poor souls
> roared and the sea mocked them, and how the poor
> gentleman roared, and the bear mocked him, both
> roaring louder than the sea or weather.   (III, iii, 88–99)

The clown anthropomorphises every component of the scene he witnessed, from the sea, through the ship, to the bear. The passage conflates both tragedies into an amalgamation of wilderness, roaring and annihilation. The sheer hideousness surrounding Antigonus (made worse by the inference that the clown watched him die without trying to help him), marks the absurd climax of horrendous events in the play, whose cathartic hideousness allows for the pastoral merriment of the following act. The allusions to consumption throughout the clown's recollection – the ship swallowed with yeast and froth, the bear's 'land-service' of Antigonus – hints towards such an idea. Comedy and tragedy meet on the shores of Bohemia where, the shepherd remarks to his son 'thou metts't with things / dying, I with things newborn' (III, iii, 110–11). Life succeeds death, and the miracle of Perdita's survival succeeds the tragic downfall of Leontes' family. The scene undoubtedly points to cyclicality and seasonality, but it also suggests a definite temporal fracture as well. As Bristol explains,

In the second half of *The Winter's Tale*, the patterns of adventure time and of the time of the Winter festival are augmented by the time of the agricultural labor and market exchange. This additional layer of time, however, is much more than the completion of an annual cursus of liturgical, natural, and practical commemorations. Spatiotemporality has been changed in fundamental and irreversible ways here.[18]

Part of what makes this spatiotemporal change irreversible is the emphasis on reflective melancholy that pervaded the play's first half. As in *Pericles*, a lengthy time lapse between Act 3 and Act 4 (sixteen years) exacerbates notions of trauma and lost time. The fourth act opens with the figure of Time itself speaking the prologue and urging us to imagine

> Leontes leaving –
> Th'effects of his fond jealousies so grieving
> That he shuts up himself – imagine me,
> Gentle spectators, that I now may be
> In fair Bohemia.
> . . .
> To speak of Perdita, now grown in grace
> Equal with wondering. What of her ensues
> I list not prophesy; but let Time's news
> Be know when 'tis brought forth.   (IV, i, 17–21; 24–7)

Time's prologue looks to the merrier events of Perdita's time in Bohemia, but it cannot erase the tragedy of its first half, made real through the vision of Leontes' shutting himself up to memorialise his downfall. The linking of father and daughter looks ahead to their eventual reunion, but the intervention of Time emphasises the distance, both temporal and affective, between the play's two realms. Camillo and Polixenes' discussion of Sicilia and its 'penitent' king (IV, ii, 6) in the next scene furthers this dovetailing.

Nostalgia and Wondrous Comic Failure

The fourth act in both plays constitutes a comic interlude that counters the sombreness of their first halves and delays the inevitably tense and emotionally fraught family reunions. While Marina endures considerable hardships (her tutors attempt to have her murdered, she is kidnapped by pirates and sold into prostitution), they serve to establish her transformative (almost transfigurative) powers as she begins to reform the patrons of the Mytilene brothel where she resides, until she catches the eye of the town's governor, Lysimachus. The exchange between Pander, Bawd and Bolt in Scenes ii and v, as well as Marina's conversation with Lysimachus (IV, vi, 66–118), despite their seedy contexts, unfold comically. More importantly, Marina displays none of the reflective torpor characteristic of her father. She recognises that she suffers under 'most ungentle Fortune' (IV, vi, 97), but she looks ahead rather than behind her, living in hope that 'the gods / Would set me free from this unhallowed place' (IV, vi, 100–1). *The Winter's Tale* undertakes a similar shift following the bear scene, as the fourth act centres on the courting of Perdita (now a shepherd's daughter) by Polixenes' son, Florizel, during a sheep-shearing festival (IV, iv). Polixenes' opposition to the courtship, along with Perdita's concealed noble identity, echo comic tropes previously developed in Shakespearean comedy. Leontes' shadow still hovers, but the act's pastoral setting, populated by rogues and clowns, provides a respite from the heavier melancholic longing of the first half. The bucolic ease of the Bohemian scenes is tempered by the spectre of tragedy at the Sicilian court and the 'sad talk' that Camillo and Polixenes engage in while the festivities take place (IV, iv, 310). Pastoral revelry momentarily delays the play's more serious concerns, but it must inevitably defer to them. Although the fourth act sets up the potential for a comic reunion of its characters, the overall dramatic situation appears more troublesome. The play has given no hint of Hermione's survival, and the strong echoes of *Pandosto*'s disastrous outcome militate against the likelihood of future merriment. In spite of such comic spirits, *The Winter's Tale* makes it clear that no single character can alleviate the traumatic forces at play. The task necessitates a series of fortuitous reversals, scheming and miraculous dramatic events to bring Polixenes, Camillo, Florizel and Perdita back to Sicily, where the persistent reminders of past trauma are to be faced and the impossibility of comic resolution is to be fully revealed onstage.

While the reunions of fathers and daughters confirm the latter's redemptive abilities in both plays, they concomitantly draw attention to the more problematic sense of wistfulness that prolonged separations have ushered in. Those anxieties are exacerbated to a breaking point once Pericles and Leontes are reunited with the wives they have abandoned. When meeting Marina, Pericles struggles to comprehend what rapidly becomes obvious to everyone else when she informs him that she 'speaks, / My lord, that may be hath endured a grief / Might equal yours, if both were justly weighed' (V, i, 89–91). When he finally understands, Pericles evokes a conflation of physical pain and joy that recalls the play's overarching mix of comic and tragic elements, as he implores Helicanus to

> Give me a gash, put me to present pain,
> Lest this great sea of joys rushing upon me
> O'erbear the shores of my mortality,
> And drown me with their sweetness.   (V, i, 196–9)

Joyous as it may be, the reunion between Marina and Pericles, and his cognitive difficulties in recognising as an adult someone he only ever knew as a newborn infant, speaks to the play's comic shortcomings. The fourteen years during which Pericles never sought his daughter undercut the emotion with which they greet each other. The scene depicts characters who, in a sense, have never met. The joy they experience comes across as genuine, but their bond harks back to past versions of themselves, to the people they were before trauma, a fact which casts their reunion under a reflectively nostalgic light. Following divine intervention by the goddess Diana, Pericles and Thaisa are reunited through a similar sharing of histories (V, iii, 1–12), and the family torn apart long ago is at last reformed, augmented even by the impending nuptials of Marina and Lysimachus. The ending is complicated by a slew of concerns, ranging from the morbid imagery of Pericles' urging to Thaisa to 'come, [and] be buried / A second time in these arms!' (V, iii, 44–5), to the potentially disturbing implications of Marina's union to Mytilene's governor (who was first attracted to her while visiting a brothel). Equally disconcerting is the dramatic discrepancy between the fourteen years of sorrow the characters have endured and the brief redemption they experience onstage; the lengthy absence cannot be overturned simply by the promises of renewed happiness professed in the final scene, nor can the full emotional impact of their suffering and reunion be conveyed to an audience after a mere two hours of stage traffic. Gower's epilogue, which brings back the incestuous king Antiochus, closes the play with a similarly mixed tone:

> In Antiochus and his daughter you have heard
> Of monstrous lust due and just reward.
> In Pericles, his queen, and daughter seen,
> Although assailed with fortune fierce and keen,
> Virtue preserved from fell destruction's blast,
> Led on by heaven, and crowned with joy at last.
>
> (V, iii, 87–92)

The epilogue is meant to celebrate Pericles and his family, but in echoing Antioch (the play's original, sinful setting), it draws attention to the play's episodic structure, to Pericles' tendency towards reflective melancholy, and to the fact that the brief reunion staged here cannot fully redeem the trauma endured. Despite the joyful reunion, there remain fourteen lost years, whose emotional potential will never be recuperated. The epilogue thus forces the audience to think back on the play and the anxieties signposted along the way.

The father–daughter reunion in *The Winter's Tale* is even more problematic given that it transpires offstage. Leontes' mournful composure is troubled by the news of Florizel's arrival to his court:

> He dies to me again whenever talked of. Sure,
> When I shall see this gentleman, thy speeches
> Will bring me to consider that which may
> Unfurnish me of reason.   (V, i, 120–3)

Leontes is made to recall the trauma of the play's first half by the arrival of Polixenes' son, before fully confronting the memory later upon witnessing Hermione's resurrection. The play thus skips Perdita's reveal altogether, having it narrated by three witnesses in the following scene (V, ii, 1–124). The encounter, emblematic of the play's complex relationships to emotional catharsis, exists only in dramatic liminality. The (non)-scene, related by anonymous lords and commented on by the rogue Autolycus, becomes a memory in itself of events that were never staged, of the non-existent relationship between Leontes and the daughter he banished as an infant to live or die as fortune would have it. Unlike *Pericles*, the play forgoes the reunion of two characters who have never met in favour of Leontes' and Hermione's (and the audience's) emotional history. The play's emotional deferral to that eventual reunion suggests that the reflective trauma at the core of *The Winter's Tale* proves unstageable, 'a sight', the third gentlemen remarks, which 'was to be seen [and] cannot be spoken of' (V, ii, 43–4). The inherent paradox of such a line reiterates the intentional failure of the final act. The reunion with Perdita is in fact one of several dramatic loose ends being tied up by the gentlemen's story as they also relate Leontes' reacquaintance with Camillo, his learning of Antigonus' horrific demise and his tearful embrace of Polixenes. As Philip Edwards points out, the scene echoes the play's overall reliance on the folk tales and fables genre, 'especially [in] the moment between narration and performance . . . seeing is believing, and only seeing is believing. Those passages of the story which are not privileged with performance are relegated to the status of old wives tales'.[19] The consecutive entrances of the three gentlemen, each contributing a portion of the retelling emphasises the fact that all of the events related here (Perdita's reunion chief among them), transfer their emotional poignancy onto Hermione's return. This is partly a move towards dramatic efficiency, limiting the repetitive moments of recognition onstage, but it also places the burden of the audience's emotional expectations squarely on the scene of Hermione's miraculous resurrection.

The play's final act mirrors its opening one in depicting Leontes being advised by his entourage to forgo an unyielding emotional stance (in this case, the mournful apathy with which he entrenches himself in grief concerning the loss of his family):

> Whilst I remember
> Her and her virtues, I cannot forget
> My blemishes in them, and so still think of
> The wrong I did myself, which was so much
> That heirless it hath made my kingdom and
> Destroyed the sweet'st companion that e'er man
> Bred his hopes out of.   (V, i, 6–12)

The speech demonstrates that the memory Leontes holds on
to is obstinately turned inward, on himself, his guilt and
his kingdom, rather than towards Hermione. Penitent as
he may be, his mourning of Hermione is as much a shrine
to her virtue as it is a cognitive and emotional cross that
he purposely bears, one which demands a constant state
of reflective longing. Paulina, who literally possesses 'the
memory of Hermione' (V, i, 50), having concealed her all
these years, sustains this behaviour as part of her elaborate
machinations to reveal that his wife was alive all along. The
conditions she imposes on the king's putative remarrying
illustrate her careful orchestrations:

> Give me the office
> To choose you a queen. She shall not be so young
> As was your former, but she shall be such
> As, walked your first queen's ghost, it should take joy
> To see her in your arm.   (V, i, 77–81)

Paulina's plan depends on persuading Leontes to move on
and take a new wife, while ensuring that he remembers
Hermione (by noting that she would approve of his 'new'/
queen). Doing so effectively merges who Hermione was
with who she now is sixteen years after the fact; once again
conflating past sorrows with present merriment. Her careful directing of Hermione's resurrection, commanding her to
move, then to touch Leontes and finally to speak, emphasises the contrast between narration and performance. As the
'dead' queen embraces her husband, Camillo and Polixenes
asks Paulina to explain the miracle they have just witnessed.
Paulina remarks,

> That she is living,
> Were it but told you, should be hooted at
> Like an old tale; but it appears she lives,

Though yet she speaks not. Mark a little while.

(V, iii, 116–19)

In a clear echo to the gentlemen's story in the previous scene, Paulina suggests that *telling* them how and why she lives would not convince her interlocutors, but rather, that *seeing* it (and eventually hearing her speak) will make a stronger, more believable case. Paulina's explanation also presents Hermione as somewhat of a hybrid of past and present selves. In this final scene Hermione is both dead and alive, both Leontes' first queen 'again in breath' and (V, i, 84) a new wife whom he must now learn to love. Hermione thus stands as both a testimony to her old, tragic story and her new, magical tale of rebirth.

Her miraculous return does not dispel the larger problems that the play's tragic events and lengthy period of missing time have incurred. When Hermione finally speaks, she all but ignores her husband:

Look down
And from your sacred vials pour your graces
Upon my daughter's head! – Tell me, mine own,
Where hast thou been preserved? Where lived? How found
Thy father's court? For thou shall hear that I,
Knowing by Paulina that the oracle
Gave hope thou wast in being, have preserved
Myself to see the issue.   (V, iii, 122–9)

Her speech, reminiscent of Leontes' self-invested opening words in Act 5, turns away from her husband. The play inverts the binary it previously established, as Hermione downplays her reunion with Leontes in favour of hearing Perdita's story. Though she 'hangs about [Leontes'] neck' (V, iii, 113) upon stepping down from the pedestal, her refusal to address him casts heavy doubts as to the blissfulness of

their reunion. Her silence implies the impossibility of comically staging such a reunion given the powerful traumatic gap
that exists between the characters. Similarly, when Leontes
closes the play, he addresses nearly everyone but Hermione,
betrothing Camillo to Paulina, pardoning Florizel and bless-
ing his nuptials with Perdita and urging everyone to retire to
more suitable quarters so as to properly unpack all that has
suddenly been revealed:

> Good Paulina,
> Lead us from hence, where we may leisurely
> Each one demand and answer to his part
> Performed in this wide gap of time since first
> We were dissevered. Hastily lead away.   (V, iii, 153–7)

His parting words convey a sense of wonderment that does
prevail throughout the last act, but they also point to rather
pressing anxieties that surfaced, most notably his failure
to acknowledge responsibility for the tragedies that have
befallen Perdita and Hermione. His request to be 'hastily'
lead offstage testifies to the impossibility of properly staging
the difficult conversations that undoubtedly follow. In refusing to stage a dialogue between Hermione and Leontes, in not
providing any hint of his contrition or of her forgiveness once
they are reunited, the play makes it clear that the melancholic
trauma it has developed is not erased. In its final moments,
the play rejects closure in favour of a reflective longing on
itself. The ending is comic in its miraculous reunions, in its
smoothing out of dramatic edges and in the promises of nuptial celebrations, but none of these can alleviate the haunting
melancholy of its past trauma, nor the wasted sixteen years
that characters have suffered. There is no indication that
Leontes and Hermione will overcome the sixteen-years that
separates them, nor is there any proof that Leontes' jealousy
(never explained) will not resurface. The conflation of tragic

and comic elements at the end of the play, and the immaterial sense of longing that accompanies it, underscores the failure of time to sooth the sorrows of the past but also intimates the unknown potential time may reveal.

Moreover, Leontes' jealous fury has claimed actual victims in Antigonus and Mamilius. Early on in the play, Hermione asks her son to tell her a story:

MAMILIUS: Merry or sad shall't be?
HERMIONE: As merry as you will.
MAMILIUS: A sad tale's best for winter; I have one of sprites and goblins.
HERMIONE: Let's have that, good sir. Come on, sit down. Come on, and do your best, to fright me with your sprites. You're powerful at it

(II, i, 23–8)

We are not privy to the tale of ghosts and goblins that he regales his mother with as the play turns their attention to Leontes' growing madness. Mamilius' innocuous remark that tragic stories are those best suited to be told in winter provides a heartbreaking commentary on his own story within Shakespeare's play, one cut short by Leontes' jealous fury. The play's wondrous final act looks elsewhere, but Mamilius' sad tale is not that easily forgotten. It lingers on, much like most of the emotional atrocities of the play's first half, and engrains itself in the new story that Leontes, Hermione and Perdita are embarking upon as they exit the stage, with promises to 'each one demand and answer to his part / Performed in this wide gap of time since first / We were disserved' (V, iii, 155–7). Each one of them will be called upon to sound out the gaps and complete their past stories before moving on to their new one. Remembering their tragic past is part of their joyous beginning. We do not hear of such tales. *Our* winter's tale has ended and we are left with a similar reflective sense of

melancomic remembering. The wistful nostalgia that concludes the play encapsulates the evolution of comic melancholy in Shakespeare and its growing disillusionment
with the genre of comedy. More so than *The Tempest*, *The
Winter's Tale* embodies the melancholic impression that
revels now are ended.

Shakespeare, Fletcher and the Comic Post-mortem

As a brief coda, I want to draw the following conclusions
regarding Shakespeare's development of comic melancholy.
First, that *The Two Noble Kinsmen*, co-written with John
Fletcher, marks a final Shakespearean engagement with the
concepts of comedy and melancholy. As Walter Cohen notes,
The Two Noble Kinsmen (along with additional Fletcher col-
laborations *Cardenio* and *Henry VIII*) marks 'a second movement within Shakespeare romance [that offers] a darker view
of violence and death than the previous romances'.[20] While
the kinsmen's story certainly ends more tragically than previous late plays, it conveys a similar sense of reflective melancholy than is found in *Pericles* and *The Winter's Tale*. In
its final moments, however, *The Two Noble Kinsmen* offers
no miraculous resurrections. Its acrimonious resignation to
death and tragedy, despite a dying wish for reconciliation,
marks a swan song of a sort for Shakespeare's comic treatment of melancholy. My second conclusion is that despite
its intricate conflation of time, memory and nostalgia, the
melancomic style of late Shakespeare seemingly loses out in
the seventeenth-century dramatic landscape as the works of
playwrights such as John Fletcher and John Ford attest to the
resurgent popularity of humours plays within an explicitly
medical framework. No longer the target of elaborate satire
onstage, as in Jonson's *Everyman* plays, comic engagements
with melancholy at the turn of century now emphasise the
proper diagnosing and treatment of the humour. Plays such

as Fletcher and Massinger's *A Wife for a Month* (performed
1624) and Ford's *The Lover's Melancholy* denote the growing dramatic importance of the medical practitioner figure,
which seventeenth-century drama, as William Kerwin points
out, increasingly comes to frame as 'physician-persuading'
and 'playwright-directing'.[21] This medicalised depiction
of melancholy is found also in *The Two Noble Kinsmen*'s
subplot involving the Jailer's Daughter (generally ascribed
to Fletcher). While the story of the duelling kinsmen marks
a final Shakespearean treatment of melancomic time, loss
and memory, the Jailer's Daughter story, concerned mainly
with the prognosis and cure of love-melancholy, offers a
synecdochic representation of the larger shift back towards
humour plays.

The Two Noble Kinsmen multiplies departures from
previous late works, notably in its focus on heterosexual
competition between kinsmen (rather than parental bonds)
and in the absence of a lengthy time interval heightening the
tragic premise. The play does not rely on the compound-
ing of tragic events over time the way previous late works
did. The play's primary source text, Chaucer's *A Knight's
Tale*, spans several years, while Shakespeare and Fletcher's
version takes place over the course of a few months. The
play nevertheless conveys a sense of longing, familiarity
and nostalgia similar to that of *Pericles* and *The Winter's
Tale*. As Lois Potter explains, the story of the kinsmen is
one seemingly as old as time since the play amounts to 'a
Jacobean dramatisation of a Medieval English tale based
on an Italian version of a Latin epic about one of the old-
est and most tragic Greek legends'.[22] The first scene offers
a concise example of the play's conflation of mirth and
melancholy. Theseus and Hippolyta's nuptials are delayed
by the arrival of three grieving queens asking Theseus to
avenge their husbands and to wage war on Thebes and
its cruel leader, Creon. The scene underscores the overall

impinging of disquieting anxieties upon joyous practices that pervades the play as Theseus agrees to delay the celebrations to attack Thebes. Theseus' defeat of Creon a few scenes later allows for the burial of the three slain kings, but this does not bring back the spirit of festivity which hovered about the play at its onset. The focus shifts to the titular kinsmen, Arcite and Palamon, made prisoners during the assaults on Thebes, who embody the play's inherent mingling of comic and tragic elements from then on.

As Michael Bristol remarks, efforts to differentiate the kinsmen prove antithetical to the play's 'essential narrative and dramatic premise, namely that the two cousins are sociological twins and that this exact social duplication is logically necessary to the depiction of social violence'.[23] The play is purposely frugal in details that could help differentiate the characters from the outset, and Bristol's assertion presents this lack of characteristic as a crucial dramatic device vested in the tragic outcome of their escalating sense of competition. Their doubling, as Helen Cooper notes, is also typical of the romance genre from which the play derives (Chaucer specifically). As she explains,

> the tight ironies of [the play's] plotting seems likely to have been one of its attractions. The dramatization of longer romances made it especially important to solve the management of episodic structures, and it was often done through the kind of organic unity privilege of parallelism and symmetry.[24]

This symmetry is also important in terms of the play's melancomic balance. The play's inherent collaborative structure, in authorship, in character and in tone, underscores the careful oscillation between comedy and tragedy that the kinsmen represent. While their doubling is initially established through their valour and the unshakeable devotion they show each other, the kinsmen's relationship rapidly disintegrates once they catch a glimpse of Emilia (II, ii, 117). The growing animosity they cultivate towards each other once they become infatuated with her finally demarcates them; from then on, Arcite's involvement in *The Two Noble Kinsmen* plays out more comically (disguised identity, athletic competition), while Palamon navigates a more tragic course of action (imprisonment and perceived madness). Their eventual fight in the final act serves as an ultimate point of convergence for both taxonomies. Though critics have ascribed distinctive passions to each kinsman in arguing for their individualities, it is more useful to conceive of their divergence in terms of a tragic–comic oscillation reaching a tipping point. This association is crucial to the play's eventual turn away from comedy in favour of the more solemn wistfulness of its final moments.

The play initiates a series of small confrontations between Palamon and Arcite that culminate in their ritualistic contest in the final act. The kinsmen trade insults, reminisce about past sexual conquests and prepare to fight in a scene parodying excessive chivalric rites. The battle is halted by Theseus, who proclaims that their feud will be settled once and for all in a duel, in which the winner will claim Emilia as his wife and the loser will be executed. In a departure from Chaucer's story (in *A Knight's Tale* the protagonists have a year to prepare for their duel) and from other late Shakespearean works, which divide moments of trauma and reconciliation with lengthy temporal gaps, the kinsmen are given a month to return home and prepare for their fight. The absence of an interval to compound tragedy ahead of a precarious resolution reduces the impact of nostalgic longing on the play. The focus remains on the immediacy of the duel. Yet the duel's structure, mirroring the kinsmen themselves, proves inherently melancomic: each outcome will prove both joyous and tragic. There are no redemptory signs in these final scenes, and Palamon's assertion that 'the glass is running now that cannot finish / Till one of us expire' (V, i, 18–19) hints at the inescapability of time's grasp and the impending emotional impact of the duel. Prior to the battle, Emilia prays to the goddess Diana, and in doing so provides the most succinct distinction of the kinsmen that the play offers:

> Arcite is gently visaged, yet his eye
> Is like an engine bent, or a sharp weapon
> In a soft sheath; mercy and manly courage
> Are bedfellows in his visage. Palamon
> Has a most menacing aspect; his brow
> Is graved, and seems to bury what it frowns on;
> . . .
> Melancholy
> Becomes him nobly; so does Arcite's mirth;
> But Palamon's sadness is a kind of mirth,
> So mingled as if mirth did make him sad
> And sadness merry. Those darker humours that
> Stick misbecomingly on others, on him,
> live in a fair dwelling.   (V, iii, 41–6; 49–55)

The assessments comes shockingly late in a play that has alerted its audience to the kinsmen's seemingly indistinguishable personhood. On one level, Emilia's description stresses the affective contrast of melancholy and mirth that they represent. On another level, her use of convoluted images, a mingling of emotions and sharp weapons in soft sheaths, reiterates the fact that Arcite and Palamon are naturally antithetical to one another; they embody the play's melancomic tone, one which the impending duel threatens to irrevocably splinter.

The climactic battle transpires offstage (V, iii, 56–92), being related by Emilia's servants. Similarly to the gentlemen's

narration of Leontes and Perdita's reunion, the manoeuvre
undercuts the play's emotional impact by withdrawing the
potential visuals of the spectacle in favour of its narrative
payoff. The final scene offers an intentional technical failure of its own, by reversing its outcome: it is reported that
Arcite, who won the contest, subsequently dies by falling
off his horse, leaving Palamon to marry Emilia. The swerve
nullifies the result of the long-touted contest and provides
one last reflection of the kinsmen's interchangeability. In
this sense, the ending pushes the paradoxically melancomic
nature of late Shakespeare even further: the winner dies, the
loser wins Emilia. The two characters are thus simultaneously deprived of and granted what they desired. Neither
joy nor sorrow can be experienced without the other in this
situation. Despite an *in extremis* reconciliation between the
kinsmen, Arcite's death seriously undermines any sense of
celebration that Emilia and Palamon's impending marriage
could induce. The play thus comes full circle, as funeral rites
delay nuptials and Theseus' closing speech echoes this precarious conflation once more:

> A day or two
> Let us look sadly, and give grace unto
> The funeral of Arcite, in whose end
> The visages of bridegrooms we'll put on
> And smile with Palamon, for whom an hour,
> But one hour since, I was dearly sorry
> As glad of Arcite, and am now as glad
> As for him sorry. O, you heavenly charmers,
> What things you make for us! For what we lack
> We laugh, for what we have are sorry, still
> Are children in some kind. Let us be thankful
> For that which is, and with you leave dispute
> That are above our question. Let's go off,
> And bear us like the time.   (V, iv, 124–37)

In a final conflation, the kinsmen are to be eternally linked in ritualistic praise and mourning. Bridegrooms will succeed mourners the way joy will eventually overtake the passing of Arcite. In the suggestion that Athens will be expected to mourn before turning towards celebrations, the play's tragic denouement lingers on, if only because we will not be privy to the eventual turn towards merriment. Nor will we be witnesses to Arcite's burial. Rather, the play ends in a state of melancomic limbo, one whose powerful stasis recalls Lartigue's still motion photography, a blurry, overexposed shadow in the dark backgrounds of the play. *The Two Noble Kinsmen* presents itself as Shakespeare's final treatment of comic melancholy. It can be understood as completing the cycle that began in *The Comedy of Errors*; whereas two brothers found themselves in Ephesus, two kinsmen effectively lose one another in Athens.

The play also suggests an endpoint for Shakespeare's engagement with comic melancholy through its subplot, generally attributed to Fletcher, concerning the malady of the Jailer's Daughter. Her scenes are not only inherently comic, but they point to the growing dramatic popularity of medico-humoral treatments of comic melancholy on the seventeenth-century stage. The Jailer's Daughter becomes enamoured with Palamon following the kinsmen's imprisonment early on. Her love-melancholy contrasts with the melancomic tones that pervade the kinsmen's story through its predication on medical theories and cures. Despite putatively tragic undertones, the Jailer's Daughter's lovesickness is meant to be comic. Like the bawds of Mytilene or the shepherds and clowns of Bohemia, she offers a respite from the more serious concerns of the kinsmen's feud. Her love-melancholy is an example of what Carol Thomas Neely describes as the rise of a subcategory of melancholy concerned specifically with women, born out of the 'dynamic interactions between women sufferers and creative doctors'.[25] Though depictions of female melancholy appear frequently in Shakespearean comedy, never before is the condition developed with such attention for its medical intricacies, a notion that suggests Fletcher's involvement in the subplot. Palamon is but a device for the play's extensive depictions of the progression, diagnosis and eventual cure of her love-melancholy. Her father informs a physician that she

> sleeps little; altogether without appetite, save often
> drinking; dreaming of another world, and a better;
> and, what broken piece of matter so'er she's about,
> the name 'Palamon' lards it, that she farces e'vry
> business withal, fits it to every question.   (IV, iii, 4–8)

The symptoms her father lists (lack of sleep and appetite, hallucinations, obsession) lead the doctor to diagnose lovesickness. ''Tis not an engrafted / madness,' he informs the father, 'but a most thick and profound / melancholy' (IV, iii, 49–51). The diagnosis, with its allusions to thickness and depth, begins at the physical (and humoral) level, as the physician subsequently explains that the condition is wreaking havoc on the daughter's physical balance:

> That intemp'rate surfeit of her eye hath distempered
> the other senses. They may return and
> settle again to execute their preordained faculties, but
> they are now in a most extravagant vagary.   (IV, iii, 71–4)

The doctor suggests that lovesickness has penetrated her body through the eyes and deprived it of its faculties, providing a diagnostic staple of early modern discourses on lovesickness.[26] Yet the scenes involving the Jailer's Daughter differ from previous humour plays in putting the focus primarily on the physician rather than the patient. The subplot is thus symptomatic of a larger dramatic shift in comic drama in the seventeenth century, what William Kerwin describes as

Jacobean theatre's creation of a 'new cultural value placed on production – as opposed to just transmission – of scientific knowledge [and] a different attitude toward performance, opening up the possibility of a brave new world of artistic independence'.[27]

The works of Beaumont and Fletcher show a renewed interest in humours on the seventeenth-century stage. Plays such as *The Woman-Hater* (1607), *The Humorous Lieutenant* (1619) and *A Wife for a Month* (1624) all focus on characters whose humours are not correctly balanced. In each work, the proposed cures hinge on correctly diagnosing the humours and administering some form of medical or scientific remedy. In *A Wife for a Month*, the usurping King Frederick vows to keep his brother, Alphonso, at bay in order to maintain his position of power. We learn early on that Alphonso is afflicted by a mournful sorrow following his father's death which makes him feel:

> Nothing but sad and silent melancholy,
> Laden with griefs, and thoughts, no man knows why
>   neither;
> The good Brandino, Father to the Princes,
> Used all the art and industry that might be,
> To free Alphonso from this dull calamity,
> And seat him in his rule.   (I, ii, 27–32)

Alphonso's melancholy plays a crucial role in the play, preventing him from opposing the immoral schemes of his brother (who attempts to claim the lovely Evanthe away from her rightful lover, Valentino). The vile king, wishing his brother 'were as sad as I could wish him, / Sad as the earth' (III, iii, 25–6), orders his henchman Sorano to poison him. Fortunately, the concoction he administers Alphonso counteracts the melancholy that afflicts him, eventually curing him of it. As Friar Marco explains in the final act, the poison's innate heat revealed itself to be

An excellent Physick,
It wrought upon the dull cold misty parts,
That clog'd his soule (which was another poyson,
A desperate too) and found such matter there,
And such abundance also to resist it,
And weare away the dangerous heat it brought with it,
The pure blood and the spirits scap'd untainted.

(V, i, 15–21)

The cure is described in terms that conflate science and spirituality (alchemy, even) and the explanation is given by a character (a friar) embodying such a nexus on the early modern stage. Though not a physician *per se*, Friar Marco represents a turn in Beaumont and Fletcher' works and in the period more generally towards more scientifically based depictions of humours, which positions physicians as 'stagers of cures and of social experiments'.[28]

Such a trend is best exemplified by plays like Philip Massinger's *A Very Woman* (c. 1619–22?) and John Ford's *The Lover's Melancholy* (1628), works in which, according to Kerwin, 'the learned doctor, steeped in ancient texts, gradually transformed into the virtuoso, the medical theorist who explored the world of nature in order to create knowledge.'[29] For him, the two plays rely on the figure of the physician to provide a dramatic test case which 'voices the hopes of reformers that physic would become part of a new social politics, in which treating disease would involve reforming social arrangements'.[30] Massinger's *A Very Woman* presents a love story in which two male protagonists, Don Martino and Don John Antonio, quarrel for the affection of Almira. Following a duel, Martino, believing he has fatally wounded Antonio, is stricken with melancholy. The doctor who attends him informs his entourage that

> There is a deeper [hurt], and in his minde,
> Must be with care provided for. Melancholy
> And at the height too, near of kin to madness,
> Possesses him; his senses are distracted,
> Not one, but all; and if I can collect 'em
> With all various ways, invention
> Or industry ever practis'd, I shall write it
> My master-piece.   (II, ii, 78–86)

The doctor is adamant that the ailment afflicting Martino constitutes a concrete threat that calls for immediate action. The physician eventually cures him through an elaborate scheme where he visits him under several disguises (IV, iii). Antonio is then reintroduced as having survived the duel and the play can proceed to its joyous resolution, with Martino vowing to 'never / Sink under such weak frailties' (V, iv, 63–7). The treatment here rests entirely on the doctor's performative abilities: only after Martino is cured can Antonio reappear. Ford's *The Lover's Melancholy* pushes the practice even further. The play revolves around a mysterious ailment afflicting Prince Palador of Cyprus, and it falls to the physician Corax to find a remedy. The doctor is quick to identify Palador as melancholic, but he must then identify the correct strain of the sickness tormenting the prince. As he explains early on,

> Melancholy
> Is not as you conceive, indisposition
> Of body, but the mind's disease. So ecstasy,
> Fantastic dotage, madness, phrenzy, rapture
> Of mere imagination differ partly
> From melancholy, which is briefly this:

A mere commotion of the mind, o'ercharged
With fear and sorrow, first begot i'th' brain,
The seat of reason, and from thence derived
As suddenly into the heart, the seat
Of our affection.

. . . .

It were more easy to conjecture every hour
We have to live, than reckon up the kinds
Or causes of this anguish of the mind.

(III, i, 108–18; 120–6)

What makes the case problematic is the fact that melancholy presents itself under various forms and types, each with specific diagnostic procedures. In order to pose the correct prognosis, Corax relies on elaborate theatrics. He organises a performance of the 'Masque of Melancholy' (III, iii. 11) in which he parades various incarnations of the disease, ending with the aforementioned lovesickness, to which Palador reacts most strongly. The explicit use of performance is seen as the surest scientific way to diagnose melancholy correctly. In the end, the prince is reunited with his beloved, professing that 'the Lover's Melancholy hath found cure; / Sorrows are changed to bride-songs. So they thrive / Whom faith; in spite of storms, hath kept alive' (V, ii, 252–4). *The Lover's Melancholy* represents the period's most overt depiction of such a phenomenon. Melancholy is intrinsically connected to comedy here and is developed mainly at the intersection of medicine and theatre. Palador enjoys a happy ending, but the star of the play is without a doubt Corax.

The cure the doctor elaborates for the Jailer's Daughter in *The Two Noble Kinsmen* echoes such a conflation of medical knowledge and dramatic *mise-en-scène*. 'It is a falsehood she is in,' the physician explains, 'which is / with falsehood to be combatted' (IV, iii, 95–6). The purported

cure revolves around the indulging of her lovesick fantasies, as her wooer is instructed to feign being Palamon in
order to satisfy her irrational craving. The doctor advises
the wooer to 'please her appetite, / And do it home; it cures
her, *ipso facto*, / The Melancholy humour that infects her'
(V, ii, 37–9). Sexual intercourse is thus introduced as the
ultimate curative agent and the doctor's stratagem legitimises the encounter by offering her a potential husband
once she is cured.[31] It should be noted, however, that the
Jailer's Daughter is not cured during the play. The physician
exits the stage with promises to her father that 'within these
three or four days / I'll make her right again' (V, iii, 105–6).
The slight delay once again suggests that the play is more
interested in the process of scientific treatment of her ailment
rather than its actual cure. As Neely puts it, the doctor's plan
'leads to a remedy that dramatizes at length the folklore
cures of the melancholy tradition'.[32] This idea underscores
the fact that the character belongs to the more comic side
of the play. The depictions of her symptoms (madness, hallucinations and so on), her interaction with the players and
the schoolmaster, and her participation in the Morris dance
(III, v, 58–161), as well as the fact that she never encounters
Palamon again once she helps him escape, suggest as much.
Love-melancholy is an accessory to the comic plot, a dramatic catalyst allowing a physician figure to cleverly diagnose it. Once the ailment is ascribed a correct treatment, the
Jailer's Daughter can exit the play. There is a certain degree
of poignancy attached to the character – in particular her
last lines to the wooer as she exits the play: 'But you shall
not hurt me . . . If you do, love, I'll cry' (V, ii, 112–13) –
but her participation overall resembles the comic interludes
of *Pericles* and *The Winter's Tale*; it develops in the same
play-world but starkly contrasts the more tragic undertones
developing out of the kinsmen's conflict.

Notes

1. Boym, *Future of Nostalgia*, 21.
2. Barton, *Essays*, 112.
3. McMullan understands 'late' as a stylistic resurgence 'not all that different from other periods in [Shakespeare's] life', *Shakespeare and the Idea of Late Writing*, 28–9.
4. Boym 3.
5. Boym xvi.
6. Boym 49. Boym differentiates reflective nostalgia from its restorative counterparts, a longing, she explains, that 'manifests itself in total reconstructions of monuments of the past', 41.
7. Boym 351.
8. Boym 29.
9. Benjamin, 'Theses on the Philosophy of History', 255–6.
10. Nevo, *Shakespeare's Other Languages*, 97.
11. Bristol, 'In Search of the Bear', 146.
12. Gillies, 'Place and Space in Three Late Plays', 182.
13. Wood, '"He Something Seems Unsettled"', 190–1.
14. Wood 187.
15. Mowat, *Dramaturgy of Shakespeare's Romances*, 14.
16. The parallel is made even stronger once Thaisa enters the Temple of Diana, becoming Emilia to Pericles' Egeon (III, iv).
17. Bristol, 'In Search of the Bear', 159; 161.
18. Bristol, 'In Search of the Bear', 163.
19. Edwards, '"Seeing is Believing"', 89.
20. Cohen, 'Shakespearean Romance', 116.
21. Kerwin, *Beyond the Body*, 273.
22. Potter, 'Introduction', 1.
23. Bristol, '*The Two Noble Kinsmen*', 88–9.
24. Cooper, *English Romance in Time*, 64.
25. Neely, *Distracted Subjects*, 69.
26. For an example, see Ferrand, *Treatise on Lovesickness*, 269–73.
27. Kerwin 170–1.
28. Kerwin 152.

29. Kerwin 133.
30. Kerwin 166.
31. The idea of sexual intercourse as a remedy for female lovesick-
    ness is a staple of early modern medical writings on melan-
    choly. See Ferrand, 335–41. See also Neely's third and fourth
    chapters, 68–135.
32. Neely 86–7.

CHAPTER 6

THE PHILOSOPHICAL AFTERLIVES OF SHAKESPEAREAN MELANCHOLY

We of the craft are all crazy. Some are affected by gaiety, others by melancholy, but all are more of less touched.

(Lord Byron)

Charlie Chaplin famously said that life was a tragedy when seen in close-up but a comedy when in long shot. Melancholy operates similarly in Shakespearean comedy. Taken individually, the depictions in each play appear problematic, even antithetical to comedy. At a distance, they form a much more congruous view of the dual revisions of melancholy and the comic genre that take place throughout Shakespeare's work. The works ultimately present melancholy and mirth as oscillating dramatic forces that form complementary dimensions of the human experience as depicted on the early modern Shakespearean stage. My interpretation does not take away from tragic melancholy and the voluminous critical body of work it has generated; rather, it enhances it by showing the comic value of early modern melancholy. This understanding also offers the opportunity to reconsider and amend some of the major theoretical engagements with melancholia in terms of the comic philosophy I have outlined here.

In this chapter, I consider the afterlives of Shakespearean comic melancholy in terms of psychoanalysis, performance theory and affect theory so as to chart out previously
unacknowledged interplay between the modern concept of
melancholia and the humour's comic heritage as developed
throughout this book. Taking as a point of departure Juliana
Schiesari's claim that 'Renaissance and postmodern melan-
cholias [are not] two different periods of dramatized loss but
rather . . . the historical boundaries of a great age of melancholia . . . whose edges are coterminous with the historic rise
and demise of the subject', I want to examine potential critical contributions that a comic understanding of melancholy
could bring to the works of Sigmund Freud, Judith Butler
and Sianne Ngai.[1] Tragic representations of melancholy, such
as in *Hamlet*, offer an ideal literary analogy for the processes
of subject formation and internalisation of loss at the crux of
psychoanalytic and performative investigations of melancholia. Comic melancholy necessitates a slight redirection in critical focus since it avoids the catharsis of death and the heroic
sense of despair that generally characterise tragic melancholics. Characters like Antonio, Don John or Jaques could be
thought of as defined by melancholy (or at least desiring to
be defined as such), but their plays do not pay them the kind
of dramatic reverence that proves crucial to Freud's use of
Hamlet in his idea of melancholic incorporation. Nor are
they simply ridiculed for their idiosyncratic affect. Comedy
allows for a clearer understanding of the inherent ambivalence of melancholy, as both an illness and as an integral
part of the human psyche, one that manifests itself frequently
even in normal states. The sense of irreparable loss that eventually appears in plays such as *Twelfth Night* or *The Winter's
Tale* is born out of comic concerns.

Despite Judith Butler's own reservations about thinking of performance theory in too close a relation to theatricality, comic melancholy does enter into fruitful dialogue

with such a discourse, particularly in terms of gender identity and social regulation. Female characters' interaction
with melancholy on the comic stage (whether we consider Viola, Portia or even Perdita and Hermione) offers
an intriguing parallel to performance theory's conceptualisation of female gender and personhood. Likewise, by
emphasising its cyclical and performative nature, comic
melancholy makes a case for the affect's productive participation in the matrix of human emotions that dovetails
with Sianne Ngai's work on negative emotions. Rather
than being a dramatic nuisance or a mere foil to merriment, Shakespearean melancholy highlights the potential
for its critical and theoretical productivity. Ultimately, the
Shakespearean melancomic connects with audiences in
ways inaccessible to tragic melancholy since it offers them
depictions of the affect that come closer to their own emotive realities.

The aim of this chapter is more to initiate critical discussions
than it is to resolve any theoretical issues. The analysis here is
in no way exhaustive, and the parallels it seeks to establish can
never exist in direct correlation with clinical or sociological
treatments of melancholia. I do not intend to completely validate or refute the arguments of the texts I examine here. The
chapter asks more questions than it answers. It experimentally
suggests potential bridges between Shakespeare's early modern
revisions to comedy and melancholy and more modern artistic
and philosophical explorations of the concept, all of which
necessitate further thinking and writing. Yet, the engagement
with Freud, Butler and Ngai also provides a closing salvo for
my consideration of the Shakespearean melancomic since the
conflation of early modern theatre and theoretical discourses
grants us a dual perception of melancholy that approximates
to Chaplin's adage. Melancholy is both a tragic close-up of
the human mind and a more joyful long shot of the human
experience.

Melancholia and the Comic Counter-Investment

Early on in 'Of Mourning and Melancholia' Freud remarks that

> there can be no doubt that anyone who has reached such an assessment of himself, and expresses it to others – an assessment like that which Prince Hamlet has ready for himself and everyone else – is sick, whether he is telling the truth or treating himself more or less unjustly.[2]

Freud was by all accounts an avid reader of Shakespeare, and it makes sense that his major work on melancholia would make use of the seminal melancholic character in trying to explain the concept properly.[3] The clinical understanding of melancholia that Freud develops, as a complex, pendular representation of the mourning process, finds strong echoes in *Hamlet*'s exploration of melancholy, notably in the idea that the condition 'behaves like an open wound, drawing investment to itself from all sides . . . and draining the ego to the point of complete impoverishment'.[4] One finds a similar (albeit understated) echo of Hamletian melancholy in Julia Kristeva's remark that 'depressive persons are affectionate, wounded to be sure, but prisoners or their affect. The affect is their thing'.[5] In psychoanalytic terms, melancholia transposes the ego conflict onto 'the battle over the object', during which it 'must behave like a painful wound requiring an extraordinarily high counter-investment'.[6] Hamlet's all-encompassing melancholy suggests a similar totalising force, one which brings about the annihilation of the Danish monarchy by the end of the play as its own dramatic counter-investment. The cathartic scene of carnage, culminating with Hamlet's body being carried heroically off the stage, signifies the strong sense of purifying release that tragic melancholy incurs.

In this sense, Shakespeare's play provides Freud with the optimal literary example of tragic heroism he perceives in melancholia. As Juliana Schiesari remarks, the 'heightened consciousness' that Freud ascribes to the melancholy man

> is dialectically aggravated through the ego's warring over the object of loss, such that the loss itself becomes the dominant feature and not the lost object . . . Freud gives us a 'clinical' picture of the pathology of melancholia; but on the other hand, by referring to Hamlet and the melancholic's visionary talents . . . he points to a cultural apotheosis of its victims, whose sense of loss and 'melancholy' is thus the sign of their special nature.[7]

Hamlet's melancholy does stand as a cultural apotheosis of early modern melancholy, and its cultural and literary notoriety allows Freud to discuss the phenomenon of melancholia in more grandiose terms than a strictly clinical view would command. The tropes of comic melancholy complicate such an understanding by moving away from the internalisation of an unconscious loss, but they also connect with Freud's psychoanalytic focus in terms of representing this loss and rendering it communicable to an audience.

Freud's clinical focus leads him to identify the dangers of melancholia. It is a source of conflict, an inner battle behaving like an open wound in the mind, one in which the afflicted individual indulges in 'insistent talkativeness, taking satisfaction from self-exposure'.[8] The inherent theatricality of Freud's remark channels Hamlet as much as it does Antonio or Jaques. In sanctioning the performance of melancholy but avoiding the disastrous outcome that its tragic counterpart demands, comedy externalises the psychic struggle that Freud illustrates. The melancholics are not validated in death but, rather, incorporated into the comic worlds the plays weave. The comedies provide the 'high

counter-investment' that psychoanalysis calls for by legitimising the emotion as integral to the comic landscape even
if it is never fully integrated into it.

In drawing attention to the fundamental ambivalence of
melancholia, Freud explains that

> ambivalence is either constitutional, that is, it is attached
> to every love relationship of this particular ego, or else it
> emerges straight out of experiences that imply the threat of
> the loss of the object . . . In melancholia, a series of individ-
> ual battles for objects begin in which love and hate struggle
> with one another.[9]

The language recalls the binary pairing of melancholy with
seemingly oppositional elements such as mirth, health or comedy itself. What Shakespearean comedy suggests is that such
dialogical associations are not so much struggles as a more
natural oscillation between complementary forces. Freud's
own assertion that, as with mourning, melancholia 'passes
after a certain amount of time without leaving any broad or
demonstrable changes' gestures toward the comic lineage of
melancholy more than in the direction of *Hamlet*.[10] For him,
melancholia remains clinical above all else, but comic theatre
enhances its communicability, while downplaying its more
threatening effects. In this sense, the transformation of melancholy into a dramatic and affective rendition of nostalgia
that Shakespearean comedy engenders epitomises the Freudian
notion of an unconscious loss. More so than *Hamlet*, the bittersweet emotional charge behind Feste's 'wind and rain' ballad,
or the powerfully understated sense of lost time that infuses
Hermione's reunion with Leontes and Perdita, are also drawn
out of the audience's unconsciousness, but nevertheless made
tangible in the mingled affective responses the plays evoke. The
legitimising of comic melancholy (into the melancomic) suggests that the focus is not so much on what is lost (consciously

or not) nor on the transformation of this loss (in the process of ego formation) but on its emotive recognition by audiences.

In situating melancholia at the level of the imaginary, the psychoanalytic tradition likewise posits parallels between mental illness and creativity, which seem predicated on the melancomic. In *Black Sun*, Kristeva writes that 'there is no imagination that is not, overtly or secretly, melancholy'.[11] While she perceives the melancholic as generally unproductive and unable to create, her discussion of literary creation as the ideal conduit by which to grasp the emotive spectrum of what she deems our 'affective experience' nevertheless gestures towards a link between melancholia and artistic creativity.[12] According to her, since our moods (particularly sadness) become 'the ultimate reactions to our trauma [and] our basic homeostatic recourses', literature can be understood as

> that adventure of the body and signs that bears witness to the affect – to sadness as imprint of separation and beginning of the symbol's sway . . . [T]hat testimony is produced by literary creation in a material that is totally different from what constitutes mood. It transposes affect into rhythm, signs, forms. The 'semiotic' and the 'symbolic' become the communicable imprints of an affective reality.[13]

The affective reality that Kristeva mentions here recalls comic depictions of melancholy, since the plays make a similar case for the inclusion of melancholy into their affective realities. The gradual infusing of melancholy into notions of setting, mood and landscape – be it Arden Forest, Illyria or even Belmont – suggests that melancholy, always existing in a multiplicity of symbolic contexts, holds 'semiotic' value as well when shaped as a stage representation of sadness. Its rhythms, signs and forms are found throughout Shakespearean comedy and its own gradual turn towards the elusiveness of nostalgic memories of loss.

The correlation between artistic creativity and the natural rhythms, signs and moods of the world around us finds itself at the core of Kay Redfield Jamison's *Touched with Fire*, which investigates potential scientific links between mental illness (manic-depressive issues specifically) and artistic genius. According to Jamison, fluctuations in the behaviour of people with manic depression are strikingly similar to the fluctuations of the natural world. 'Seasonal cycles are particularly important,' she writes, 'and these are discussed in the context of the scientific evidence for seasonal patterns in moods and psychosis, as well as illustrated by the seasonal patterns of artistic productivity.'[14] Jamison's study far exceeds the aims of this book, and her empirical look at the work of several writers who suffered from mental illness and wrote about it, like any biographically focused argument, is not compatible with Shakespeare's work.[15] Yet her discussion of the influence of natural rhythms on both artistic creation and human emotions is worth considering in conjunction with Shakespearean comedy and its development of the melancomic. Life, Jamison notes, 'is proportioned by time – years, months, days, minutes – into events that tend to recur at regular intervals . . . such oscillatory processes serve to regulate life on the cellular level, biochemical, physiological, and probably psychological level as well'.[16] This consolidation of nature, science and emotion is crucial to the development of comic melancholy on the Shakespearean stage as I have shown here, not just in the oscillation between iconic dyads of light and dark, life and death or mirth and melancholy but in the 'transitional and fluctuating aspects' of such processes as well.[17] The end result (if there is such a thing) of the dual revisions of comedy and melancholy found in Shakespeare is a portrait of the human experience not unlike the world as it is perceived by sufferers from manic depression, according to Jamison: seen simultaneously through 'a glass darkly [and as] a shattered pattern of views seen through a prism or kaleidoscope: often brilliant but generally fractured ... [T] he weaving together of these contrasting experiences', she concludes, 'from a core and rhythmic brokenness is one that is crucial to both the artistic and manic-depressive experience'.[18] This brokenness comes close to our general affective reality as presented on the early modern stage; it echoes both the fundamentally idiosyncratic presence of melancholy in plays such as *The Merchant of Venice* as well as the inherent technical failure of later works such as *Pericles*.

Gender, Subjection and Performing the Melancomic

Judith Butler makes extensive use of Freudian melancholia throughout her work on gender performance and subjugation. For Butler, gender, understood as the performing of 'a series of acts which are renewed, revised, and consolidated through time', is a fundamentally melancholic process of internalising and ambivalently incorporating an unconscious loss into the psyche.[19] 'What is exteriorised and performed', she writes of gender identity, 'can only be understood through reference to what is barred from the signifier and from the domain of corporeal legibility.'[20] Butler is particularly interested in the creation of female gender, which, in Lacanian terms, becomes a melancholic masquerade predicated on loss. In Lacan, the mask symbolises

> the taking on of attributes of the object/Other that is lost ... The mask thus conceals this loss, but preserves (and negates) this loss through its concealment. The mask has a double function which is the double function of melancholy. The mask is taken on through the process of incorporation which is a way of inscribing and then wearing a melancholic identification in and on the body; in effect, it is the signification of the body in the mood of the Other who has been refused. Dominated through

appropriation, every refusal fails, and the refuser becomes part of the very identity of the refused, indeed, becomes the psychic refuse of the refused.[21]

In the rejection (or refusal) of the lost Other, women claim their gendered identity through the wearing of a melancholic identification. For Lacan, this is due to their lack (loss) of the masculine symbol of the Phallus; their identity is created in reaction to a male understanding of gender. Butler emphasises the social dimension of such a process and, in doing so, adamantly claims that gender performance is not coterminous to theatricality since

> in the theatre, one can say, 'this is just an act,' and de-realise the act, make acting into something quite distinct from what is real [and] maintain one's sense of reality in the face of temporary challenge to our existing ontological assumptions about gender arrangements [which] allows strict lines to be drawn between the performance and life.[22]

Rather, Butler contends, gender is constituted by daily acts of social repetition forming 'at once a reenactment and reexperiencing of a set of meanings already socially established'.[23] Hence, gender is not theatre because it is constantly being performed (as opposed to repeatedly performed) as part of the regulatory matrix of social subjection. Butler's view of gender identity revolves around a turn of the self not unlike Ficino's idea of the scholar being 'fixed at the centre' in melancholic contemplation.[24] She writes that power's subordinating effect in the subject 'is relentlessly marked by a figure of turning, a turning back upon oneself or even a turning *on* oneself'.[25] Bringing in Foucault's idea of subjection, Butler argues that 'the peculiar turning of a subject against itself that takes place in acts of self-reproach, conscience, and melancholia . . . works in tandem with processes of social regulation'.[26] Gender exists internally, at the psychic level, but is performed outwardly into the matrix of power and sub-jection. Despite Butler's disassociation with theatre, female comic characters in Shakespeare can be thought to have a similar relationship with melancholy; in being denied access to the masculine ideal of melancholy, female characters claim their stage identities in their reactionary performance of the notion.

In *Gendering Melancholia*, Schiesari suggests that early modern melancholy can be understood 'as a particular dis-course that encodes subjectivity in terms of this history of great men and great deeds . . . it is not so much that a mel-ancholic syndrome cannot establish itself vis-à-vis the young girl,' she concludes, 'but that the syndrome is in itself part and parcel of a melancholic discourse that has in effect privileged male subjectivity in terms of loss itself'.[27] According to her, if women do not have access to the proper transformative pro-cesses of melancholia, there is a need to delineate and 'legiti-mate other modes of feminine self-representation'.[28] Female melancholy thus situates itself 'at the level of the symbolic, where and only where a collective rearticultion of women's loss can take place'.[29] Schiesari astutely notes the inherent masculinity of melancholy discourses in the Renaissance (in a tradition spanning from Ficino to Freud). While Shakespear-ean comedy by and large abides by such a dual representa-tive standard (contrasting masculine, genial melancholy with female hysteria or greensickness), the plays examined here validate Schiesari's idea that the perpetual mourning associ-ated with female melancholia 'points to a resistance to patri-archy that would serve as the radical basis for a collective refiguring of women's identities but also suggests the possi-bility of rethinking a symbolic of loss that would displace a patriarchal symbolic'.[30]

Thinking back to Butler's use of melancholic loss in the process of gender formation, female characters' reaction to melancholy becomes a crucial identity marker onstage.

Shakespearean comedy abounds with scenes contrasting masculine and feminine expressions of sadness, in which female characters both underscore their inaccessibility to melancholy and actively seek to avoid being ascribed the feminised label of hysteria or green sickness. Portia, Viola and Rosalind all begin their respective plays afflicted by sorrows but, as opposed to their masculine counterparts, they rapidly spring into action to improve their lots. Their sense of agency can be understood as a stand against what Schiesari terms the 'patriarchal symbolic' of early modern melancholy. Shakespearean heroines seem aware that any claim to melancholy would incur a treatment not unlike The Jailer's Daughter in *The Two Noble Kinsmen*. The ways in which female characters discuss, react to and intervene against male melancholy become a way for them to assert their gendered identities.

Taken together, Butler and Schiesari's understandings of gender, performance and melancholia gesture strongly towards Shakespearean comic melancholy. When it comes to gender performance, Butler maintains that 'one is simply not a body, but, in some very key sense, one does one's body and, indeed, one does one's body differently from one's contemporaries and from one's embodied predecessors and successors as well'.[31] A similar claim could be made that one does one's emotions on the early modern stage when considering notions of embodiment and performance of melancholy charted throughout this book. As was the case with the 'affective reality' that early modern theatre communicates to its audiences, the performance of melancholy (and gender) is directed primarily at the audience. It echoes Katherine Maus's notion of the 'radically synecdochic' nature of the early modern stage, which 'seems deliberately to foster theatregoers' capacity to use partial and limited presentation as a basis for conjecture about what is undisplayed or undisplayable'.[32] Butler's contention that, while the idea of being female is a falsehood, 'to be a woman is to become a woman, to compel the body to conform to an historical idea of "woman," to induce the body to become a cultural sign',[33] dovetails with the inherent suggestion in Schiesari's argument that early modern women come to define themselves through a resistance to masculine ideals of melancholy and character.[34] The dynamics of comic melancholy in Shakespeare, at the nexus of theatre, philosophy and identity, represent the 'dialect of vision and concealment' that informs Renaissance drama.[35]

In discussing the 'social temporality' of gender acts, Butler draws attention to the importance of

> the *appearance of substance* . . . a constructed identity, a performative accomplishment which the mundane social audience, including the actors themselves, come to believe and to perform in the mode of belief. If the ground of gender identity is the stylized repetition of acts through time, and not a seemingly seamless identity, then the possibilities of gender transformation are to be found in the arbitrary relation between such acts, in the possibility of a different sort of repeating, in the breaking or subservient repetition of that style.[36]

Identity, when performed in a Butlerian sense, is not just the identity of an actor, but 'a compelling illusion [and] an object of belief', transpiring in 'real' time (hence, Butler's differentiating the process from a theatrical model that understands 'the gendered self to be prior to its acts').[37] Butler's notion of gender performance is anything but theatrical. Yet, given the parallels already established here, we find such illusions throughout Shakespearean depictions of comic melancholy. The osmotic quality of Arden Forest, the inherent technical failure at the end of *Pericles* and even the tenuous oaths of joyful reunions professed in *The Comedy of Errors* and *Love's Labour's Lost* are all predicated on similarly compelling affective illusions the audience is asked to believe in.

Comedy integrates melancholy as part of its overall dramatic mood and landscape. As seen in Chapter 4, melancholy achieves spatial relevance (what Benjamin envisions as melancholic topography) by establishing 'the psychic conditions for regarding "the world" itself as contingently organised through certain kinds of foreclosures'.[38] In other words, melancholy becomes a self-perpetuating prism through which to perceive the world we inhabit, a view not unlike Jamison's idea of 'rhythmic brokenness'. In its comic form, it provides the audience with a way in which to view their world that, while it is modelled on their own affective and performative realities, is always distant and never fully integrated into them. Butler's positioning of it as a middle ground between social and psychic realms, offering 'potential insight into how the boundaries of the social are instituted and maintained, not only at the expense of psychic life, but through binding psychic life into forms of melancholic ambivalence', suggests that, in its theoretical as well as Shakespearean dimensions, melancholy oscillates between the human emotions more than it partitions them.[39]

Much like Freud's, Butler's understanding of melancholia remains too firmly within the realms of critical theory, psychoanalysis and what I would term social anthropology to fully dovetail with the development of comic melancholy in Shakespeare. Her careful distancing of the performative acts she elaborates from notions of theatricality is compelling, yet their very language and ideas are theatrical, especially when considering the notion of melancholy from its comic (and melancomic) perspectives rather than its tragic one.

The Ugliness of Comic Melancholy

Sianne Ngai's *Ugly Feelings* offers another critical avenue in which to consider the afterlife of Shakespearean comic melancholy: that of affect theory and its recuperative efforts towards negative emotions. At the onset of her study, Ngai professes her interest in what she terms the 'aesthetics of negative emotions . . . affective gaps and illegibilities, dysphoric feelings, and other sites of emotional negativity', which she groups under the label of 'ugly' feelings, so as to 'explore similarly ambivalent situations of suspended agency'.[40] Her book stands at the nexus of the aesthetic and the political since, as she explains, the feelings she examines 'are marked by an ambivalence that will enable them to resist, on the one hand, their reduction to mere expressions of class *ressentiment* and, on the other, their counter-valorisation as therapeutic "solutions" to the problems they highlight and condense'.[41] Ngai is quick to exclude melancholy from the negatively perceived affects whose critical productivity she aims to reaffirm. As she explains it, the feelings examined throughout her book (such as irritation, anxiety and paranoia) are usually thought of as 'minor and unprestigious', unlike melancholy and other elevated emotions which she categorises as 'morally beatific states'.[42] *Ugly Feelings* focuses instead on uneasy emotions, affects that 'are explicitly amoral and noncathartic, offering no satisfaction of virtue, however oblique, nor any therapeutic or purifying release'.[43] Moreover, though she relies extensively on literary and cultural examples to support her claims, she explicitly avoids 'the more recognizable "emotional" genres [found in] canonically major forms and genres like the Homeric epic and Shakespearean tragedy'.[44] The critical productivity of the affects she aims to recuperate, she explains, is far more potent outside of the literary canon because, as she puts it, 'something about the cultural canon itself seems to prefer higher passions and emotions – as if minor or ugly feelings were not only incapable of producing "major" works, but somehow disabled the works they do drive from acquiring canonical distinction'.[45]

It makes sense, given her investment of political agency into negative affects, for Ngai to distance her study from melancholy in its canonical form. The Freudian tradition of analysis, predicated on the iconicity of Hamlet's ailment, as a cathartic (if not morally beatific) state, is counterproductive to the aims of her book. Comic melancholy, on the other hand, can be understood in similar terms to those which Ngai poses in her introductory chapter. In the golden age of genial melancholy that was the Renaissance, its comic treatment could be dismissed as unprestigious, if not minor. As seen time and again in this book, Shakespearean comic melancholy is fundamentally non-cathartic and often offers no sense of release whatsoever. The stubbornness of Shakespearean melancholics, the overwhelming force of the affect in certain characters, as well as their refusal to temper their behaviour all gesture towards Ngai's notion that the feeling they are meant to convey proves 'diagnostic rather than strategic [and] diagnostically concerned with states of inaction in particular'.[46] The comic inaction of characters such as Antonio or Jaques and reaction and actions of the characters around them suggest as much. Comic melancholy often denies any sense of release or satisfaction, but instead clings on to the plays it inhabits. If anything, from *The Merchant of Venice* to *The Winter's Tale*, melancholy is one of the dramatic elements that remain with the audience at the end of the play. It would be an exaggeration to claim that comic melancholy belongs in Ngai's project of politically-charged aesthetic of negative emotions. Yet the framework she establishes underscores the critical productivity of a comic sense of melancholy as developed in Shakespeare, one whose overlooked potential in terms of affect theory brings it closer to being an ugly feeling.

Lastly, Ngai's redefinition of tone in the context of negative emotions is worth considering, especially in conjunction with later Shakespearean comic works and their reliance on the melancomic. For Ngai, tone implies

> a literary or cultural artefact's *feeling tone*: its global or organizing affect, its general disposition or orientation towards its audience and the world . . . The formal aspect of a literary work that makes it possible for critics to describe a text as, say, 'euphoric' or 'melancholic,' and, what is much more important, the category that makes these affective values meaningful with regard to how one understands the text as a totality within an equally holistic matrix of social relations.[47]

The idea of a regulatory matrix brings us back to Butler and to her own parallels with comic melancholy. The affect is crucial to the plays' orientation towards the world of their audiences. Its meaning is acquired through its non-cathartic nature and its eventual (ambivalent) incorporation into the comedies it haunts. Late comedies achieve what Ngai, in the context of Adorno's notion of 'aura', describes as 'the idea of a distance attained not from feeling but by feeling'.[48] In plays such as *Pericles* and *The Winter's Tale*, melancholy is both defused and empowered by the lengthy time intervals that split both plays asunder; their final tableaux are those of emotionally powerful distance. Furthermore, the imperceptibility of tone, as explained by Ngai, mirrors that of the melancomic in later plays. 'Tone is a feeling which is perceived rather than felt,' she writes, 'and whose very nonfeltness is perceived. There is a sense, then, in which its status is fundamentally negative, regardless of what the particular quality of the affect is.'[49] The melancholic tone of the Shakespearean comedies examined attests to the emotion's 'ugliness', whose idiosyncratic nature is ripe with affective and critical possibilities. Following Sylvan Tomkins's notion of analogue amplification, comic melancholy, through Ngai, can be understood as a 'mechanism that magnifies awareness

and intensifies the effects of operations associated with other
biological subsystems . . . capable of very great combina-
tional flexibility with other mechanisms that it can conjointly
imprint and be imprinted'.[50]

My focus throughout this book has remained largely on
the plays themselves and on the prismatic effect they exert on
melancholy and comedy alike. This chapter raises more questions than it answers, and there remains work to be done in
exploring the philosophical afterlives of Shakespearean melancholy. Its connections to psychoanalytic, performative and
affective theories, however, are apparent. The very ethos of
melancholy still resonates sharply in our post-modern world,
and a consideration of its comic dimensions can help its ongoing integration into our affective, social and artistic realities.
We may write, think or talk of melancholy, as Burton would
suggest, to avoid being melancholy, but we can only dodge
it for so long. A comic perspective helps us to appreciate its
communicative flexibility. Melancholy is as much a part of
comedy as it is of the human condition. The melancomic
in Shakespeare gestures towards Simon Critchley's idea of
'mirthless laughter', which he identifies as

> the essence of humour. This is the *risus pursus*, the highest
> laugh, the laugh that laughs at the laugh, but laughs at that
> which is unhappy . . . this smile does not bring unhappiness,
> but rather elevation and liberation, the lucidity of consola-
> tion. This is why, melancholy animals that we are, human
> beings are also the most cheerful. We smile and find our-
> selves ridiculous. Our wretchedness is our greatness.[51]

Much like mirthless laughter, Shakespearean melancholy
invites us to laugh without mirth, to find ourselves ridiculous
by finding insistently melancholic characters ridiculous. We
find in ourselves echoes of Viola, Rosalind and Perdita, of
Antonio and Antipholus, even of Feste and Jaques. In experiencing their melancholy and reflecting upon it (perhaps

longingly after exiting the performance), we bring about our 'lucidity of consolation'.

I began this book by discussing the induction to *The Taming of the Shrew* and its idea that a comedy might have health benefits for those whose blood is congealed by too much sadness. As I conclude, it is important to keep in mind Sly's answer to the purported medical advice: 'Marry, I will let them play it' (Induction, II, 133). My analysis of Shakespeare's comedies brought attention to the emotionally charged underpinnings that complicate each play's comic development of melancholy. Yet such works remain, in the end, comedies. They may elicit strong contradictory emotions but they eventually release us from their spell. All they ask is that we play along for a little while and remember from time to time. Comic melancholy is funny, sad, nostalgic and life-affirming all at once. It is a sad clown, a still photograph and a stormy landscape. Like an old fool, impervious to wind and rain, its familiar song reminds us that melancholy, like foolery, does indeed walk the orb like the sun.

Notes

1. Schiesari, *Gendering Melancholia*, 2.
2. Freud, 'Of Mourning and Melancholia', 206. In a footnote on p. 218, Freud cites *Hamlet*: 'Use every / man after his desert, and who shall 'scape whipping?' (II, ii, 529–30).
3. Schiesari, 26–7, for an overview of the psychoanalytic tradition of 'rereading the Renaissance'.
4. Freud 212.
5. Kristeva, *Black Sun*, 14.
6. Freud 218.
7. Schiesari 11.
8. Freud 207.
9. Freud 216.

10. Freud 212.
11. Kristeva 6.
12. Kristeva 42.
13. Kristeva 22.
14. Jamison, *Touched with Fire*, 6.
15. See Jamison's third chapter, 'Could it be Madness – This? Controversy and Evidence' (49–100), for a review of the scientific arguments for and against the idea of a 'relationship between mood disorder and achievement, especially artistic achievement', 88.
16. Jamison 130.
17. Jamison 34.
18. Jamison 125.
19. Butler, 'Performative Acts and Gender Constitution', 523.
20. Butler, *Bodies that Matter*, 234.
21. Butler, *Gender Trouble*, 67.
22. Butler, 'Performative Acts and Gender Constitution', 527.
23. Butler, 'Performative Acts and Gender Constitution', 526.
24. Ficino, *Book of Life*, 6.
25. Butler, *Psychic life of Power*, 3.
26. Butler, *Psychic life of Power*, 18–19.
27. Schiesari 67–8.
28. Schiesari 69.
29. Schiesari 93.
30. Schiesari 17.
31. Butler, 'Performative Acts and Gender Constitution', 521.
32. Maus, *Inwardness and Theater*, 32.
33. Butler, 'Performative Acts and Gender Constitution', 522.
34. Schiesari 26–32.
35. Maus 29.
36. Butler, 'Performative Acts and Gender Constitution', 520.
37. Ibid.
38. Butler, *Psychic Life of Power*, 143.
39. Butler, *Psychic Life of Power*, 167–8.
40. Ngai, *Ugly Feelings*, 1.
41. Ngai 3.
42. Ngai 6.

43. Ibid.
44. Ngai 10.
45. Ngai 11.
46. Ngai 22.
47. Ngai 28, my emphasis.
48. Ngai 87.
49. Ngai 76.
50. Tomkins, *Exploring Affect*, 53.
51. Critchley, *On Humour*, 111.

WORKS CITED

Adelman, Janet, 'Male Bonding in Shakespeare's Comedies', in Peter Erickson and Coppélia Kahn (eds), *Shakespeare's Rough Magic: Renaissance Essays in Honour of C. L. Barber* (Newark: University of Delaware Press, 1985), pp. 73–103.

Alulius, Joseph, 'Fathers and Children: Matter, Mirth, and Melancholy in *As You Like It*', in Joseph Alulius and Vickie Sullivan (eds), *Shakespeare's Political Pageant: Essays in Literature and Politics* (Boston: Rowman & Littlefield, 1996), pp. 37–60.

Aristotle. *De Poetica* 5, in Richard McKeon (ed.) and Ingram Bywater (trans.), *The Basic Works of Aristotle* (New York: Random House, 2001), pp. 1455–87.

—, 'Problem XXX', *Problems: Books 20–38*, ed. and trans. Robert Mayhem (Cambridge, MA: Harvard: University Press, 2011), pp. 273–312.

Babb, Lawrence, *The Elizabethan Malady: A Study of Melancholia in English Literature from 1580 to 1642* (East Lansing: Michigan State University Press, 1965).

Bacon, Francis [1625], 'Of Travel', in *Bacon's Essays* (New York: Carlton House, 1950), pp. 132–5.

Barber, C. L., *Shakespeare's Festive Comedies: A Study of Dramatic Form and its Relation to Social Context* (Princeton: Princeton University Press, 1959).

Barton, Anne, *Essays, Mainly Shakespearean* (Cambridge: Cambridge University Press, 1994).

Bath, Michael, 'Weeping Stags and Melancholy Lovers: The Iconography of *As You Like It*, II, I', *Emblematica* 1: 1 1986, pp. 13–52.

Baudelaire, Charles, *Curiosités Esthétiques, L'Art Romantique et Autres Œuvres Critiques (1846)*, ed. Henri Lemaitre (Paris: Garnier Frères, 1962).

Beaumont, Francis, and John Fletcher [1615–25], *The Nice Valour, or The Passionate Mad-Man*, ed. George Walton Williams, in *The Dramatic Works in the Beaumont and Fletcher Canon. Vol. VII*, ed. Fredson Bowers (Cambridge: Cambridge University Press, 1982), pp. 425–513.

— [1624], *A Wife For a Month*, ed. Robert Kean Turner, in *The Dramatic Works in the Beaumont and Fletcher Canon Vol. VI*, ed. Fredson Bowers (Cambridge: Cambridge University Press, 1982), pp. 355–482.

Beecher, Donald, and Massimo Ciavolella (ed. and trans.), 'Introduction', in Jacques Ferrand, *A Treatise on Lovesickness* (New York: Syracuse University Press, 1990), pp. 3–166.

Benjamin, Walter, 'Theses on the Philosophy of History', in Hannah Arendt (ed.), *Illuminations: Essays and Reflections* (New York: Schocken, 1968), pp. 253–64.

—, *The Origin of German Tragic Drama*, trans. John Osborne (London: Verso Books, 1998).

Bergson, Henri, 'Laughter', in Wylie Sypher (ed. and trans.), *Comedy* (Garden City: Doubleday Anchor, 1956), pp. 61–190.

Bevington, David (ed.), *The Complete Works of Shakespeare*, 4th, updated edn (New York: Longman, 1997).

—, *The Comedy of Errors*, in *The Complete Works of Shakespeare*, 4th, updated edn (New York: Longman, 1997), pp. 2–4.

—, *The Merry Wives of Windsor*, in *The Complete Works of Shakespeare*, 4th, updated edn (New York: Longman, 1997), pp. 252–4.

Bingen, Hildegard of, 'Book of Holistic Healing', in Jennifer Radden (ed.), *The Nature of Melancholy from Aristotle to Kristeva* (Oxford: Oxford University Press, 2000), pp. 79–86.

Bloom, Harold, *Shakespeare and the Invention of the Human* (New York: Riverhead, 1998).

Bodin, Jean [1576], *Six Bookes of the Commonwealth*, trans. M. J. Tooley (Oxford: Basil Blackwell, 1955).

Boym, Svetlana, *The Future of Nostalgia* (New York: Basic Books, 2001).

Brayton, Daniel, 'Shakespeare and the Global Ocean', in Lynne D. Bruckner and Daniel Brayton (eds), *Ecocritical Shakespeare* (Burlington: Ashgate, 2011), pp. 173–90.

Bright, Timothy, *A treatise of Melancholy containing the causes thereof, and reasons of the strange effects it worketh in our minds and bodies: with the physicke cure and spirituall consolation for such as haue thereto adioyned afflicted conscience* (London: Printed by William Stansby, 1613), Early English Books Online, <http://eebo.chadwyck.com> (last accessed 9 February 2018).

Bristol, Michael, '*The Two Noble Kinsmen*', in Charles H. Frey (ed.), *Shakespeare, Fletcher, and The Two Noble Kinsmen* (Columbia: University of Missouri Press, 1989), pp. 78–92.

—, 'In Search of the Bear: Spatiotemporal Form and the Heterogeneity of Economics in *The Winter's Tale*', *Shakespeare Quarterly*, 42:2 Summer 1991, pp. 145–67.

—, 'Shakespeare's Sonnets and the Publication of Melancholy', in Paul Yachnin and Bronwen Wilson (eds), *Making Publics in Early Modern Europe: People, Things, Forms of Knowledge* (New York: Routledge, 2010), pp. 193–211.

Bulman, James, *The Merchant of Venice: Shakespeare in Performance* (Manchester: Manchester University Press, 1991).

Burton, Robert [1621], *The Anatomy of Melancholy*, ed. Holbrook Jackson (New York: New York Review, 2001).

Butler, Judith, 'Performative Acts and Gender Constitution: An Essay in Phenomenology and Feminist Theory', *Theatre Journal*, 40:4 December 1988, pp. 519–31.

—, *Bodies that Matter: On the Discursive Limits of 'Sex'* (New York: Routledge, 1993).

—, *The Psychic Life of Power: Theories in Subjection* (Stanford: Stanford University Press, 1997).

—, *Gender Trouble: Feminism and the Subversion of Identity*, 2nd edn (New York: Routledge, 1999).

Butler, Samuel [1667–9], *Characters*, ed. A. R. Walker (Cambridge: Cambridge University Press, 1908).

Cohen, Walter, 'Shakespearean Romance', in Stephen Greenblatt, Walter Cohen, Jean E. Howard, Katharine Eisaman Maus, Gordon McMullan and Suzanne Gossett (eds), *The Norton Shakespeare Romances and Poems* (New York: Norton, 2008), pp. 103–20.

Cooper, Helen, *The English Romance in Time: Transforming Motifs from Geoffrey of Monmouth to the Death of Shakespeare* (Oxford: Oxford University Press, 2004).

Cox, John, *Much Ado About Nothing* (Cambridge: Cambridge University Press, 1997).

Daniel, Drew, *The Melancholy Assemblage: Affect and Epistemology in the English Renaissance* (New York: Fordham University Press, 2013).

Davies, Stevie, *Shakespeare: Twelfth Night* (New York: Penguin, 1993).

Du Laurens, André, *Discourse on the Preservation of Sight of melancholike diseases; of rheumes and of old age*, trans. Richard Surphlet (London: Imprinted by Felix Kingston, for Ralph Iacson, dwelling in Paules Church yard at the signe of the Swan, 1599), Early English Books Online, <http://eebo.chadwyck.com> (last accessed 9 February 2018).

Dutton, Richard, *Ben Jonson: To The First Folio* (Cambridge: Cambridge University Press, 1983).

Edmondson, Paul, 'Melancholy and Desire in *Twelfth Night, or What You Will*', in Christa Jansohn (ed.), *In the Footsteps of William Shakespeare* (Piscataway, NJ: Transaction Publishers, 2005), pp. 141–58.

Edwards, Philip, '"Seeing is Believing": Action and Narration in *The Old Wives' Tale* and *The Winter's Tale*', in E. A. J. Honigman (ed.), *Shakespeare and his Contemporaries: Essays in Comparison* (Manchester: Manchester University Press, 1986), pp. 79–93.

Enterline, Lynn, *The Tears of Narcissus: Melancholia and Masculinity in Early Modern Writing* (Stanford: Stanford University Press, 1995).

Everett, Barbara, 'Or What You Will', in R. S. White (ed.), *New Casebooks: Twelfth Night* (New York: Palgrave, 1996), pp. 194–213.

Ferrand, Jacques, *A Treatise on Lovesickness*, ed. and trans. Donald Beecher and Massimo Ciavolella (New York: Syracuse University Press, 1990), pp. 203–366.

Ficino, Marsilio [1489], *Marsilio Ficino: The Book of Life*, trans. Charles Boer (Irving, TX: Springs, 1998).

Fineman, Joel, 'Fratricide and Cuckoldry: Shakespeare's Doubles', in Murray Schwartz and Coppélia Kahn (eds), *Representing Shakespeare: New Psychoanalytic Essays* (Baltimore: Johns Hopkins University Press, 1980), pp. 70–110.

Fiorentino, Giovanni [1598], 'Il Pecorone', in Leah S. Marcus (ed.), *The Merchant of Venice: Authoritative Text, Source and Context Criticism, Rewriting and Interpretations* (New York: Norton, 2006), pp. 84–99.

Floyd-Wilson, Mary, *English Ethnicity and Race in Early Modern Drama* (Cambridge: Cambridge University Press, 2003).

Ford, John [1628], *The Lover's Melancholy*, ed. R. F. Hill, The Revels Plays (Manchester: Manchester University Press, 1985).

Foucault, Michel [1961], *History of Madness*, ed. Jean Khalfa, trans. Jean Khalfa and Jonathan Murphy (London: Routledge, 2009).

Freedman, Barbara, *Staging the Gaze: Postmodernism, Psychoanalysis and Shakespearean Comedy* (Ithaca: Cornell University Press, 1991).

Freud, Sigmund, 'Of Mourning and Melancholia', *On Murder, Mourning and Melancholia*, trans. Shaun Whiteside (London: Penguin Books, 2005), pp. 205–18.

Frye, Northrop, *A Natural Perspective: The Development of Shakespearean Comedy and Romance* (New York: Columbia University Press, 1965).

Galen, 'On the Natural Faculties', in Robert Maynard Hutchins (ed.) and Arthur John Brock (trans.), *Hippocrates/Galen* (London: Encyclopaedia Britannica, 1952), pp. 167–215.

—, *On Antecedent Causes*, ed. R. J. Hankinson (Cambridge: Cambridge University Press, 1998).

—, 'On the Affected Parts, Book III (Chapter 10)', in Jennifer Radden (ed.), *The Nature of Melancholy from Aristotle to Kristeva* (Oxford: Oxford University Press, 2000), pp. 67–8.

—, 'On the Causes of Diseases', in Ian Johnston, *Galen on Diseases and Symptoms* (Cambridge: Cambridge University Press, 2006), pp. 157–79.

Gillies, John, 'Place and Space in Three Late Plays', in Richard Dutton and Jean E. Howard (eds), *A Companion to Shakespeare's Works: Volume IV: The Poems, The Problem Comedies, Late Plays* (Oxford: Blackwell, 2003), pp. 175–93.

Granville-Baker, Harley, *Preface to Shakespeare* (Princeton: Princeton University Press, 1946).

Hampton, Timothy, 'Strange Alteration: Physiology and Psychology from Galen to Rabelais', in Gail Kern Paster, Katherine Rowe and Mary Floyd-Wilson (eds), *Reading the Early Modern Passions: Essays in the Cultural History of Emotions* (Philadelphia: University of Pennsylvania Press, 2004), pp. 272–94.

Harrison, William [1577], *The Description of England*, ed. Georges Edelen (Ithaca: Cornell University Press, 1968).

Heffernan, Carol Falvo, *The Melancholy Muse: Chaucer, Shakespeare and Early Medicine* (Pittsburgh: Duquesne University Press, 1995).

Hippocrates, 'Nature of Man', *Hippocrates*, Vol. 4, trans. W. H. S. Jones (Cambridge: Harvard University Press, 1984), pp. 1–42.

Hoeniger, David, 'Musical Cures of Melancholy and Mania in Shakespeare', in J. C. Gray (ed.), *A Mirror up to Shakespeare: Essays in Honour of G. R. Hibbard* (Toronto: University of Toronto Press, 1984), pp. 55–67.

—, *Medicine and Shakespeare in the English Renaissance* (Newark: University of Delaware Press, 1992).

Holderness, Graham, 'Comedy and *The Merchant of Venice*', in Martin Cole (ed.), *New Casebooks: The Merchant of Venice* (New York: St Martin's, 1998), pp. 23–35.

Hramova, Tatyana, 'The Mystery of Two Jacques in Beckett and Shakespeare', *Notes and Queries*, 58:1 (2011), 122–5.

Jamison, Kay Redfield, *Touched with Fire: Manic-Depressive Illness and the Artistic Temperament* (New York: Simon & Schuster, 1993).

Johnson, Samuel [1765], *Preface to Shakespeare's Plays* (Whitefish, MT: Kessinger, 2010).

Jonson, Ben [1598], *Every Man in His Humour*, ed. Robert S. Miola (Manchester: Manchester University Press, 2000).

— [1599], 'Everyman Out of his Humour', *Ben Jonson's Plays in Two Volumes: Volume One*, (London: Dent, 1967).

Kerwin, William, *Beyond the Body: The Boundaries of Medicine and English Renaissance Drama* (Amherst: University of Massachusetts Press, 2005).

Kitzes, Adam H., *The Politic of Melancholy from Spenser to Milton* (New York: Routledge, 2006).

Klibansky, Raymond, Erwin Panofksy and Fritz Saxl, *Saturn and Melancholy: Studies in the History of Natural Philosophy, Religion and Art* (Cambridge: Thomas Nelson and Sons, 1964).

Knowles, Richard (ed.), *A New Variorum Edition of Shakespeare's As You Like It* (New York: MLA, 1977).

Ko, Yu Jin, 'The Comic Close of *Twelfth Night* and Viola's *Noli me Tangere*', *Shakespeare Quarterly*, 48: 4 Winter, 1997, pp. 391–405.

Kristeva, Julia, *Black Sun: Depression and Melancholia*, trans. Leon S. Roudiez (New York: Columbia University Press, 1989).

Levin, Harry, *Playboys and Killjoys: An Essay on the Theory & Practice of Comedy* (Oxford: Oxford University Press, 1987).

Lewis, Cynthia, *Particular Saints: Shakespeare's Four Antonios, their Contexts and their Plays* (Newark: University of Delaware Press, 1997).

Lopez, Jeremy, *Theatrical Convention and Audience Response in Early Modern Drama* (Cambridge: Cambridge University Press, 2003).

Lyly, John [1591], *Endymion*, ed. David Bevington (New York: Manchester University Press, 1996).

— [1591], *Midas*, in *Gallathea/Midas*, ed. George K. Hunter (Manchester: Manchester University Press, 2000).

Lyons, Bridget Gellert, *Voices of Melancholy: Studies in Literary Treatments of Melancholy in Renaissance England* (London: Routledge, 1971).

McCarthy, Kathleen, *Slaves, Masters and the Art of Authority in Plautine Comedy* (Princeton: Princeton University Press, 2000).

Mack, Maynard, 'Engagement and Detachment in Shakespeare's Plays', in Jay Halio (ed.), *Twentieth-Century Interpretations of As You Like It: a Collection of Critical Essays* (Englewood, NJ: Prentice Hall, 1968), pp. 112–15.

McMullan, Gordon, *Shakespeare and the Idea of Late Writing: Authorship in the Proximity of Death* (Cambridge: Cambridge University Press, 2007).

Magnusson, Lynne, '"To gaze so much at the fine stranger": Armado and the Politics of English in *Love's Labor's Lost*', in Paul Yachnin and Patricia Badir (eds), *Shakespeare and the Cultures of Performance* (Hampshire: Ashgate, 2008), pp. 53–68.

Malone, Edmond, 'An Attempt to Ascertain the Order in which the Plays Attributed to Shakspeare Were Written', in Samuel Johnson and George Stevens (eds), *The Plays of Shakspeare*, Vol. 1, 2nd edn, 6 vols (London, 1778).

Marshall, Cynthia, 'The Double Jaques and the Construction of Negation in *As You Like It*', *Shakespeare Quarterly*, 49: 4 Winter 1998, pp. 375–92.

Massinger, Philip [c. 1619], 'A Very Woman', in *The Plays and Poems of Philip Massinger*, ed. Philip Edwards and Colin Gibson, Vol. 4 (Oxford: Clarendon, 1976), pp. 201–97.

Maus, Katherine E., *Inwardness and Theater in the English Renaissance* (Chicago: University of Chicago Press, 1995).

Mazzio, Carla, 'The Melancholy of Print: *Love's Labour's Lost*', in Carla Mazzio and Douglas Trevor (eds), *Historicism, Psychoanalysis and Early Modern Culture* (New York: Routledge, 2000), pp. 186–227.

Melchiori, Giorgio, *Shakespeare's Garter Plays: Edward III to Merry Wives of Windsor* (Newark: University of Delaware Press, 1994).

Mentz, Steve, *At the Bottom of Shakespeare's Ocean* (London: Continuum, 2009).

Miola, Robert, 'The Plays and the Critics', in Robert Miola (ed.), *The Comedy of Errors: Critical Essays*, Shakespeare and Criticism 18 (New York: Garland, 1997), pp. 3–51.

Montaigne, Michel de, 'How we cry and laugh for the same thing' [1572–4], *Michel de Montaigne: The Complete Works*, trans. Donald M. Frame (New York: Alfred A. Knopf, 2003), pp. 208–11.

—, 'Of Sadness' [1572–4], *Michel de Montaigne: The Complete Works*, trans. Donald M. Frame (New York: Alfred A. Knopf, 2003), pp. 6–9.

Morton, Timothy, *Ecology without Nature: Rethinking Environmental Aesthetics* (Cambridge, MA: Harvard University Press, 2007).

Mowat, Barbara A., *The Dramaturgy of Shakespeare's Romances* (Athens, GA: University of Georgia Press, 1976).

Muir, Kenneth, *Shakespeare's Comic Sequence* (Liverpool: Liverpool University Press, 1979).

Neely, Carol Thomas, *Distracted Subjects: Madness and Gender in Shakespeare and Early Modern Culture* (Ithaca: Cornell University Press, 2004).

Nevo, Ruth, *Shakespeare's Other Languages* (New York: Methuen, 1987).

Newman, Karen, *Shakespeare's Rhetoric of Comic Character: Dramatic Convention in Classical and Renaissance Comedy* (New York: Methuen, 1985).

Ngai, Sianne, *Ugly Feelings* (Cambridge, MA: Harvard University Press, 2005).

Paster, Gail Kern, *The Body Embarrassed: Drama and the Disciplines of Shame in Early Modern England* (Ithaca: Cornell University Press, 1993).

—, *Humouring the Body: Emotions and the Shakespearean Stage* (Chicago: University of Chicago Press, 2004).

Patterson, Steve, 'The Bankruptcy of Homoerotic Amity in Shakespeare's *Merchant of Venice*', *Shakespeare Quarterly*, 50: 1 Spring, 1999, pp. 9–32.

Paulson, Ronald, *Don Quixote in England: The Aesthetics of Laughter* (Baltimore: Johns Hopkins University Press, 1998).

Peele, George [1595], *The Old Wives Tale*, ed. Patricia Binnie (Manchester: Manchester University Press, 1980).

Pendergast, John S., *Love's Labor's Lost: A Guide to the Play* (London: Greenwood, 2002).

Plato. *The Laws*, trans. Trevor J. Saunders (Harmondsworth: Penguin, 1922).

—, 'Timaeus', in John M. Cooper (ed.) and Donald J. Zeyl (trans.), *Plato: The Complete Works* (Indianapolis: Hackett, 1997), pp. 1224–92.

Potter, Lois (ed.), 'Introduction', *The Two Noble Kinsmen* (London: Thomas and Nelson, 1997), pp. 1–130.

Radden, Jennifer, 'Melancholy and Melancholia', in David Michael Levin (ed.), *Pathologies of the Modern Self: Postmodern Studies in Narcissism, Schizophrenia, and Depression* (New York: New York University Press, 1987), pp. 231–50.

— (ed.), *The Nature of Melancholy from Aristotle to Kristeva* (Oxford: Oxford University Press, 2000), pp. 95–105, 119–21.

—, 'Melancholy, Mood and Landscape', in *Moody Minds Distempered: Essays on Melancholy and Depression* (Oxford: Oxford University Press, 2009), pp. 180–7.

Sacker, Austin, *Narbonus: The Laberynth of Libertie* (London, 1580). Early English Books Online, <http://eebo.chadwyck.com> (last accessed 9 February 2018).

Schalkwyk, David, *Shakespeare, Love and Service* (Cambridge: Cambridge University Press, 2008).

Schiesari, Juliana, *Gendering Melancholia: Feminism, Psychoanalysis and the Symbolics of Loss in Renaissance Literature* (Ithaca: Cornell University Press, 1992).

Schleiner, Winfried, 'Jaques and the Melancholy Stag', *English Language Notes*, 17 March 1980, pp. 175–9.

—, 'Orsino and Viola: Are the Names of Serious Characters in *Twelfth Night* Meaningful?', *Shakespeare Studies*, 16 (1983), pp. 135–41.

—, *Melancholy, Genius and Utopia in the Renaissance* (Wiebaden (GER): Harrassowitz, 1991).

Schoenfeldt, Michael C., *Bodies and Selves in Early Modern England: Physiology and Inwardness in Spenser, Shakespeare, Herbert and Milton* (Cambridge: Cambridge University Press, 1999).

Sebald, W. G. 'Constructs of Mourning', in Sven Meyer (ed.), *Campo Santo*, trans. Antha Bell. (London: Hamish Hamilton, 2005), p. 210.

Segal, Erich (ed.), 'The MENAECHMI: Roman Comedy of Errors', in *Oxford Readings in Menander, Plautus and Terence* (Oxford: Oxford University Press, 2001), pp. 115–26.

Shapiro, James, *A Year in the Life of William Shakespeare: 1599* (New York: Harper, 2005).

Shaw, George Bernard, *Shaw on Shakespeare*, ed. Edwin Wilson (Harmondsworth: Penguin, 1968).

Sidney, Sir Philip, 'The Defence of Poesy' [printed 1595], *Sidney's 'The Defence of Poesy' and Selected Renaissance Literary Criticism*, ed. Gavin Alexander (London: Penguin, 2004), pp. 1–54.

Spivack, Charlotte, *George Chapman* (New York: Twayne, 1967).

Spizer, Leo, *Essays in Historical Semantics* (New York: S.F. Vanni, 1948).

Starobinski, Jean, *A History of the Treatment of Melancholy from Earliest Times to 1900* (Basel: Geigy, 1962).

The Stoic Reader: Selected Writing and Testimonia, trans. Brad Inwood and Lloyd P. Gerson (Indianapolis: Hackett, 2008).

Stott, Andrew, *Comedy*, 2nd edn (New York: Routledge, 2014).

Sullivan, Erin, *Beyond Melancholy: Sadness and Selfhood in Renaissance England* (Oxford: Oxford University Press, 2016).

Taylor, Gabriele, 'Deadly Vices?' in Roger Crisp (ed.), *How Should One Live? Essays on the Virtues* (Oxford: Oxford University Press, 1998), pp. 157–72.

Tempera, Mariangela, '"Now I play a merchant's part": The Space of The Merchant in Shakespeare's Early Comedies', in Michele Marrapodi and Giorgio Melchiori (eds), *Italian Studies in Shakespeare and His Contemporaries* (Newark: University of Delaware Press, 1999), pp. 152–64.

Theophrastus. *Characters*, ed. and trans. James Diggle (Cambridge: Cambridge University Press, 2004).

Tofte, Robert, 'Alba: The Month's Minde of a Melancholy Lover', in Felicia Hardison Londré (ed.), *Love's Labour's Lost: Critical Essays* (New York: Routledge, 2001), pp. 41–2.

Tomkins, Sylvan S., *Exploring Affect: The Selected Writings of Sylvan S. Tomkins*, ed. E. Virginia Demos (Cambridge: Cambridge University Press, 1995).

Topsell, Edward. *The historie of foure-footed beastes Describing the true and liuely figure of euery beast, with a discourse of their seuerall names, conditions, kindes, vertues (both natural and medicinall) countries of their breed, their loue and hate mankinde, and the wonderfull worke of God in their creation, preseruation, and destruction. Necessary for all diuines and students, because the story of euery beast is amplified with narrations out of Scriptures, fathers, phylosophers, physitians, and poets: wherein are declared diuershyerogliphicks, emblems, epigrams, and other good histories, collected out of all the volumes of Conradus Gesner, and all other writers to this present day* (London, Printed by William Iaggard, 1607). Early English Books Online, <http://eebo.chadwyck.com> (last accessed 9 February 2018).

Trevor, Douglas, *The Poetics of Melancholy in Early Modern England* (Cambridge: Cambridge University Press, 2004).

'The Two Menaechmuses', in T. E. Page (ed.) and Paul Nixon (trans.), *Plautus*, Vol. 2 (Cambridge, MA: Harvard University Press, 1951), pp. 363–487.

Udall, Nicholas [1552], *Ralph Roister Doister*, ed. John S. Farmer (London: the Early English Drama Society, 1907).

Walton, J. Michael and Peter D. Arnott, *Menander and the Making of Comedy* (Newport, CT: Praeger, 1996).

Watson, George, *Heresies and Heretics: Memories from the Twentieth Century* (Cambridge: Lutterworth Press, 2013).

Wells, Marion A., *The Secret Wound: Love-Melancholy and the Early Modern Romance* (Stanford: Stanford University Press, 2007).

Withworth, Charles, 'Rectifying Shakespeare's Errors: Romance and Farce in Bardeditry', in Robert Miola (ed.), *The Comedy of Errors: Critical Essays* (New York: Garland, 1997), pp. 227–60.

Womack, Peter, *Ben Jonson* (Oxford: Basil Blackwell, 1986).

Wood, David Houston, '"He Something Seems Unsettled": Melancholy, Jealousy and the Subjective Temporality in *The Winter's Tale*', *Renaissance Drama*, 31 (2002), pp. 185–213.

Woodbridge, Linda, 'Payback Time: On the Economic Rhetoric of Revenge in *The Merchant of Venice*', in Paul Yachnin and Patricia Badir (eds), *Shakespeare and the Cultures of Performance* (Farnham: Ashgate, 2008), pp. 29–40.

INDEX